Slab Life

By Nick Cansfield

Also by Nick Cansfield.....

Err ... nothing actually

Nick Cansfield

Dedications:

Sir Gary Waddock
James Rowe

1 - Jake Cole
2 - Nick Arnold
3 - Cheye Alexander
5 - Will Evans
7 - Shamir Fenelon
8 - Manny Oyeleke
9 - Scott Rendell
10 - Matt McClure
11 - Bernard Mensah
12 - Nicke Kabamba
14 - Shaun Okojie
15 - Josh McQuoid
16 - Jake Gallagher
17 - Jim Kellerman
18 - James Rowe
19 - Adam McDonnell
20 - Chris Arthur
20 - Lewis Kinsella
21 - George Fowler
22 - Callum Reynolds
26 - Fabien Robert
27 - Bobby-Joe Taylor
34 - Lewis Ward

Shahid Azeem
Mark Butler
Steve Gibbs

And to my wife – you're the best
(when you let me go and watch the Shots)

Nick Cansfield

In Memorium

Peter Cansfield

31 December 1940 to 16 February 2018

My Dad

Bill Tootill

28 October 1960 to 8 December 2016

My very good friend

Rest in Peace

Author's note

This book is self-published.

On the plus side, this means I can write whatever I like without an editor going through and taking out anything that they don't think should appear in print.

On the down side, this means I can write whatever I like without an editor going through and taking out anything that they don't think should appear in print.

And the stuff that an editor might take out because they don't think it is appropriate is likely to include anything that is rude or likely to cause offence. So, I need to state that all opinions and views are mine, and I have absolutely no intention to cause any offence to anyone. This is my ramble through the season as I saw it. I admit to being somewhat biased towards my football team.

I'd also like to say that I assume no responsibility or liability for any errors or omissions in the content of this book. Everything quoted is accurate to the best of my knowledge, but I can offer no guarantee to its accuracy or completeness.

Of greater concern is that there may be some grammatical or punctuation errors within my book. Any incorrect uses of commas, hyphens or other punctuation, and any spelling or typing mistakes will all be mine. If you do spot anything that should be corrected, please don't hesitate to let me know, and who knows – it may be corrected if there was ever to be a second edition.

Nick Cansfield

Acknowledgements

Readers will be able to get a rare insight into my world through these pages and find out more about my friends, the people who are important to me and one of the greatest (but not necessarily most successful) football clubs in the world.

The acknowledgements page is a slightly indulgent opportunity to name check some of these people. So, huge thanks to my lovely wife, for putting up with my obsession for the Mighty Shots. I do, however, need to remind you that the Shots were in my life before you were. Just saying....

To my children Matt and James, I promise you there could have been many worse things that you could have been born into than supporting the Shots.

To my best friend Gary, I thank you for your time and effort in proof reading my amateurish efforts, but more than this my friend, I thank you for your friendship since you first went away for a week camping with my wife.

I would also like to thank Steve from Number 11 for introducing himself to me at our street party. What a wonderful meeting and I thank you for your friendship over this season, and, hopefully, over many more to come.

This is also too good an opportunity for me to miss in thanking other Slab dwellers for their companionship and easy friendship. Charlie, Andy, Alan, Midlands Bill, Steve from Bournemouth, Big Jack, Dave, Adie, Tim, Pete, Sue, Heather, Dave, Richard and everyone else who at one time or another comes and stands on our little slab of concrete in the corner of the ground.

And a special mention to Sergeant Jason Holford, the best advert for policing in Hampshire.

The Recreation Ground is a very special place, and it is you, the wonderful people that particularly make it so.

But most of all, this is the right place to acknowledge Bill Tootill, who was such a good friend to me over 35 years, during which time we travelled the length and breadth of the country, following the Shots. Bill was so cruelly taken from us in December 2016. There's not many days that go by when I don't think of you, my friend.

And these thoughts are extended to other supporters who we have lost over the last couple of years. Rest in peace and try and put in a good word for the Shots if you get the chance

Nick Cansfield, October 2018

Introduction

Gary and I were enjoying a quiet evening in a local pub, when I suddenly said, "I think I should write a book". I'm not entirely sure why I said it, and I'm not entirely sure why those specific words might have come out in that particular order. Certainly, it wasn't anything that I had previously given any thought to, but at that particular moment it seemed like a good idea and, given the number of books that continue to be published, obviously it can't be that hard. Could it?

Gary, always a voice of sound common sense, asked me what seemed like a very intelligent question, namely, what I was going to write about. I said that I had no idea, and we started one of our rambling discussions, that start nowhere and generally tend to go nowhere, but they keep us amused. Often for several hours at a time. Eventually, I suggested there could be a book in 'anti-supporting' a team for a season. Gary didn't know what I meant and asked me to say more. I suggested that maybe you could have a book where the first few chapters would talk through all the various football clubs that we didn't like, and all the reasons why we didn't like them as we tried to work out which one we disliked the most. And once we had worked out whether this was going to be Reading or Crawley Town, we could talk about all the reasons that we didn't like them, which could easily cover several chapters. And then we could buy a season ticket for their away end so that we could go and watch every game of their season from the opposition's terrace, cheering them on to defeat, relegation and humiliation. Gary quite liked the idea and thought that it was 'novel' which I thought was amusingly appropriate. Unfortunately, it took a while, and it took someone else, to point out the obvious flaws in this idea. Firstly, it would mean having to go and watch either Reading or Crawley every week. Secondly, Gary isn't allowed out on Saturdays, so I would have to go and watch them all on my own, and thirdly, because I would be watching Reading or Crawley every week, I wouldn't be able to go and watch the Mighty Shots. And so, we had to bin this idea, but maybe it could be an option for that difficult second book....

I've been regularly going to the Rec since my first game in late 1979 or early 1980 when my friend, Matthew, was round for the day. His Mum came to pick him up because he was going to the Recreation Ground in the evening to watch the Shots, and I asked whether I could go with him. For an early teenager going to his first live football match, standing in the East Bank for an evening match was an awesome experience, and I was immediately hooked. Like most habits, I initially thought I was in control of it. But out of nowhere, I eventually came to realise that I was an addict, and there was nothing I could do about it, other than to turn up on the terraces every week for my next fix.

There have been quite a lot of low points along the journey, but there have been one or two high points. Most lower league fans would understand that you need to suffer the multiple lows in order to enjoy the occasional high. Life must be so dull for the glory-hunting armchair Man City, ManUre or Chelsea fan, as the only emotion they will ever experience is disappointment. Every game they play they expect to win, so the pleasure in doing so is never going to be as intense as it is for the Shots. Winning a trophy is their only measure of success, and if they don't win one, then they are going to be disappointed. As José Mourinho said towards the end of the 2017/2018 season, "Manchester United don't celebrate finishing second".

It takes a Leicester fan to really understand how good winning the league can feel, and that's the emotion that can only come from supporting one of the less fashionable teams. The joy of the Shots winning at Wolverhampton to gain promotion to League 1 in 1987, the joy of winning promotion back to the football league in 2008, or the joy of beating West Ham United at Upton Park in 2011 are experiences that no one but a genuine fan who has supported their team through thin and thin, will ever really understand and fully appreciate. But Shots fans are realistic enough to know that these miracles only happen rarely, and we are realistic in our aspirations. We want to be entertained, and we want to feel that we are getting value for money for our entrance fee. Beyond that, it doesn't really matter than much.

Of course, we want to win most of our games, and of course we want to win all of our home games, but it's far more important that we play entertaining football, and keep fans coming through the turnstile. This is why Ian Ridley's decision to include an element of Steve Claridge's pay deal at Weymouth being linked to the size of the crowd, was so clever. More fans equates to more income. More money equals more options to recruit better players, or more players, when needed, and it becomes self-perpetuating, in a way that throwing money at chasing glory could never be.

Just look at the number of teams that have tried to buy their success and failed. I find that the money that teams like Eastleigh, Forest Green Rovers and Billericay have (arguably) wasted trying to buy success is completely immoral. But then, the amount of money that exists in the Premier League is equally immoral. It's a game. That's all it is. It's 11 players against 11 players, and given the issues that exist in the world, there really is no argument for paying players hundreds of thousands of pounds a week, let alone millions. Football, abetted by Sky has, in my opinion, taken a very, very wrong turn.

Some sports work reasonably well on TV, like cricket. When you're watching cricket, you get to see things that you can't when you are watching within the ground, but with football, it is the other way round. Your viewing experience could never be as good as the real experience of standing on a terrace being able to see and hear everything that is going on.

The Shots were originally formed in 1926, and except for four years, we spent our entire life in what is now called League 2. There is a wonderful quiz question about which team has won the most matches in Division 4, to which the answer is Aldershot. League 4 existed between 1958 and 1992, and apparently we also scored more goals than anyone else during this time. We did get promoted in 1973/74 and spent two seasons in League 1, but we soon returned to our spiritual home. We also temporarily visited League 1 from 1988 to 1990 after we won the play-offs in the first year that they were in place. This ended badly and we were soon relegated, and found ourselves in serious financial difficulties which eventually led to the Shots being kicked out of the league in March 1992. Our results were expunged for the season as if we hadn't existed. But against the odds, we reformed in the Ryman Division 3 – effectively league 9 - and gradually progressed back to where we had previously been. Terry Owens and Graham Brookland were the Chairman and Secretary as the Shots progressed, and while we might have originally had a dream of returning to the league within ten years, we achieved it in 16, under the stewardship of 'Sir' Gary Waddock. Our first home league game when we reached League 2 back in 2007 was a 1-1 draw against Bournemouth. I wonder what happened to them over the last ten years.

The Shots were bought by a Polish lottery winner, Kris Machala, and Shots fans learned the hard way that the Polish lottery wasn't quite as generous as the Euro Millions as unfortunately Kris soon ran out of money. This sparked a collapse, and the Shots were relegated in the 2012/13 season, and entered administration, suffering a ten-point deduction in the next year, our first back in the National League. We had a few difficult years until Sir Gary Waddock was re-appointed as the Shots manager in the 2016/17 season.

Life as a Shots fan in 2017 and 2018 is undoubtedly good. Personally, I didn't think relegation was the end of the world. Of more concern was the fact that the Board of Directors had allowed us to rack up considerable debts which forced us into administration. Given our history, this was disastrous for Shots fans. Living within our means so that we have a club to support is more important than playing in a higher league. Our life in the Ryman Leagues was tremendous fun, and we made a lot of friends along the way. I would still follow the Shots if we returned to these leagues, and as I say, the only thing that really matters is that we play attractive football, and that we are competitive in every game that we pay money to go and watch.

Since Sir Gary Waddock took us back into the Football League in 2007/2008 we have had managers who did not understand what the fans wanted. Kevin Dillon, Dean Holdsworth, Andy Scott and Barry Smith are all, I'm sure, very good men, and potentially good football men, but they didn't really understand that the only thing Shots fans want is to be entertained with end to end action and excitement. So, when we heard that Sir Gary had been appointed, we were delighted. Sir Gary has always played an attacking brand of football where we will always (unfortunately) have the potential to concede goals, but we will always score goals, and these will come from any of the players on the pitch. I love Sir Gary's approach to the game, and I'd be delighted if the club gave him a lifetime contract.

He was a legend at QPR where he had a very successful playing career and is equally a legend at Aldershot where he has had arguably his most successful managerial spells. He re-joined at the beginning of last season, and after a relatively indifferent start, we really kicked on from Christmas, after which we only lost one game in the last five months of the season, scraping into the last play-off spot. Unfortunately, we went out in the first round of the play-offs, but it was undoubtedly a very exciting year.

And so, we prepared ourselves for the new season with some excitement and a potentially realistic expectation of achieving the play-offs. What was never in doubt, was that we would be riding a rollercoaster, and we strapped ourselves in and got ready for the ride.

Street Party

Saturday 22 July 2017

In a quiet cul-de-sac on the border of Hampshire, Surrey and Sussex, our village community was holding its annual street party. It's a nice area, and the people are all very friendly and neighbourly, but like many roads in the south of England, people tend to keep themselves to themselves and, after 15 years, I am slightly ashamed to admit that I don't know too many of my neighbours.

After making up a nice Mediterranean salad to take with us, we strolled over to meet the neighbours. Someone had put some serious thought into this street party, with three industrial sized BBQs ready to cook the obligatory burgers and hot dogs, and some rather splendid draft Moondance from the wonderful Triple F brewery in Four Marks. Unfortunately, my Mediterranean salad was incomplete as there had been a shortage of watermelons this year, which I was led to believe was due to our Spanish friends milking the opportunity to make some extra cash by extending the pepper season.

After saying hello to a few of the people we knew, this chap came up and introduced himself to me as Steve from number 11. He tentatively asked me whether I supported Aldershot Town Football Club, at which point my poor wife sighed exasperatedly, not wanting to believe that there was another fan living so close to us. After I confirmed that I indeed did, he then asked me if I remembered having a drink with him at Dartford a few years earlier. Steve from Number 11 reminded me that this was the game when our striker, Brett Williams, scored a wonderful goal towards the end of the game to rescue a point after our Goalie had been sent off earlier on.

I struggled to remember too much of the game, to be honest, however, I've only been to Dartford's new ground once and I flushed with embarrassment as I recalled the conversation that had taken place before the game. I had travelled to the game with my very good friends Bill and Gary. Some of my friends are slightly odd, and these two are no exceptions. Gary had been treating us to stories about the research he had been undertaking into the Thames Ironworks and Shipbuilding Company.

Over to Gary for a brief synopsis ...

"Based in the East End of London, this company had a long and interesting history which had nothing to do with Mr Isambard Kingdom Brunel who had nothing to do with building HMS Warrior".

"For one thing, IKB was dead before construction started, and for another, the whole shebang was a Royal Navy thing. HMS Warrior was designed by the imaginatively titled 'Chief Constructor of the Navy', Isaac Watts".

"Thames Ironworks were awarded the contract to build HMS Warrior, after making a successful bid. It marked one of the first Admiralty contracts undertaken by them, and, when complete, HMS Warrior was the largest warship in the world".

"She was built (rather hurriedly it should be said, in just over a year) because the sneaky Frenchies had wrapped a load of iron around a wooden ship and called it ironclad just so they could say they'd launched the first open sea ironclad in the world, which, if you are interested, was Le Gloire, in 1859. Warrior was the first one that was completely designed to be an ironclad, and therefore should, quite correctly, be called the first ironclad".

"Possibly of more interest is the fact that the Thames Ironworks social club football team eventually became West Ham United. And of even more interest is that the Mighty Shots beat them in one of the best football games ever, in the first round of the League Cup, back in 2011."

I nearly missed this game as we were on a family holiday in Crete when it was scheduled to be played. Fortunately, some local hoodlums came to my rescue, by organising some riots in London, which resulted in the game being postponed, and we were home for the re-arranged date.

Gary would, I'm sure, want me to point out that, contrary to the belief of some Americans, they did NOT launch the world's first ironclad warship. I guess this could be contrary to a similarly held belief by some Americans, but they didn't build the world's first steamship either. Even the propeller that (Swedish) Ericsson invented for them was not the first as some claim. And Gary is very keen to point out whenever the subject comes up, that it most definitely wasn't the best propeller.

Gary seamlessly manoeuvred the conversation into other nautical subjects and before we knew it we were talking about the impact of containerisation on the world. Yes. On the way to a football match, we were actually talking about the impact of containerisation. At this point, Bill, eager to demonstrate how well read he was offered a view that containerisation had been a major contributing factor to the Allies winning the Second World War. Not true, said Gary, and he started to tell Bill that containerisation didn't really take off until the 1950s. And thus began a discussion which lasted all the way up the M3, around the M25 and on to the M20 to Dartford.

We were amongst the first to arrive at the ground – mainly because I was driving as fast as possible to try and scare Gary into a change of subject. After parking outside the ground we went into the bar in the relatively new Prince's Park stadium and ordered some refreshments. I tried on several occasions to steer the conversation in other directions, but sadly to no avail. At one stage, a couple of Dartford fans sat on our table, and as Gary paused for breath, I politely enquired if they had a view on the subject, thinking that given they were so close to the River Thames, and the shipbuilding industry of the past, that they may have had a passing interest. "Piss off" came the response, and they upped and moved away to sit with their own kind. Although this rejection felt somewhat unfair, I fully understood where they were coming from, and slightly envied the ease with which they could move tables.

Anyway, it turns out that Steve from Number 11 had been one of the Shots fans who joined our table in the seats vacated by those locals who struggled to find the interest and desire to join our conversation, but who, as I recall, smiled politely at us. He obviously had remembered me, and his wife, Kerry, suggested that I looked more memorable than her husband, who she described as 'non-descript' and 'very generic looking'. I wanted to take this as a compliment and started to puff my chest out, but Mrs C brought me crashing down to earth by suggesting that it was probably my unkempt hair that she was talking about.

Personally, had I come across us a few years later, I would have walked in the other direction. Dick and Mary from the other side of the road would have been a good bet for conversation. As would Richard and Nicola, or indeed almost anyone else. But instead, Steve from Number 11 showed his poor judgement, and chose me.

But all was good. Steve and I got on really well, and we agreed that from now on we would travel together to away matches. This was quite important to me. Partly because Mrs C refuses to come to football matches with me and partly because Gary isn't allowed out at weekends. Another option, Steve from Bournemouth, looked as if he might have been a promising travelling companion, but after we lost the first leg of the play-off against Tranmere at the end of last season, he changed his mind about travelling to the away leg. Given I had already bought the tickets, this didn't bode well for the coming season, or his confidence in our ability to come back from a 3-0 deficit.

Bill, who I had travelled the length and breadth of the country with over the previous 35 years, died last December. This was a terrible and unbelievable shock, and it still saddens me that his lovely wife, Gill, and their children Laura and Rob, have been so cruelly robbed of such a good man who loved them so deeply.

On a more selfish note, it robbed me of my regular travelling companion. Bill was wonderful. If Bill said he was coming to a game, you could immediately start planning for it. Gary is pretty reliable, but unfortunately is only rarely allowed out to play on Saturdays, but Bill was always up for an away match, and could always be relied upon. So I was delighted to make Steve from Number 11's acquaintance and I had high hopes of developing a new friendship as we travel the length and breadth of the country over the next few years.

Wednesday 2 August 2017

I read a tweet from Anthony Baston, who said "Well, that's brought my pre-season excitement down a peg or two" as he re-tweeted the club message saying "Striker @IdrisKanu9 has joined @theposhofficial for an undisclosed fee. We wish Idris well for the future". I guess there's a limit to what you can fit into 140 characters, but this did feel particularly brief.

The official announcement didn't give much more away, saying: "Aldershot Town forward Idris Kanu has joined Peterborough United for an undisclosed fee. The 17-year-old who joined the Shots from West Ham United last summer made 32 appearances in 2016-17 and scored 4 goals. We thank Idris for his efforts and wish him well for the future"

I remember Iddy's first game, at home against Solihull Moors last season, when he came on as a substitute towards the end of the game as a raw 16-year-old. He seemed to have an astonishing level of confidence as he ran at seasoned defenders with no fear. I couldn't wait for Deano's video footage to be uploaded so that I could show my friends what an impressive player we had signed.

Iddy had chosen to leave West Ham in order to further his career at Aldershot and he had chosen the Mighty Shots when ManUre were allegedly after his signature. We felt this was a sign of his maturity in recognising that playing men's football would do his longer-term career more good than being included in some Premiershit Club's collection of players who would never actually get to play a competitive game of football. And proof, if it were needed, that Sir Gary is very highly thought of in football circles. To attract someone of Kundai Benyu's ability on loan for a 6-month period last season was massive, and, to get Iddy to sign for us as well has given Shots fans some increased confidence for the future after what has been a number of depressing years.

Iddy was so exciting, it was difficult at times to remember just how young he was, and for the fans to keep calm when he kept the ball for a few seconds too long or sent a pass astray. But the lad has massive potential. He has pace, strength, agility, and most of all, wonderful confidence.

As 'New Recruit' posted on the Shots chat room, "I will always remember that first touch on his debut. Standing in the Eastbank I heard the North Stand gasp". Now, I'm not sure I've ever heard the North Stand gasp as most of the time all they seem to do is whinge and moan, but the Slabbers certainly did gasp and look at each other in amazement as Iddy nutmegged an experienced Solihull right back and made him look stupid right in front of us within a few seconds of coming on as a substitute in the second half. Wow…

We saw him improve throughout the season, and while we knew that sooner or later he was going to move on to bigger and better things, we were hoping for another season so that he could get into the Football league with the Shots. It's not to be. Thank you for the memories, Iddy – and good luck for the future. We'll watch your career with interest.

One of the downsides of a settled squad is that there is little news provided by, or expected from, the club during the summer months. As soon as the news broke, the Shot's chat room was busier than ever. Well – nearly busier than ever...

The most popular discussion during the summer months was the need to replace the guttering over the disabled section in the North Stand. As an Old Age Slabber, I am used to standing in the rain, but I admit this is through choice (one day I must try and find out why). Supporters confined to a wheelchair don't have access to the same choice - and there really is nothing worse than being under a downpour if you don't want to be.

Many ideas were discussed about why the issue existed, but 'Ancient Shot' seemed to have spent far too much time thinking about it when he suggested that a "110mm (4") downpipe should drain 47 square metres of roof with no problem (except in torrential rain)". Ancient reckoned that "Replacing the guttering with 154mm (6") downpipes would store a bit more before it disappeared down the downpipe.

Although he admits to not having counted them, Ancient's conclusions was that there aren't enough downpipes. Good advice one might think, but Richard Petty countered by suggesting that it was their diameter that was the problem, and they aren't large enough to cope with the amount of water that the guttering is having to deal with. Richard suggested that remove the existing guttering completely and replacing it with a substantially wider aluminium Box Gutter running the whole length of the north stand would definitely solve the problem, although highlighted that there would be a pretty substantial cost associated with it.

This was as good as it got during the summer, and while we had made a couple of signings early on, with Manny Oyeleke rejoining at the end of last season, Bobby-Joe Taylor (from

Maidstone) and Shaun Okojie (Corinthian Casuals), there was no major news coming from the club.

With hindsight, this wasn't such a bad thing. Shots fans are resilient characters, and the opportunity created by Iddy's transfer was immediately spotted by 'Dalinz' who suggested that we can now afford to repair the gutters in the disabled section, with maybe enough change to get a new burger van".

Good news indeed…..

Halifax versus Aldershot

Saturday 5 August 2017

Match day!

It was the first game of the season, away at Halifax today. I didn't go. I thought about it. Several times, but I'd not yet confessed to Mrs C that I'd be out pretty much every night the following week, so something would need to give. I should say fairly early in this tome, that my wife doesn't understand me. Or more specifically, my wife doesn't understand my passion for football. And even more specifically, my wife doesn't understand my passion for lower league football. And if we want to get right to the point, she doesn't understand my passion for Aldershot Town FC.

Although she will never admit it, she does try. In fact, she buys me a season ticket every year, and she understands that with the season ticket comes permission to attend all the home games. Well, maybe except for Boxing Day. And any other game that clashes with something that she has organised for us to do. But all other games are fine… Except for away games. And especially away games in the North. But I can live with that because this season, the Conference had more southern than northern teams, so I figured I'd be able to get to quite a few of the away games without too much bother, and that suited me fine.

There was a risk that my cricket team would need me today, but fortunately our Captain managed to get 11 people with varying degrees of skill at batting, bowling, fielding or indeed, just being able to stand up for 42 overs, which meant he wasn't desperate enough to need me. One of my friends turned up for a game when we were short, and when asked what he did, he replied saying that he could run, and he could catch. "Ah, an all-rounder" said our Captain enthusiastically.

I've found in previous years that it's very difficult to try and focus on a game of cricket when I know the Shots are playing. Either that or I am just totally rubbish at cricket anyway. Clearly this isn't the case though, as I did score 35 not out once. A few weeks after this, Harry, our First XI Captain came up to me and explained that the First XI were a player short for the weekend. My chest puffed out as I imagined how the tale of my 35 not out had been told within the Club, but Harry brought me crashing down to earth by asking if one of my then 12 year old children would be available to play.

I'll admit that this hasn't been my finest season though. My batting average currently stands at 0. I hadn't got a bowling average, as our Captain, 'Mad Max', won't let me bowl, and I am too scared to ask him if I could have a go. I am also the first to admit that I'm not very good at fielding. A cricket ball is very hard, and it really hurts when it's been well struck by a cricket bat. I guess I'm a bit of a coward at heart.

My Great Uncle Jim used to be quite good at cricket. Or at least he used to tell us a story that he once bowled Don Bradman out, so we used to think he was quite good at cricket. The truth was not quite so impressive. Uncle Jim used to work on the Cruise Liners during the 1950s as an Engineer and he was once aboard when the Australian cricket team were travelling to or from the

UK. With very little to do during the six-week journey, the young men used to get up to the same type of mischief that young men today would get up to, and this invariably involved lots of alcohol. Uncle Jim managed to bowl out the Don, on an indoor carpet-wicket because on that particular night he was even more drunk than Uncle Jim was.

What my team does like from me though, is that I turn up when and where requested, and I don't complain too much. As a bonus, I'll even write a match report for the local paper, and the better players can gain a little notoriety from their occasionally commendable performances. I'll also bring one or two of my boys along to join in if needed – something that no one else in the team does, and my kids are significantly better than most of the other players. Matt took 5 wickets on his debut for the Adult team aged 14, and James has at least three 50s to his name.

Fortunately, I wasn't required today, so it was an opportunity to watch the game on the radio. I managed to get the shopping out of the way before 3pm and settled down to spend a couple of tense hours listening to the excellent Rob Worrall and our legendary former goalkeeper, Nikki Bull. Bully played 267 games for the Shots between 2002 and 2009 and was a huge favourite with the fans, winning the player of the year award on three occasions. I still remember the first time very clearly. In the last home game of the season that we won the Ryman Premier (2001/2002), Bully with his hair dyed red and blue picked up the Player of the Year award before the game started. We were winning 3-2 when we won a penalty. The whole stadium started chanting "give it to Bully". Regular penalty taker, Roscoe Dsane joined in with the spirit of the game, and held the ball up for Bully, and as he slowly walked up the ground, he anxiously looked towards our manager, Terry Brown, for permission. Terry appeared to be about to put his head in his hands before reluctantly agreeing that Bully could take it. He needn't have worried as Bully confidently slotted the ball into the bottom right hand corner of the net to score his only goal for the club.

Roscoe Dsane was one of my favourite Shots players. He made 110 appearances for the Shots and scored 48 goals before being diagnosed with tendonitis in his knees and having to give up full time football. The name Terry Brown will be familiar with all followers of non-league football. Terry was our manager when we managed to secure promotion into what is now called the National League. Terry is a legend in non-league football, and after leaving the Shots, had a lot of success taking AFC Wimbledon into the football league. Shots fans, and Wimbledon fans will forever remember Terry's name with fondness as he is one of the nicest men to have lived. My friend Izzy bumped into Terry in her local pub and thought she would ask him for his autograph for me. She only had a bar tab, but this was OK, and Terry wrote "Dear Nick, you are shit at fantasy football, love Terry". Harsh, I thought, given I had won our fantasy football league the previous year, but this started something, and every time I bumped into a 'celebrity' I asked them for their autograph, below similar words. Shane Ritchie and many others were very happy to oblige, but Ben Fogle did ask if I would mind if he said, "Dear Izzy you are 'rubbish' at Fantasy Football". That's how posh he is ....!

Being Aldershot, the league table always looks quite promising at the beginning of the season. This year however, AFC Fylde were top of the league before a ball had been kicked in anger. Personally, I think adding in the FC, or in this case, AFC, before the name of the team is cheating, and they should be deducted points. Fylde begins with an 'F', and not an 'A'.

I lost the BBC Radio Surrey commentary for 5 minutes in the second half and had to listen to a dour Yorkshireman describing the game on BBC Radio Leeds. My word he was dull, but it did serve to remind me of just how good Rob is.

We won 2-0. We had to weather a bit of Halifax spirit in the first 5 or 10 minutes, before we started to assert ourselves and this pushed Halifax deeper and we were able to take control. Although goal-less at half time, the 298 Shots fans who made the journey didn't stop singing and could be heard through the game in the background. In the second half, Shamir Fenelon scored a lovely goal, and after what was described as a perfectly good goal was disallowed for off-side, we scored from a penalty that should probably not have been given towards the end of the game.

A perfect start for the Shots – winning away from home and keeping a clean sheet. It was also nice to see the team putting in a great performance without Idris, Kundai, and Bernard Mensah who was still (fortunately) a Shots player but sat out of the game with a slight injury. Taking 298 away fans to Yorkshire is also a cracking achievement, and it make me think - had Bill and I been able to go, we would have rounded it up to 300.

I'm still waiting for my friend Mike, a 'Fax fan in Yorkshire to reply to my messages. It could be that he doesn't like me gloating – I'll have to send him another message to make sure.

Aldershot versus Torquay

Tuesday 8 August 2017

I managed to leave work promptly in order to pick up Gary and head to Aldershot in time for a beer and bite to eat before the match. I mentioned to Gary while we were in the car that I had had a funny conversation with Jack, the groundsman at my cricket club, who had been in the merchant navy for many years. After I had mentioned Gary's observations, Jack had been quite violent in his assertion that containerisation had ruined the enjoyment that he received from the best job he ever had in the Merchant Navy. I wasn't entirely sure what he meant – one to follow up at another time if I could be remotely bothered. Sadly, however, Gary was. He started telling me about a new book he was reading called 'The Shipping Revolution' by a gentleman by the name of Robert Gardiner. He didn't know that this was going to be about containerisation, but he was way too excited when he started reading and found out that it was. Why he thought I would be remotely interested, I do not know.

Steve from Number 11 had said that he would get to the pub for 6.45pm, and he arrived bang on time. My high hopes for Steve from Number 11 continue to look well placed. Unfortunately, Gary and I were in the middle of an in-depth discussion as to what affliction to your big toe would hurt the most – gout or gonorrhoea. Neither Gary nor I have suffered from gonorrhoea, so it was difficult for us to answer the question. Gout hurts.

Gout can hurt an awful lot, but neither of us were too sure as to whether gonorrhoea hurts or not, and if it did, whether it would hurt more than gout. Steve, on joining the conversation wondered if it didn't hurt because it sent you mad, but Gary had to correct him and said that he was getting his sexually transmitted diseases muddled up. Steve apologised and said he would do more research for next time.

We made our way down to the ground, stopping in the shop to pick up my season ticket before heading to the Slab. But to our dismay the Slab was closed. The club put something out on Twitter saying that it was due to lack of stewards. This is where the Health and Safety rules are bonkers. Apparently, you need to have stewards guarding every entrance and every exit into every stand in a football ground and unfortunately we have quite a lot of them. Entrances and exits that is. We also usually have quite a lot of stewards, but seemingly tonight there was more entrance and exits than stewards…

Any Shots fan will tell you that the Slab is like a retirement home for retired football fans. The average age of Slab dwellers is around 60 and there is very little bad language, let alone aggression. Except when we sing "Oooh it's a corner…" Not that this is a particularly aggressive song, but it does irritate some of the Slab dwellers. I don't think this is the reason that Roy moved to the North Stand, but it might be. But it does irritate Charlie, which makes it even more fun for us.

We've been singing this little ditty in the hope that it will catch on for around 30 years, but unfortunately it hasn't done so yet. We once managed 13 singers in an away game at Bristol Rovers about 17 years ago, but that was only because seven or eight drunks came wandering into the ground and didn't really know what we were doing, got carried away and joined in with us. Generally, though, it has often been just a combination of Gary, Bill or me singing, and since Bill died, it's often just Gary and I. And, as I told you before, Gary doesn't do Saturday games, so often it's just me. But it's a lucky tradition, and we can't ever stop it now because we would be failing in our memories of Bill.

I once posted a plea on the Shots chat room asking if we were to go up the East Bank for a game, would people join in with us if we asked nicely. A couple of posters said they would be happy to do so, but when push came to shove, and we won a corner, the more usual rendition of 'Come on you Shots' rang out over the top of us.

So, with the Slab out of bounds, we had to make a decision – North Stand, High Street End, North Stand East side or the East Bank? We decided to head for the High Street End of the North Stand, partly, because this is our designated meeting point in the event that the Slab is closed (as it was a couple of times last season), but if I'm honest, it was mainly because it is less far to walk and most Old Age Slabbers aren't quite as lively on their feet any more.

Soon we were joined by Steve from Bournemouth, his son Big Jack, and Bill's son, Rob. All seemed to be in fine fettle, and we settled down to watch the game. It generally takes me a few games to really get into the season, but today was a bit of an exception. The standard for exciting attacking football had been well and truly set last season, and our hopes were high. And while we don't necessarily expect to win every game, we do expect to have a certain level of entertainment, and tonight set the bar very high.

We were attacking the High Street End in the first half (always a good sign), and Shamir Fenelon scored in the fifth minute. It was a slightly odd goal in that the Torquay goalie pulled off a fine save and Shamir jumped over one of their players to tap in the ricochet. From where we were standing – level with Shamir at the time he struck the ball - we wouldn't have been surprised to see it called offside. One to watch on the video highlights later. But it was given, and thank goodness for that because three minutes later, Torquay scored from a free kick with a beautiful shot from 20 yards out that curled majestically around our wall. As Big Jack said – two goals scored before a corner kick has been given.

But we didn't have long to wait for a corner, and our small group was in fine singing voice, chanting 'Oooh it's a corner' lustfully as the Shots attacked towards our end. The Shots had lots of possession, and lots of attacking intent, making their 'keeper pull off a number of top draw saves – how he managed to swivel his body through 90 degrees while airborne to get fingers to Matt McClure's rocket of a shot, I will never know. Already a contender for one of the best saves of the season.

Second half, and a wonderful break by Shamir down the right wing saw him cross the ball and Bobby Joe Taylor had the simplest of tap-ins. 2-1 to the Shots, and we were looking dominant. Then came the game changing moment. Halfway through the second half, Torquay made a double substitution, bringing Jake Gosling and Jon-Paul Pittman into the fray. A corner from Gosling in front of the Slab was headed in by Pittman, who looked to have escaped his marker, and the referee gave the goal. Our Captain, Callum Reynolds, then walked over to the linesman and after a seemingly quite polite discussion, Callum seemed to have convinced the linesman to raise his flag. We have no idea what Callum said, but it was presumably along the lines of "Did you not see their player over the far side?" To which the linesman's reply might have been "Oh yes, now that you mention it, I did. I had better put my flag up."

The referee and linesman had a four-minute consultation, before the referee decided to go with the linesman and gave a free kick to Aldershot instead. Torquay players and fans were understandably slightly irritated by this, but fair play to both, they didn't let it get to them and they continued to focus on trying to get back into the game.

We kept going, and managed to win a corner, from which Shaun Okojie bundled the ball in at the far post. 3-1 and the Shots were good value for a win. But just as the fourth official held up the board to signal five minutes of injury time, Pittman stooped to head in at the far post, to make it 3-2, and give us a nervous final few minutes, through which we managed to hold on and clinch the victory. The only sour point was the performance of the referee who was over-zealous in handing out yellow cards. There were seven in a game where I can't remember any particularly bad tackles. This was not the game I was watching!

A crowd of 2,662 was great to see, as was over 300 travelling fans from Torquay. I have a bit of a soft spot for Torquay. They are a similar sized team to us, with a similar size fan base. The fans I know are all great, and the team try and play good football. They had a couple of decisions go against them, but throughout the 90 minutes they kept going, and I don't think I saw a bad tackle, or some of the poor gamesmanship that we see so regularly from football teams. Well, generally any team from Barrow, or from any team that is managed by a former Crawley Town manager that Shots fans will be familiar with. Torquay have had a tough few years but have had some great ex Aldershot players such as Brett Williams and Tim Sills and I wish them well.

We had seen a cracking game of football. We had brilliant entertainment throughout the 95 minutes, and a brilliant result (for us). Two games played, five goals scored, and the Shots are top of the league, level on points with Dagenham and Redbridge.

And it was great to hear that Steve from Number 11 was up for the away game next Tuesday at Maidstone. He was looking to be an exceptionally good find. Even if he hadn't yet understood the importance of singing along with us, we still had five of us singing, which is considerably higher than most games from last season. I wonder if we can maintain that level of noise and commitment.

Aldershot versus Guiseley

Saturday 12 August

Here we go again. I always have slightly mixed feelings about the beginning of the season. Personally, I love the way the fixtures come fast and furious, with two each week, but I'm also mindful that this isn't the same for everyone in my household. But today was a home game and it's covered under the 'Rules of Granting a Season Ticket'. Unfortunately, and much to his disappointment, Steve from Number 11 had a family do to attend in London, so I said I'd text him updates during the game. Bill and I also used to have this arrangement, and it worked really well. Some days, I notice Bill is missing from the terrace, and still reach for my phone when we score or something exciting happens. Like when we win a corner.

Today, my son James had said he would like to come with me. This is great news. James is a lifelong Shots fan, having attended numerous games over the first 18 years of his life. I do still worry that the away cup match at Middlesbrough in January 2013 seemed to put him off for a while, so every time he shows an interest in coming, it does please me.

I still vividly remember us sitting in front of the TV watching the draw being made for the fourth round of the League Cup, and we were shouting various Oooohs and Ahhhs out loud. Manchester

United – "Yes please" will play Accrington Stanley - Groan. Morecambe "No, no, no!" will play Newcastle "phew". At some stage, my wife came in to see what the commotion was about. We explained that this was the draw for the fourth round of the League Cup, which was a bit of a rarity for the Shots. The last time we had reached this far was in 1986/7 when we drew at home against Barnsley before losing the replay. While I had been at the home game, I was unfortunately unable to make the away trip. Never again! It was also something like only the sixth time that the Shots had reached the fourth round since 1926, so we explained that we were going, and how excited we were that we didn't know whether it was going to be a home game or an away game – and if it was an away game we could be going anywhere in the country. My wife, still not understanding our obsession with football said, "hang on a minute, you could end up going anywhere – even Middlesbrough", to which James and I said that we didn't care, because we were going. Surely enough, a few seconds later the TV said, "Middlesbrough will play..." and we knew before he pulled out the next ball, that it was going to be us.

Middlesbrough is a very long way from Hampshire and with a detour to Harrogate to pick up my friend Richard, we made it to the Riverside in good time to have a pre-match beer and to narrowly avoid a fight with some eight-year-olds who were swearing and throwing snowballs at us. It wasn't a bad game, but it was soul destroying to concede in the 98th minute of the game. If only Dean Holdsworth hadn't tried to get us to hold up the ball in the corner area for the last 10 minutes of the game. We were level with a good Championship side because we had tried to play football with them. I really don't like it when we try to close out the game so early before the finish – and inevitably it back-fired.

Fortunately, the Slab was open for the Guiseley match today, and we were able to catch up with Charlie and Andy. However, the away end wasn't opened – probably because it wasn't required with a small (although enthusiastic) group of only 34 away fans in attendance, and these fans joined us on the Slab to watch the game. Their early cheers didn't last long as the Shots ran amok, scoring six goals. Both sides had a goal disallowed but man of the match, Matt McClure, scored twice, and further goals were scored by Callum Reynolds, Jim Kellerman, Shamir Fenelon and James Rowe. So far this season, the goals are coming from all over the place, which is often the sign of a really good team. Matt had a sniff of a chance of a hat-trick near the end when he rose to meet a cross, but it was slightly too high for him and he couldn't quite direct it towards the goal. The first goal from Matt was of particular note as he collected the ball in front of the dug-outs on the half way line before running purposefully towards the High Street End and unleashing a spectacular effort from 25 yards out that would have beaten any goal-keeper in any team as it bounced in off the far post.

We did wonder whether the Guiseley number seven, Kevan Hurst would get stuck in at all, and whether he would risk unsettling his wonderfully bouffant hair with a header, but we didn't get the chance to find out as Aldershot made the afternoon a long one for the Lions. Nicky Bull said on the radio commentary he thought that Guiseley would prefer to play through half-time without taking a break so that they could end the game 15 minutes earlier.

Another very likeable team with genuine fans, and the ones I spoke with agreed that travelling a 500-mile round trip to see your team stuffed 6-0 was much better than being an armchair fan and watching ManUre on the TV. I wish them well for the season, but I fear they are unlikely to survive another season in the National League on today's showing.

I am not convinced about away fans being allowed into the home end though. As it was, there weren't very many of them and we comfortably won but had that been different there's not much fun in being taunted at close range when you're losing. There are other places within the Rec where you can stand to give and/or receive abuse from the opposition, but the Slab really isn't one of them.

I began to regret promising Steve from Number 11 that I would text him updates. With so many goals, near misses, disallowed goals and corners to text, it must have cost me a fortune and no doubt contributed to a future RSI problem, but these are, ultimately, welcome problems.

Three games played, and we are top of the league on nine points. Fantastic! And James had a good day too, so hopefully he'll be coming again soon.

Maidstone versus Aldershot

Tuesday 15 August

A Tuesday night away at Maidstone was definitely an achievable journey, and one worth bunking off work early to get to. I've seen us play Maidstone away before. In fact, the very last away win for the Aldershot FC team before our unfortunate demise was away at Maidstone (who were playing at Dartford) in early 1992. I recall the celebrations when the final whistle went, and can still visualise our Captain, Ian McDonald, saluting the away fans for travelling to the game. This was a sentiment which was totally reciprocated as the team were playing in very difficult circumstances, often without pay, and still trying to give their all.

I picked up Gary and Steve from Number 11 and we had a good run to Maidstone, arriving just before 6.00. Plenty of time to park up and head to the White Rabbit for a lovely pint or two of Spitfire where we met up with Bill from the Midlands and Heather for a chat before heading to the Gallagher stadium.

When we visited towards the end of last season, they were building a new stand at one end of the ground, which reduced the attendance, but we recorded a superb 2-0 victory on our charge towards the play-offs. Last year was great. When he knew that Maidstone were being promoted, my friend Colin (aka Napoleon) said that he would come along to the game. When tickets went on sale, I asked him if he still fancied it and he said that he did. I e-mailed him to advise that I had booked the tickets and was slightly surprised to receive a reply saying he had booked a hotel for us! Fortunately, my wife was very understanding, given this had suddenly escalated from an away game an hour further away than a home game to a weekend away. Memories of last year therefore involved considerable quantities of beer, and only a vague recollection of this particular hostelry.

Maidstone's artificial pitch is an extraordinarily dark colour, resembling the colour of grass afflicted by a slime mould, and the weak floodlights made viewing the other side of the pitch difficult. I'm in two minds about whether artificial pitches should be allowed or not, however people with more knowledge than I have clearly state that they are not permissible in the Football League, so I don't understand why they are allowed in lower leagues. I guess it must relate to opportunities to make money from using the pitch more regularly, but if this is the argument, then surely it applies equally in Leagues One and Two?

Anyway, our record playing games on artificial pitches is not as good as our record for playing on grass, so clearly there are differences, including how the ball bounces, and if it is different to grass then clearly playing on it regularly gives the home team an advantage, and that doesn't feel fair.

Some 400 Shots fans were packed into one corner of the new stand which was clearly not designed to hold this many people. It did feel quite claustrophobic, and we were relieved that there wasn't a fire alarm which would require us to evacuate quickly, as I'm sure this would have been traumatic...if not downright pointless.

Periodically throughout the game we could see the head of a rather strange man poking out from within the leaves of one of the big trees on the other side of the big new stand on the outside of the Stadium. This did strike us as being slightly odd. He was a middle-aged man and if he was remotely interested in the football, he could have had a good view of the whole pitch from inside the stadium. Tickets were readily available and, really, they weren't that expensive. I wondered if it might have been Hampshire's finest football police chief, Sergeant Jason, and maybe he had recently transferred to Special 'Branch', but this little quip was greeted with a certain degree of disdain.

The game was good. It started off fairly evenly and then the Shots' superior quality began to tell, and we started to dominate, pushing Maidstone increasingly deeper. It was probably a tale of two keepers in the end, with the Shots keeper, Jake Cole, pulling off two remarkable saves and the Maidstone keeper going slightly better with three or four. Our dominance increased into the second half and a tactical masterstroke saw Sir Gary bring on Jake Gallagher who scored within a few minutes of coming on.

We won a fair number corners during the game and it was a pleasure to hear Steve from Number 11 joining in our singing, with increasing enthusiasm. Unfortunately, in the middle of the second half, Maidstone changed their tactics and started to bring the game to us and, rather than exploiting the gaps, we started to try and soak up the pressure. This rarely works, and while we thought we had seen the game out when the Maidstone striker Delano Sam-Yorke blasted a shot straight up into the moonlit sky in the 94th minute, more time was allowed and they equalised a minute or two later with pretty much the last kick of the game.

Disappointment for the Shots fans but a point is a point, especially away from home. There was a nasty crash on the M20 driving home and we later found out that a car, full of Shots fans, had been written off after a tyre blew. Fortunately, everyone was unhurt but it sounded like it could have been worse as it skewed across all three lanes of the motorway twice before hitting the central reservation. This puts the results of a football match into context and reminds us that it is only a game.

And things could always be worse...I was looking on the Leyton Orient chat room before the game, and noticed a thread entitled 'Joke Teams.' Someone using the title 'Nice Username' had posted "Not being funny, but how are teams like Solihull and Maidstone even at this level? If we keep winning until October, the EFL should just reinstate us, it's literally embarrassing." If this wasn't funny enough, 'Beradogs' had replied with "Is that possible? Perhaps it's worth making an initial enquiry with the football league." 'Nice Username' said he thought it would be possible, and that they would just take the place of whichever team was bottom of League Two. At least 'Beradogs' had the good sense to point out that this might not actually be fair, although he did suggest it would be more of a question of "...how much better we are than the teams in this league." Oh, how I laughed when I heard the result – 'part-time' Bromley 6 – 'too good for this league and promote us in October' Orient 1.

Gary once again regaled us with what he thought were entertaining nautical stories on the journey home, including the history of the USS Monitor. Monitor was the first American iron-hulled ship and was built in 1862 during the American Civil War. It took 101 days to build this ship and the urgency was because the Confederates were building their own ironclad warship, named Virginia. Soon after, the two iron-clad ships fought each other in an inconclusive four-hour battle. It would appear that Monitor subsequently foundered while being towed during a storm on her way to North Carolina, and her seafaring days had lasted not much longer than the time taken to build her. She was rediscovered in 1973 and has been partially salvaged with her guns and other relics on display in a museum in Virginia. I recall Gary being much more fun when he was working in the porn industry.

I have to add, however, that this was a more comfortable conversation than the one where Gary was trying to work out how bad my obsessive compulsive disorder is. Just because I pointed out, when we were defending a free kick in the second half, that I wished Bobby Joe Taylor (shirt number 27) and Callum Reynolds (shirt number 22) who were third and fourth in the wall would swap positions so that the wall was in ascending order of shirt number...

Thursday 17 August

Great news – James did really well in his A levels and has been formally accepted into Reading University. Actually, this is mixed news, but he has promised me that he will not under any circumstances become a plastic Reading fan. I'm still not sure whether I completely trust him, but he did remind me that he had come back from a boy's week in Malia a couple of weeks ago with no tattoos, broken bones or sexually transmitted diseases; that he hadn't lost his passport or money, and that he hadn't wastefully spent all of the Euros I had given him. Maybe there is some hope, but the more games I can get him to before he goes the better. Or maybe not. The result of the Maidstone game isn't likely to have had a positive effect on him!

I do recall that my wife and I were admonished by his primary school teacher a number of years ago. We were told that the kids had been talking about their football teams in the playground, and when James' pals said that they supported ManUre and Chelski, James quite rightly asked them why. Seemingly, they had replied along the lines of "because they're the best", at which point, 5-year-old James started pointing at them and singing "Glory Boys, Glory Boys, Glory Boys". While I was hugely proud of the effect that my brainwashing was having, their teacher was, unfortunately, somewhat less impressed.

Boreham Wood versus Aldershot

Saturday 19 August

Unfortunately, I wasn't able to make the short trip to Boring Wood today, but Steve from Number 11 went, and took his family with him. While lunching in Wetherspoons, Steve from Number 11 sent me a text with a promise to return my earlier favour by sending me updates. I had high hopes that I would receive a few updates and thought that we might edge the game given our performances so far this season.

The first text said 'Pretty flat here. No atmosphere and like pre-season. They had one difficult free header and Rowe just ballooned over. Little so far.'

Sadly, this was pretty much the most enthusiastic text of the afternoon.

· 'Wood having the better of it. We can't retain possession.'

· 'They just missed a free header and then in the next phase Jake made a good save. Under the cosh.'

· 'Wood have scored. Looked absolutely miles offside but it was coming.'

· 'Jake another good save. So nearly in. Getting battered.'

· 'They've scored another. Free kick outside the area and took an awful deflection leaving Jake flat footed. Shocking performance by the Shots. The 3g pitch really changes the nature of the game too.'

- 'We've just hit the crossbar. Everything going wrong.'

- 'Half-time 2-0.'

- 'Five gone of second half and we look more organised.'

- 'Alexander screamer 2-1!!!!!'

- 'Jake saved down to his right. Close.'

- 'Another Jake save.'

- 'They've just hit the post…'

- 'We stink.'

- 'Full-time lost 2-1. Officiating was poor. We were worse.'

So, there you have it. Aldershot News and Mail eat your heart out, and I'll compare Steve from Number 11's review with the one in the Non-League Paper in the morning.

It's no wonder the atmosphere was pretty flat. 462 Shots fans did indeed outnumber the 347 home fans in a crowd of 809, but they were in an open terrace where it is very difficult to create any noise. We know this from our attempts to sing on the Slab. Still, it was more home fans that Boring Wood had in their last home match when the total crowd numbered a rather paltry 319. It really does make you wonder how they could compete with other teams in the league without an owner putting a lot of money in.

'Tubetrot' posted on the chat room that it was the worst performance since the Shots played at Dover in an FA Cup match a few years ago. I remember this game as Terry Owens, the founder of the new club had kindly offered to pay for a coach to try and encourage more fans to attend the game. It captured the Shots fans' imagination, and several more coaches were subsequently booked much to the distress of Terry's bank balance. Unfortunately, Kent Police obviously had some concerns about the numbers arriving in Dover and made us wait for what felt like hours at Ashford services before our seven coaches could continue towards Dover. We got there in time for the start, but it was a woeful performance, on a freezing cold day, and we went down 2-0.

While this was one of our worst performances, Tubetrot obviously hadn't attended the 7-0 away defeat at Swindon in the FA Cup in January 1984 (after winning 3-1 at Fratton Park in the previous round); the 8-0 thrashing at home against Sheffield Wednesday in October 1989 (after we drew at Hillsborough) or the 10-1 thrashing away at Southend United (aka the Thames Estuary Galacticos) in November 1990.

These were pretty rough days, but in my experience, nothing could ever compare to the shocking performance away at Woeking in October 2006. We were live on Sky against our local rivals who play in red and white shirts. Unfortunately, the referee wouldn't let us wear our red and blue quartered home shirts or our white away shirts, so for the ultimate embarrassment, we had to wear Woeking's away shirts. I can't recall a pass from one Shots player to another throughout the evening – and we were live on TV. It couldn't get any worse than that.

'Alf W' thought Jim Kellerman played well but Steve from Number 11 wasn't quite so sure. Personally, I'm really warming to Jim, who joined us from Wolves last season. He wasn't a regular first team player last year, but against Guiseley, I thought he probably had his best game in a Shots shirt. He seemed to be everywhere, and really up for the game. Jim is only 20 and seems to be ever-improving.

To be fair though, most Shots fans were agreed that we were pretty poor throughout, and that a 2-1 defeat flattered us. Hopefully we can put this behind us and look forward to getting back to winning ways against Chester next Saturday. I'm hoping to make this game, but Gary, Mr Tickle and I are heading to Yorkshire on Thursday for the first day of the Headingly Test match, and we'll be travelling back on the Saturday. It might come down to how much of an excess there is at the cricket.

Normally I wouldn't worry too much about it, because Gary's heavy drinking days are way behind him, and Mr Tickle is a total lightweight. However, Napoleon has just told us that this weekend will be doubling up as his stag weekend, and I think he said that he had managed to get hold of 18 tickets for the cricket, so who knows what might happen.

It will be great to catch up with the Northern crowd, many of whom I used to work with before I changed jobs a few years ago. Cricket weekends are a brilliant way for us to keep in touch, and I understand that my friend Sleesy is coming. Sleesy is a wonderfully bad influence. I know I am easily led, but I always seem to end up very drunk when I see Sleesy. I had been telling my wife that he was a bad influence for a number of years before she eventually got to meet him. She told me that she thought I had him wrong as he was a lovely chap. I said I wasn't arguing about whether he's a lovely chap or not – I had been talking about what a bad influence he is!

Sadly, the Shots are not going to be invincible this year. We never will be, but when you win the first few games, your hopes rise, and if we want to be champions come April, we expect to come away from teams such as Boring Wood with at least a point.

As a result of this defeat, we've dropped down to third in the league. Interestingly, the top two teams in the league have both got artificial pitches, which could disqualify them from promotion, so I guess this means that we are technically still top!

I woke up on Sunday morning to be greeted with an e-mail from my Barnet supporting friend, Stephen. He said 'I saw your boys yesterday. Thought them very poor indeed in the first half and couldn't understand why you were going so well. Second half you got your passing game together and gave the impressive Wood a game of it, scoring a super goal bringing you back into the game. Your play-maker Rowe - who I would have taken off at half time - came into his own after the break. He's clearly a class act. I also liked your flying wing backs. Your team generally lacks height and I wonder whether you will be bullied by more physical teams in that league? You also lack a cutting edge in the final third, although the substitutes made you more dangerous.'

Not a bad summary, although I'm not going to take any nonsense from a Barnet fan. We know we had an off day, and we know that we've got two or three players who are injured at the moment. I'd still much rather be watching the Shots than watching Barnet.

But if Stephen was watching the game, it means there were actually only 346 home fans

England versus the West Indies

Thursday 24 August 2017

Listening to the radio as I got into my car and set off this morning, I learned that the draw for the third round of the League Cup, or the newly titled Carabao Cup, had taken place in Beijing at 4.20 in the morning, UK time. For crying out loud, football is about normal people going to watch their team play. You are pandering to armchair fans with more allegiance to a 'brand' than they have any affinity with a football team. The football authorities have got this so wrong.

I cancelled my Sky subscription a couple of years ago. Partly because I was getting increasingly frustrated at annual price increases that were three times the size of my pay rises, and partly because I begrudge spending so much money on watching the TV. If they charge me £80 a month, then that's over £1,600 of gross income a year. That's a lot of money. My main reason though is that Sky is putting so much money into the Premiershit, and all that happens is that all the teams have more money, so transfer fees and wages are over-inflated. Some of the money that you read about in the press is completely immoral, and I don't want to be contributing to it.

Football has completely lost the plot – even the head of their Trade Union is reported to earn £2 or £3 million a year.

I hadn't heard of Carabao before so I needed to Google it. Seemingly, it is '...an energy drink that was inspired by the fighting spirit of an individual.' But their website tells me that '...it is more than a global energy drink. It is the empowerment to accomplish personal goals. Carabao symbolises the spirit of individuals who fight for the cause they believe in. Not by force, but with determination, hence the slogan: "The Fighting Spirit of Carabao".' It goes on to say that '...energy drinks have become popular with the young, trendy urban population. By positioning these drinks as trendy and fashionable, many companies have forgotten the original purpose of an energy drink. Many of these so-called energy drinks have now become soft drinks. Carabao believes that energy drinks were created with a purpose: to provide replenishment for lost energy.'

I'm not entirely sure how a global energy drink is going to help me to accomplish my personal goals, but then again, there's quite a lot of the 21st century that seems lost on me.

And so, without the aid of any energy drinks, we set out on our annual cricket trip to Yorkshire. The precedent for this started about 15 years ago, when I used to go to quite a few of the London test matches, at either Lords or the Oval, with the previously mentioned bad influences and after consuming a couple of gallons of beer I was always, rather unsurprisingly, the worse for wear on returning home. I recall three consecutive matches that I attended within a couple of months of each other. When I returned home and tried to work out why the lock on the front door had unexpectedly shrunk to a quarter of its former size, I had moments to take in my mother-in-law opening the front door to find out what the commotion was about, before I fell onto my face in the hallway.

Now, it would be no exaggeration to say that in the mother-in-law department, I have really come up trumps. I love my mother-in-law, and I think she loves me too. However, this reciprocal arrangement was beginning to get sorely tested. Well, very clearly it was being sorely tested on one side as she wondered who her daughter had ended up with. And so, I realised, that if I ever wanted to keep in touch with Sleesy, I would need to stay away over-night, and I could pretend that I didn't get hopelessly misled and hopelessly drunk.

And after 15 years, this has grown from, maybe 3 or 4 of us, to a crowd of 18 this year, and it's a delight to be able to see Sleesy, and spend some time with Napoleon, Pete, Neil and some other people who I have been close to in a work context in the past, but don't see very regularly these days.

The other benefit of the Headingly Test match is that the tickets are only £35 each, compared to the £95 that Gary and I paid to go to Lords a few weeks ago. Lords is a wonderful experience, but by the time you add on the train fare and beer at £5.10 a pint, it becomes an expensive day out. And you can only get two tickets, so while it's a very pleasant day out, it's very different to our Northern excursions.

I picked up Mr Tickle and Gary and we stopped off at the Hogs Back Brewery to pick up a present to Napoleon for having us. Obviously, flowers were in order for Josephine but clearly something of a more practical nature was required for Napoleon - especially something of a practical nature that we could share.

The traffic was pretty busy, and it seemed that there were roadworks all the way up the M1, but, as the designated driver, it became clear that these were the very least of my problems. These started with Mr Tickle, a Company Director in his 50th year thinking it would be a jolly ruse to write rude words in the light covering of dust on the rear of my car. We avoided fisticuffs but I did have to man-handle him into the car before things turned nasty. I found out quite a lot about Mr Tickle that I hadn't known before. Instead of deferring to Gary on the grounds of age and disability, Mr Tickle insisted on sitting in the front of the car, a decision I was to rue for many hours and many miles. As soon as he took his seat, he started emptying his pockets and depositing his stuff all over the car. He had his keys, his glasses, some lunch and, among other items, a large builder's tape measure. These went into the side door pocket, the centre console and any other potential receptacle he could find.

Now, I'm not overly car proud, but, as previously described, I do have a mild form of some variety of obsessive compulsive disorder. It's not strong but it's pretty real, and one of the things that bothers me is people putting things in different pockets and cupboards in my car. I had to pull over to ask him, quite assertively in the end, to refrain from distributing his personal effects in places that would ensure that he will never remember to pick them up, and we compromised that he could have the centre console as his personal little storage space. This didn't stop him playing with various buttons that were within his reach and a few terse words were exchanged before we settled down to enjoy the journey. I like to think that playing some warming tunes from the fabulous David Gedge and The Wedding Present was instrumental in calming him down, but Gary wasn't so sure that this might have been a co-incidence, and more likely to have been linked to the rather rapid evaporation of the cider that Mr Tickle had bought from the brewery.

But we did manage to get on our way, and it proved to be a fairly slow journey due to the heavy traffic and multiple road-works. The only excitement happened about half-way when there was a beep and one of the warning lights lit up on the instrument panel on the dashboard. We discussed what the possible options might be in order to determine if it was serious or not.

I'm not very good with cars, or indeed with anything that has any mechanical or electrical parts, and I always worry when I get a beep or a warning light. Gary was slightly more relaxed about it, which may be because he hasn't driven a car since he was 13 when he drove one of his neighbour's cars into a rather deep pond. Obviously different times so long ago, but clearly an incident that made Gary think that he didn't want to learn to drive, and the brewing industry has enjoyed considerable success as a result of his decision.

Given Mr Tickle was sitting in the passenger's seat (or the co-pilot's seat as we sometimes like to call it) he was tasked with looking in the manual to try and discover what the problem was. This was when we realised that Mr Tickle was of no use to humankind whatsoever. It took a while before a frustrated Gary, sitting in the back seat, decided that it might help if Mr Tickle were to look in the cunning, helpful guide that was included at the back of the manual called 'the index'.

After about 20 minutes, Mr Tickle found Chapter 4, and read page 219 which confirmed that the beep had been due to the Tyre Pressure Monitoring System – the good old 'TPMS'. I have no idea why car manufacturers, or indeed any other manufacturers have to come up with acronyms to describe things that they make up. I still recall the Sony products that were the first to boast of their marvellous ANSS and the APSS capabilities, whatever they were.

Mazda have outdone themselves with my car though, and the index provided handy tips on the AFS, ABS, BSM, DRSS, DSC,

FSC, HBC, HLA, LDWS, MRCC, RCTA, SBS, SCBS F, SCBS R, SRS, and my personal favourite, the i-ELOOP. The manual tells me that '…if the vehicle is driven while i-ELOOP charging is displayed, a beep sound is heard. Make sure the message is no longer displayed before driving.' Further investigation indicated that, apparently, the i-ELOOP re-directs the energy discarded by breaking into items run by electrics within the car. It's a Regenerative Braking System – and someone has decided to call it an i-ELOOP. I think this all part of a master plan to make people like me struggle even more to understand the modern world. A whole new language has developed since I was a kid, and I'm not sure I understand very much of it, and I question how much of it is actually for the benefit of humankind.

We pulled over at the next Services, and I put some air into the tyres. Seemingly the TPMS is quite sensitive as the tyres are supposed to be between 33 and 35 psi, and while three of the tyres were at 34, one had dropped to 32. I drove off while Mr Tickle was still engrossed in the manual, and I asked him whether there was anything I needed to do in order to switch the light off the dashboard.

Mr Tickle read 'To allow the system to operate correctly, the system needs to be initialised with the specified tyre pressure. Follow the procedure and perform the initialisation.' I'm not sure this was helping us too much, but he continued 'For vehicles with the 'type A *1 instrument cluster', check the vehicle condition or have the vehicle inspected at an expert repairer, we recommend an Authorised Mazda Repairer (presumably this would be an AMR?) according to the indication.'

We suggested that Mr Tickle look to see whether mine was indeed a 'type A *1 instrument cluster', but this proved harder than we thought. Eventually he read on a few pages and discovered some text which he excitedly read to us 'While the vehicle is parked, press and hold the TPMS set switch and verify that the tyre pressure warning light in the instrument cluster flashes twice and a beep sound is heard once.' This was genuinely exciting news. All we had to do was find the TPMS switch which we eventually found to the right-hand side of the dashboard. When we next stopped because of the heavy traffic, I pressed the button and the light went off. This was especially good news for me as I am not very good at coping with lights on the dashboard that are on when they shouldn't be. And, I haven't got a clue about what to do with them, so this normally means I have to take the car to the garage.

With this little problem sorted, I asked Mr Tickle to put the manual back in its holder, and then put it back into the glovebox, together with the CDs that I had been holding while Mr Tickle tried to solve our problem. Clearly this was a job to which Mr Tickle wasn't particularly well suited as he didn't put it back in its correct place. CDs were put underneath the manual with some facing outwards and some facing sideways. None were in the same order which they were in before. I told Mr Tickle that his behaviour was not conducive to long journeys in my car with me, and, much to Gary's amusement, told Mr Tickle that he would either be in the back seat or on a train for the return journey.

Gary was clearly on my side when he wrote in his blog that 'Nicktor waved a few CDs impotently around in the air, spluttering a few choice words regarding Mr Tickle's disregard for normal social behaviour and starting to recite the rules that bind the common man with bonds that stop them killing each other.' Mr Tickle, on reading Gary's blog said "I'm not so sure I like being called a common man. Particularly from a 10-pound Pom who spent most of his life in Australia".

The cider had caught up with Mr Tickle by now, and for the next hour or so, Gary and I enjoyed the music and each other's company as the miles passed, with Mr Tickle quietly snoring within a deep sleep. Unfortunately, this was never going to last as Mr Tickle was going to have to wake up at some point, but when he did, a cunning game of I-spy helped to ease us through the next few miles. Mr Tickle's "I spy with my little eye something beginning with 'R'" lasted for about 17 miles before we gave up and Mr Tickle told us that it was …. 'railings', of all things.

We arrived at the Butcher's Arms in Hepworth about an hour and a half later than we had expected, but we had about 45 minutes to wait for Napoleon and Sleesy, so we settled into a corner of the pub with a very pleasant pint and a few nibbles. Well, Gary had a few olives, and I had a bowl of chips and a few onion rings. Conscious that Josephine was cooking us a meal later that evening, Mr Tickle decided to have the largest steak on the menu, together with chips and all the traditional trimmings.

Fortunately, the plates were cleared by the time Napoleon joined us, and he entered the pub just in time to hear Mr Tickle's impression of a pig. He had been 'entertaining' us with his animal impressions on the journey. He thought his pig was his best, but I'm not sure we agreed. It could have been an impression of a pig in an abattoir maybe, but it most certainly was not a good impression of a happy pig. It was, however, a much better impression than that of his horse, which in itself was an improvement on his seal. And the less said about his seal the better.

And so, we headed back to Napoleon's house for dinner with a large container filled with Hogs Back Bitter looking forward to an evening of wonderful company and very pleasant conversation.

England versus the West Indies - continued

Friday 25 August 2017

Breakfast is generally a rather splendid occasion on our cricketing weekends. Without wanting to introduce any stereotypes, in my experience - and I can only talk from my experience - northern men are different to us southerners.

Take Neil, for instance. Neil is a wonderful chap. A regular church-goer and Leeds United season ticket holder. One might think that these two would be mutually exclusive, but Neil manages it. Genuinely, you couldn't hope to meet a warmer, gentler, nicer human being. But at his house the kitchen is very much his wife's domain and he does not interfere. Even when he has invited twelve friends over for breakfast he wouldn't dream of entering the kitchen to help his wife. Neil is much more at home sitting down with a beer and entertaining his guests while she sweats in the heat of the kitchen.

Napoleon did at least enter the kitchen. But then Josephine had gone out for the day, and it was his kitchen. But it was clear from the off that he didn't spend very much time in this kitchen and he didn't know where anything was. Steve from the squash club (there does seem to be a disproportionate number of Steve's in my life) had come round to cook breakfast and seemed to be more at home in Napoleon's kitchen than Napoleon himself was and with a little bit of help rustled up sausage, bacon, eggs, toast, mushrooms, tomatoes and beans for eight people.

A splendid effort indeed, although if one were to offer any constructive feedback, one might want to suggest that the bacon could have been grilled rather than fried. The sausages were the posh ones that have 99% meat content which never taste as nice as normal ones; the eggs were floating in too much oil (I do prefer a slightly crispy bottom); the mushrooms had no parsley; the hash browns weren't crispy enough and the toast was made from granary bread. Apart from that, we agreed it was perfect.

We then all managed to squeeze into Napoleon's extraordinarily large car and drove to Brockholes station to await our train. This really is the most wonderful station and was originally opened in 1850. How Dr Beeching managed to miss it is anyone's guess. Rather than removal, it has been transformed into a scene that you would like to find on the front of a jigsaw puzzle. There is only one set of rails which take trains between Sheffield and Huddersfield, and the station house has been privately purchased and turned into someone's home.

We were going to Huddersfield before we changed trains to Leeds and then on to Headingly where we arrived shortly after the match had started and we saw that England were batting first.

We had assumed that England had lost the toss as the weather, while warm, was overcast and cloudy which everyone knows, can cause balls to move all over the place at Headingly.

Our group, under Napoleon's leadership fractured as we left Headingly Station. Because we were walking slower than the others we assumed that everyone had taken their seats, so having bought ourselves some refreshments we entered the Truman stand to find that only two of our party were there. Seemingly the rest had decided to head to a pub in preference to going to the cricket. This does remind me of an incident which happened a number of years earlier when (again Sleesy was involved) we went to Lords to watch England v New Zealand. We had arranged to meet in the pub so that the tickets could be distributed and entertained ourselves with some wonderful conversation over a few pre-match drinks, while we waited for everyone to assemble. Time flew by, and eventually someone remembered that we were going to the cricket match. Someone else pointed out that it was nearing 1pm, and that therefore we might as well stay in the pub for another half an hour. It was at this point that we realised that there was a television in the pub and the Landlord kindly allowed us to switch it on. As the picture came to life, the newscaster told us that one of the Kiwi batsmen, Chris Cairns, had set a new world record for the greatest number of sixes in a session of test match cricket. And unfortunately, we had missed it. Since then, I've always tended to head straight to the ground.

Back at Headingly, people in our party were in and out, collecting refreshments or going to the toilets to make space for more refreshments, and we took the opportunity to move seats on a regular basis so that we could all talk to each other. While Gary was getting his post lunch coffee, I suggested to Steve from the squash club that we should try and get our Aldershot chant going when Gary returned. I was visualising a whole stand singing 'Oooh it's a boundary' which I thought might make Gary wonder.

We tried it, and very soon it was beginning to gain momentum with 4 or 5 of us in our small group singing. I thought this was a fantastic start, and while the others thought it was a rather pathetic effort, I did have to tell them that generally it was only me singing, so to get 4 or 5 of us was indeed a success. Gary soon returned, and within a few minutes, Ben Stokes stroked a boundary towards where we were sitting. 'Oooh it's a boundary' we screamed, to find that Gary was slightly less than astounded. He simply joined in. It could have been because of the coffee.

We had a lot of debate about how many verses needed to be sung. At Aldershot, we only ever sing two verses, which is generally because that's how many we can get in before we're drowned out by the more customary chant of 'Come on you Reds'. However, Steve from the squash club was adamant that adding a third verse would allow more momentum to be gained. I have to admit that this was a rather splendid idea, and before the end of the days play we had smashed our 2001 record against Bristol Rovers with at least 15 of us singing. These included, Gary, Pete, Mr Tickle, Steve from the squash club, Yorkshire Pete, Napoleon, Neil, Gary, a couple of guys from the row in front of us who I think were with our party but I didn't catch their names, Sleesy (eventually and very reluctantly), three lads from Lancashire who were sitting a couple of rows behind us and, of course, me.

One of the conversations I was listening to was between Yorkshire Pete and Mr Tickle (who had been brought up in the Hull area). They were talking about the 'Comfort' and 'Twirlies'. Seemingly these are people who would weekend in the Hull area, which, when pronounced in a thick Yorkshire accent would become people who "'Come for t' weekend. If they arrive before the local hostelries are open for business, then they are deemed to have come too early, or "Twirly". Hence, we have "Comfort" and "Twirlies".

The day was delightful, but as with all good things they do have to come to an end and, at stumps, we made our way out of the terrace with Napoleon leading us on our way.

Unfortunately, while Napoleon may have had a plan, he didn't share it with anyone, and he charged off in the direction of…actually, no one knew which direction he was heading off in. Sleesy had disappeared to the toilet and as we know, Gary is unable to charge anywhere, but this is where we fully appreciated the darker side of Napoleon's character. His interpretation of 'leave no man behind' seemed to be 'leave ALL men behind,' and by the time I had caught him up, I asked how many people we had started the day with. "18," he replied. I had to ask him the obvious follow up question which was "How many people have you got now?" Napoleon counted, and then checked his counting as obviously 18 is quite a big number. "Six" he confidently replied, which had me asking whether this was an acceptable level of loss.

We waited for a few more chums to appear and once we had reached 12, we headed towards the pub where some had watered before the cricket started. We weren't the only ones with this idea, and the bar was busy, but we met up with another four of our party who had left early to secure a seat in the pub. Pete and Simon went to the bar and were soon at the front of the queue. At this point Napoleon decided that he couldn't be bothered to queue any longer and headed off to another pub nearby. With two of our party at the bar, two in the toilets and five sitting outside, we did suggest that this would rather split our group, but Napoleon is a leader who, like his namesake, doesn't waiver with his plans, and off he went.

Having decided to head back to Headingly Station in order to get the train back to Leeds, Neil and Simon finished their drinks and we said our goodbyes and were already looking forward to meeting up next year. Shortly after, we received a phone call ordering us to make our way to the bus stop as Napoleon was about to board a bus. We had a good view of the bus stop from our seats and couldn't see any buses. While we knew they might be a different colour in Yorkshire, presumably they would still be great big things that would be difficult to miss. The order was very clear: 'Leave your drink if you haven't finished it as we are boarding a bus right now.'

We made our way across the road, rather surprised to see Napoleon getting into a taxi with another four of our party. After some deliberation, we decided that we would get a taxi ourselves, and head towards Leeds station and then catch our train to Huddersfield. We managed this without fuss (or further loss), and after running across the station to board the train at platform 16B, we jumped on the train, straight into the arms of Neil and Simon, and Napoleon and the rest of our party.

Much to our irritation, Napoleon was feeling very satisfied with his leadership skills, but even he had to admit that the tannoy announcement that greeted us soon after boarding, advising us of a broken-down freight train and a delay to our departure "for the foreseeable future" was not part of his plan. We discussed how long 'the foreseeable future' was, and we agreed that as we couldn't put a time to it, it felt that it was probably not particularly good news.

Fortunately, the AA were called to get the freight train moving, or give it a tow, and we were able to head to Huddersfield where we fell out of the train and straight into the Head of Steam, the beer garden of which is on the platform. Clearly, we hadn't had enough to drink as Napoleon ordered another round. Mr Tickle was already struggling to stay awake, but it wasn't long before we were ordered to drink up as we were leaving. Yorkshire Pete was heading home at this point, but he warmly shook our hands and told us that we had done Aldershot proud with our singing.

We left the pub to see Napoleon with four of our party boarding a taxi to take us to Holmfirth, closer to where the majority of people lived. Sleesy, Mr Tickle, Gary and I decided to hail another cab, and instructed the driver to follow Napoleon. The driver told us that he had followed the driver of the other cab a few days ago, and he had taken two and a half hours to get to Manchester airport and back, while our driver proudly told us he had managed the journey in 90 minutes. He said that there was therefore no way he was going to follow him anywhere. We said that this was fine, and we didn't mind if he wanted to follow him from the front, plus there would be the added entertainment of being able to gesticulate at Napoleon as we went by. The only downside of this plan was that our driver didn't know exactly where we were going, but we thought that this was probably a small problem as Holmfirth isn't a particularly big town.

At some point in the day, Napoleon had indiscreetly advised us that he had planned for us to go to a beer festival in a pub called the Nook later in the evening. We felt that, having been drinking since 11.00 in the morning, this wasn't exactly an essential need, and that maybe some food was called for, but you can only ever have one leader.

With a screech of tyres, we overtook Napoleon's taxi quite quickly, and we sat back holding on to whatever handles there were to enjoy what turned out to be a very quick journey to Holmfirth. We found the pub quite easily and bought some further refreshments before taking our seats while we waited for our valiant leader to catch up with us. He duly did and decided that the other bar was more to his taste, but we refused to move. We told Napoleon that we were hungry and he disappeared, reappearing a few minutes later proudly clutching some menus for the Bengal Spice restaurant which was 50 yards around the corner, advising us that he had booked a table for ten minutes time. He told us that we could take our drinks with us to the Bengal Spice and we made our way, slightly unsteadily, up the hill. Of our original 18, we were now down to five, but Napoleon hadn't seemed to notice. These seemed to be acceptable losses on the day.

We ate what was probably the worst curry that any of us had ever had and after settling the bill, Napoleon told us that we had to head back to the Nook for some much-needed refreshment. At this time the four of us mutinied. We flagged down a passing taxi and made our way back to Napoleon's house where we were asleep before he returned some time later.

Aldershot versus Chester

Saturday 26 August 2017

Breakfast was an all-together quieter affair, with Napoleon kindly sharing his 'fresh' French croissants that he had brought back from France a week ago with us.

Gary was writing some notes to go into his blog. "Don't forget to include the suicide whippets," said Sleesy.

"Don't mention the Swedish," said Mr Tickle. "Or Mucky Jane. Or the Swedish for Mucky Jane."

"Don't let Mr Tickle do his seal impression again – even if it is only in your blog," I added.

"Don't forget my interesting fact that, contrary to popular belief, the Great Wall of China can't actually be seen from outer space, but the Sulphur Slag heaps of Kazakhstan can." said Sleesy.

"Are you writing a blog?" asked Napoleon. "How many followers do you have?" Gary proudly said that he had three – his wife, his mother, and me.

We said that we needed to hit the road relatively early in order to get back to Aldershot for 3pm, and ideally to get back to

Aldershot for around 2pm in order to meet Steve from Number 11 in the Victoria before-hand.

We said our goodbyes, shared manly man-hugs, and climbed into the car.

I was very clear with Mr Tickle that he was going to be sitting in the back seat for this journey and after much protestation, he eventually complied. Gary is a much better-behaved co-pilot, and so we headed off. But it wasn't long before Mr Tickle realised that there was a pocket in the back of the seat and there were some neatly folded supermarket carrier bags there. Now we have to pay 5p for a carrier bag it obviously makes sense to have a supply in the car, particularly as the car is the mode of transport which gets you to the supermarket. So, Mr Tickle got all the neatly folded bags out and, much to my irritation, he started playing with them. I generally tend to have about six bags, and I have noticed that if I put them on top of each other, I can fold them in half, and then fold them three times which gives me a nice neat supply of bags to take into the shop with me and this doesn't take up too much room in the car pocket. There was no need for Mr Tickle to unfold them, and I had little confidence that he would fold them back with the same level of neatness.

We reached the M1, and started heading south, but motorway signs told us that we were required to divert to the A1(M). My road atlas is in the back-pocket of the other front seat and Mr Tickle was asked to look at where we were and what the best options where. We soon gave up on this idea. Remarkably for the Managing Director of, admittedly a small company, it would appear that Mr Tickle cannot read a simple road map.

We continued down the A1(M), making good progress which enabled us to make a quick pit stop to use the facilities and for

Gary to grab his regular morning coffee and a small bag of peanuts for a little treat. Mr Tickle, on the other hand, bought himself a three-course meal. He put his coffee on the roof of the car while he thought about how he was going to eat his feast. I was more concerned about how he was going to eat his feast while we were continuing to drive south, cradling a cup of coffee between his knees and a drink of something purple between his feet. This felt like a recipe for a rather messy disaster but Mr Tickle thought he had a neat solution by using all of my carrier bags as table-cloths and rubbish bags. At 5p each, he should really treat them with a little more care and respect. Fortunately, Mr Tickle only comes on our cricket trips every other year. I'm becoming increasingly pleased about this, and in two years' time, it will be his turn to drive, so I can wreck his car.

We did manage to get to Aldershot in time for the kick off, but sadly not in time to join Steve from Number 11 for a pre-match beer.

Aldershot were superb in the first 45 minutes. Chester played deep and didn't venture into the Aldershot half, but it made it hard for us to get past their packed midfield and defence, and eventually we managed to score. Except I missed it due to being interrupted by Sergeant Jason who thought that the moment before Aldershot scored was a good opportunity to say hello to me. I did, however, see us hit the woodwork three times and we had a very good shot which looked to us as if it had bounced off the crossbar into the goal, but it wasn't given. I asked the photographer Eric Marsh, who had a particularly good view, and he thought it hadn't crossed the line, but we still felt hard done by. Missing the goal was preferable to the end of last season when Sergeant Jason came to say hello to me and decided to forcibly handcuff me to a chair in the South Stand bar before the game. With hindsight, I should have asked him to keep me there as it poured with rain and we lost 3-0 against Tranmere Rovers.

It turned out that it was very much a game of two halves and Chester changed their tactics during the break. But, out of nowhere, the referee gave them a penalty from which they scored. This felt a harsh decision and I'm not sure whether the referee had a good sight of any alleged contact or not. Certainly, the linesman did not flag for anything, and he had a much better view.

Unfortunately, this goal gave Chester a bit of confidence and, with this, they started to venture into our half. They had a cross into the penalty area from just in front of us that was several feet off-side but not given, and then a few minutes later exactly the same thing happened from which they scored.

We pushed everyone forward to try and get an equalizer, but every time we got close, the referee found an excuse to blow the whistle and give the advantage back to Chester. A very disappointing end to the game, and a disappointing end to our weekend. I had been hoping that we could get a little revenge on Chester for inflicting an 8-2 thrashing on us a couple of years ago, but we can't win all of the games, and Tickle does seem to be a bit of a jinx whenever he comes.

We've still got a club, a team, and a manager that we can be very proud of.

I was also rather pleased to be able to head home to see my wife and to detox and catch up on some sleep.

Eastleigh versus Aldershot

Monday 28 August 2017

I decided I should give this one a miss. Having spent three days away on a boy's trip, and with football dominating the next three Saturdays, I felt that I should demonstrate that football is not more important than spending time with my wife. Of course, it is very close, but I also needed to edit the 2,500 photographs that I had taken at Wings and Wheels the previous day.

And, if I'm honest, I was not in the greatest mood. As I went to our local supermarket in the morning, I discovered that I only had four carrier bags in my back-seat pocket rather than the customary six, which meant I had to buy another two to fit my shopping in. I've lost count of the number of bags that I've bought since the 5p rule came in and this was a completely unnecessary purchase, solely required because Mr Tickle is a nuisance. On the bright side, I am up to the tune of a notebook, a pen, a few coins and a builder's tape measure, so it's not all bad – except my DIY ability is such that I would not know how to use a builder's tape measure. But I did wonder whether I could cover the cost of the carrier bags through a cheeky e-bay sale...

While it's disappointing that the Vulcan is no longer appearing at Wings and Wheels and the Battle of Britain Memorial Flight and the World War 1 fighters were absent this year, there was still much to get excited about, including a couple of Spitfires, a Hurricane, a P51 Mustang, an ME109 and my personal favourites, the Flying Fortress, the Eurofighter Typhoon and the legendary Red Arrows.

And listening to the cricket in one ear, and the football commentary in the other, I settled down for a tense afternoon. Steve from Number 11 had texted me to say that he had had to sit in their new stand, and he caught up with Heather who we met at Maidstone.

The commentator was telling us that Eastleigh had scored 7 points at home from their opening three games, which were against Sutton, Tranmere and Dagenham. We were going to have to be on form today, and Eastleigh are always one of our bogey teams, so my fingers had to be firmly crossed.

The game got off to a slow start, and the highlight seemed to be Steve from Number 11's Kit-Kat melting in the heat. However, all of this changed with Manny Oyeleke twisting his knee on their dreadful pitch, and then Kodi Lyons-Foster, making his debut for the Shots, receiving a straight red for allegedly diving in with his studs up on one of the Eastleigh players. Rob Shot and Tim Sills on the radio said they thought it should have been a yellow card, and they said it was not too dissimilar to the tackle that Craig McAllister had made on Kodi earlier in the game. For some reason, we didn't seem to be getting the rub of the green this season.

BBC Radio Surrey coverage was intermittent and at one stage I was forced to listen to BBC Solent where the summariser was Wayne Shaw, who gained notoriety for his pie eating during Sutton's Cup match against Arsenal last year. Mr Shaw was quite difficult to listen to, and I found his calling the commentator 'mate' in every contribution that he made really irritating. Tim Sills, Rob's co-commentator on Radio Surrey, on the other hand was brilliant. Tim is rightly a Shots legend, having scored 51 goals in 126 appearances for the Shots between 2003 and 2006. Most memories of Tim involve goals from unstoppable bullet headers. A wonderful player for the Shots, and a great co-commentator. I look forward to listening to him the next time I can't make a game.

Nick Arnold was taken off on a stretcher after 70 minutes which continued to add to our injury problems and then Scott Rendell was fouled and, unsurprisingly, the referee gave Eastleigh a free kick. In the circumstances, I guess it's a point gained, and again, we can remind ourselves that life would be much worse if we supported Eastleigh.

Well done to man of the match Callum Reynolds who put in a performance comparable to Super Ray Warburton according to some, and who received a very rare accolade of 10/10 from Dr Jim Royle.

'Super Ray' only played for the Shots for a couple of years, from 2003 to 2005, when he was at the end of his career, but he was immense, and is remembered as another legendary former player. Not only did he lead by example, he was one of the few senior players that I can recall who was able to 'coach' the more junior players in real time during matches, and was in many respects, very similar to John Terry.

Well done to all the players, and to the 542 Shots fans that made the short trip. Only another 1,800 photos to go....

Aldershot versus Sol-Lee-Hull Moors

Saturday 2 September 2017

Unfortunately, Steve from Number 11 wasn't allowed out this afternoon. His wife, Kerry, had decided that a BBQ with the families who went to their antenatal group some ten years ago was more important.

He asked my advice as to whether this was potential grounds for divorce. I'm not sure it is, but it feels like grounds for a bit of an argument at the very least, knowing that he holds a little bit of the moral high ground (we both know from bitter experience that holding the moral high ground is an unusual feeling, and while it's nice while it lasts, it's guaranteed not to last for very long). Steve from Number 11 did sound slightly irritated so I thought I could console him, knowing that there is another home game next Saturday followed by our planned trip to Ebbsfleet the Tuesday after. Steve replied saying he needed to think about how and when he was going to break this news to his wife, which reminded me, that I needed to do the same.

Steve from Number 11 wanted to hold a wildcat strike (in the style of Arthur Scargill). Given the deeds of the houses in our estate prevents us from having for sale boards and caravans, I think it is unlikely we will be allowed to have a burning oil drum at the entrance to our close, and while legislation allows for up to six pickets, it's pretty clear that it would only be Steve and myself.

And only then if we're allowed to.

I pointed out that my life coach and mentor, Big Al, did have a saying that "you needed to fight fire with napalm".

I've only needed my life coach and mentor a couple of times. The most memorable was when I had arranged to meet some friends for a pre-match beer in the Crimea some time ago. At the last minute, Matt said he wanted to come to the game. Deep down, I knew that my wife would expect me to arrange to meet my friends inside the ground, but I thought that given the lad was 7, it would be good for his development to mix with other adults, and that he would be fine.

A week or so later when, co-incidentally, I was on the phone to Big Al, I received a text from my wife asking me why I had taken our son to the pub and asking why I had told him to keep quiet about it. He's a clever lad and he realised that Mum probably wouldn't approve of him visiting the pub, all by himself. However, asking a 7-year-old to take the blame for going into the pub in the first place would be more difficult to get an acquittal from. Big Al came up trumps, by suggesting that I replied with "what would you rather I had done, you silly woman? Leave him outside on the pavement? He's only 7 for goodness sake!" Fortunately, she saw that this was intended as a slightly humorous response, and immediately replied asking if I was talking to Big Al. His reputation is as large as he is.

I noticed on the Shots' chat room in the morning that Shots fan Tim Perei, died last week. Tim was one of the colourful characters on the Slab, regularly sporting a wide brimmed

Middlesex Cricket Club sun hat and what looked suspiciously like golf shoes. He often stood in the middle of the Slab with one or two of his pals, but if they weren't at the game, he was very happy to chat to anyone, and share his views on the game and the officials. Tim had only recently turned 50. A terrible shame to lose another Shots fan at such a young age. Rest in peace, Tim.

Before leaving home, James and I watched the first half of Billericay against Didcot. We were cheering on Didcot, but alas it wasn't to be. Glen Tamplin seems to be quite a colourful chap who is desperate to make a name for himself. Four ex-Premiershit players playing for a team in the Ryman Premier is quite unusual. I hope Mr Tamplin has some very deep pockets, because if his wage bill really is the reported £35,000 a week, he needs to know that it is going to need to be a lot bigger if and when Billericay get promoted. In the meantime, it will make them disliked by fans of many other clubs. Most genuine football fans really don't like hobby clubs.

I did smile when I read that Mr Tamplin had ordered a new Ferrari which he was having painted in Billericay colours. My friend Bill used to have a Mark 3 Cortina. There were a few rust patches around the wheel arches so he got a small tin of paint and wrote Aldershot slogans over the rust. Not sure this would look quite so good on a new Ferrari but we thought Bill's Cortina looked pretty cool. Mind you, I had a bright orange Talbot Sunbeam at the time, so pretty much anything else would have looked impressive. Well, maybe except for an Austin Allegro.

Although we wanted Billericay to lose, this was never likely to happen given the financial gulf between the two clubs, but it was nice to see Jake Robinson score a hat-trick for Billericay. Jake played for the Shots on loan from Brighton back in 2005 and scored four goals in ten league games. He returned when he was released by Brighton in 2009 and scored four in 19. Not a big return, but a fabulous player who could also create opportunities for other players. We thought he would go on to bigger and better things, but he played for Shrewsbury Town, Torquay and Northampton in League Two before dropping back into the Conference for a handful of games with Luton in 2012/13 and then Conference South for a couple of seasons with Whitehawk where he scored 38 goals in 90 games before taking what is, presumably, a big money move to Billericay.

And so, after the warm up act, it was off to Aldershot, and we arrived on the Slab at eight minutes to three. James thinks that we should aim to get there for about 30 seconds before kick-off and doesn't like my preference for getting there early in time for a pre-match beer. He's off to university at the end of this month, and he doesn't like beer. I'm not sure how he is going to make any friends but I'm sure he will work something out. Every game we go to together, we have a battle of wills to see how late we can leave it and he was happy with arriving eight minutes early today. The Slab was pretty empty.

The Shots are currently having a major injury crisis – we were only able to name four substitutes for the game today. Two of these were loanees who joined from Ipswich during the week on one month 'emergency' loans and two were members of the youth team who hadn't played a game before.

We were having our own injury crisis on the Slab. Andy told me that Bill from the Midlands had pulled some ligaments playing football. One would have thought he would have stopped such exercise many moons ago, but seemingly not. And seemingly this injury was enough to prevent him driving down to the game.

Charlie was also absent for the second consecutive game. He had previously been talking about taking a holiday with his brother in Ireland but his brother had broken a rib and they had been forced to postpone it. Hopefully his brother was feeling better and they had gone to Ireland and there's nothing else we need to worry about. The Union of Referees were on the Slab today, and that's always a mixed blessing. Whilst it's nice to see them, and good to have an expert view on contentious moments in the game, all referees seem to be part of the same masonic lodge and, shouting abuse or questioning any decisions by the referee is very much frowned on. Charlie and I both got a sound telling off towards the end of last season for questioning a decision which we were told was entirely consistent with some rule or other.

Given the number of players out injured, the Shots played magnificently. Callum Reynolds was again superb in marshalling the defence, and Bobby-Joe Taylor didn't stop running at the Solihull defenders and caused them no end of trouble. Our goal came from a beautiful move, when BJT took a short corner and played a neat one-two with James Rowe before putting a pinpoint cross towards Shamir Fenelon. Sadly, Shamir pulled his hamstring as he scored, and had to go off injured in only the 10th minute. Besides a couple of spells when Solihull exerted some pressure, it was mainly the Shots in dominant form all afternoon, and had we been able to get the ball on target then we might have been able to rack up another six goals. I'd sent Steve from Number 11 a total of 40 texts during the game which is testament to a very good game of football.

Aldershot versus Dover

Saturday 9 September 2017

I was talking to Dominic in the office earlier in the week to congratulate him on Hereford's 8-0 demolition of Godalming in the FA Cup. Dominic was disappointed that he'd had to miss the game but was keenly looking forward to seeing who Hereford had drawn in the next round.

We noticed that there is a club called FC Romania who have been drawn against the winners of Maldon and Tiptree and Hayes and Yeading in the Second Qualifying Round of the FA Cup. It took us a while to work out whether FC Romania were playing the winners of Maldon and Tiptree against Hayes and Yeading, or whether they were going to be playing the winners of Maldon versus Tiptree who were then going to be playing the winners of Hayes versus Yeading, but we soon resolved this and started researching a Hertfordshire club called FC Romania.

They were started about ten years ago, and, unsurprisingly, with the exception of the Club Secretary, their Board of Directors and all their players are Romanian. Who knew?

I first came across Dover back in 1996 when we drew them in the Second Qualifying Round of the FA Cup. My wife and I were living in Maidstone at the time, and this was going to be a relatively local game for me to get to - except she had booked us into the Registry Office to get married on the same day. After huffing and puffing for a few minutes, my then fiancée suggested that I could still go to the football in the afternoon after the wedding ceremony in the morning. Being the fool that I am, I believed that she was making a genuine offer, but clearly this was never going to happen, and indeed it didn't. And we lost.

I have to admit that Dover is one of those teams I don't really like. In part, this is because my experiences of visiting their ground have not been very positive, but also because they always seem to play a particularly boring style of football. I recall the game at Aldershot towards the end of last season when they were trying to consolidate their position in the play-offs. They came with 10 defenders and their sole purpose was kicking the ball to Ricky Miller up front whenever they could. There was no style and no finesse, and no real attempt to play football. I can understand this level of defensiveness for a team that is at the bottom of the league, hoping for damage limitation when they're playing away to a team at the top of the league but, surely, if you have ambitions for getting into the play-offs and potentially promotion, you really should be a bit more ambitious., Even their fans were hugely critical as losing against us was key to them not making the play-offs.

Unfortunately, our injury crisis was worsening, and Bobby-Joe Taylor was going to miss today's game after turning his ankle getting out of his car. Picking up an injury getting out of your car has to be one of the more unusual ways of picking up an injury, but maybe not the most. Shots legend Darren Barnard tore his knee ligament and was side-lined for five months in his Barnsley days after he slipped in a puddle of his puppy's wee on the kitchen floor, but even that is not as odd as Rio Ferdinand picking up a tendon strain in his Leeds days whilst he was watching the TV. Knee strains seem quite popular injuries amongst footballers. I remember hearing that the Aston Villa full back Alan Wright once strained his knee by stretching to reach the accelerator in his new Ferrari. Having said that, I think it is probably unlikely that Bobby-Joe's injury was connected to a Ferrari.

I was going to suggest to Steve from Number 11 that he bring his football boots with him. Obviously, Charlie wouldn't be allowed to take his zimmer frame onto the pitch and Gary wouldn't get very far with his walking stick. Steve from Number 11 is a good ten years younger than me and he goes jogging, so I assume he is slightly fitter than me too. We were having a chat in the pub before the game and Steve from Number 11 admitted that he was just getting over a hamstring injury and his knee was now hurting. I don't think he has a Ferrari either. Hopefully there would be someone else in the crowd who could play if needed because the Slab injury crisis is really beginning to mirror that of the team.

It was nice to see Charlie back on the Slab, and reassuringly any concerns about his health and well-being were misplaced as he had indeed been on holiday with his brother in Ireland over the previous two weeks.

Today Dover came with a game plan. They played deep and let us boss the midfield and they hardly ventured into our half in the first thirty minutes. We totally dominated and played some pretty football, but we couldn't break through their defence. Dover then caught us on the break, and we went in at half-time a goal behind. Similar to last season, but with no Ricky Miller capable of scoring 40 goals a season, they had two strikers, something which provided them with more options, and while they were still trying to catch us on the break, they had players who looked fast and interested.

It was also seemed that Cheye was injured for the majority of the second half, and we looked very vulnerable on the quarter of the pitch in front of the Slab where Dover were attacking the High Street End, which is indeed where their second goal came from.

Our game relies on our pace and solid, accurate passing between the players but today we had very few options with Shamir Fenelon, Bernard Mensah and Bobby-Joe Taylor injured, and James Rowe closed down very quickly. We tried hard and we didn't give up. Each man put in a huge shift, but too many players were missing and too many players were carrying injuries which meant that we were exposed, and with our lack of creativity…well, let's just say that it wasn't one of our better days.

I'd have given the man of the match award to Jim Kellerman who had another fabulous game. He was everywhere trying to make something happen, but it wasn't to be our day and we didn't do enough to test their goal-keeper.

I did suggest at the beginning of the game that we were going to lose because the match sponsor was a local vicar. While I have nothing against vicars per se, I still vividly recall the awful season that we suffered after the Dalai Lama blessed our pitch. We finished bottom of the league and were relegated from League Two so maybe religion is best kept away from the Recreation Ground. Aldershot Town FC is our own religion, and everyone knows you can't follow two.

So, we went home disappointed and, I have to say, rather soggy, following some rather inclement weather but knowing we have the chance to put things right on Tuesday when we travel to Ebbsfleet.

Ebbsfleet versus Aldershot

Tuesday 12 September 2017

'Webbed feet' were promoted to the Conference National League last season but we have some history with them in previous years. Before changing their name in 2007, they were known as Gravesend and Northfleet. Maybe Ebbsfleet does sound better to some, but I can't help thinking it sounds dull, modern and bereft of tradition.

They beat us in the semi-final of the FA Trophy in the year we got promoted (2007/2008). I recall going to the first leg away where we lost 3-1. We were so good that season that at the time it didn't seem to matter. We were confident that we could over-turn this in the second leg. We were 1-0 up and bombarding their goal but they caught us on the break and scored an equaliser in the 90th minute. It wasn't to be, but at the beginning of the season I'd have happily settled for League Champions and the League Cup, snappily called the 'Setanta Shield'. Expecting a Wembley appearance and the FA Trophy on top would have been plain greedy.

We played them away a short while later and drew 2-2 at their ground in the league, but I don't think we've played them since, so a little bit of payback is called for. But then again, we said that about Chester.

Ebbsfleet also gained a degree of national press attention at this time when they were owned by the web-based venture 'MyFootballClub'. For £35 a year, fans could buy a share in the club and have the opportunity to vote on player transfers, budgets and ticket prices among other things. This was quite popular in the first year with 32,000 members joining the scheme, but only 9,000 renewed and by 2013 the idea had been abandoned and replaced with Kuwaiti investment. I felt for their manager, Liam Diash, at the time. There was no real animosity between the Shots and Gravesend. I had admired some of their players and we often had pretty good games between our sides. Until they knocked us out of the FA Trophy that is. It's tough to get knocked out in the semi-finals of a cup competition where the final is played at Wembley. Normally we don't know about this as we generally get knocked out in the first or second round, but to get so close and miss out at the last moment isn't great. Although, I have to say it is still far better than not getting to the semi-finals in the first place. And losing in the final isn't all that much either, to be honest.

Either way, Steve from Number 11 and I were keen to go, and I left work early to pick him up before we headed east. We had a pleasant journey with very little traffic on the roads which meant that we arrived and parked up in Ebbsfleet International Railway Station (Car Park C) shortly after 5.00. This meant we had more time than usual to enjoy any pre-match entertainment that we could find.

The Ebbsfleet bar was not due to open until 7.00 which took us by surprise, but we saw a couple of other Shots fans who advised us that they were heading to the George and Dragon to the left of the ground, and we started to follow. Steve from Number 11 thought it advisable to ask a Steward for confirmation of our directions, and one told us that the pub we were heading to was a very long way up a steep hill and that we would be better off heading for the Rose and Crown which was in the other direction. We retraced our steps and sought confirmation from another Steward at the other end of the Ground. "Where's the nearest pub?" We asked? "Turn around and go back the way you've come. The George and Dragon is only five minutes over the bridge."

With this indecision over, we strode purposefully over the bridge to find the George and Dragon a five-minute walk over it, which, while it did have a bit of an incline, could not really be described as a 'very steep hill.' We entered to find a number of Shots fans already in situ, and Steve from Number 11 ordered us refreshments and a couple of extraordinarily large pork pies. I like a pork pie, but these were each big enough to feed a family of four for their Sunday lunch and I'm not sure we really needed one each.

As I sat down next to Howard and Sara I noticed that many others were tucking into a box of fish and chips which they had presumably picked up at the fish and chip shop next door and brought with them. Now that really would have hit the spot. I first met Howard and Sara at an away match at Port Vale in our relegation season from League Two. I'd had (on this occasion, totally co-incidentally) a meeting in Stoke the next day which had been in my diary before our game was re-arranged. The footballing gods were smiling down on me and I was able to leave the office at lunch-time on the day of the match, which meant that my colleague Andy and I were in the pub in Port Vale shortly after 4.00. Spending three and a half hours in a pub before a game when your able to claim costs on expenses is a long time and, consequently, we had a wonderful afternoon. Some 160 Shots fans made the trip and we were greeted in a similar fashion to that described by Tony Hawks as he travelled across Ireland with his fridge.

"Where are you in the league?"

"Bottom."

"How many games are left this season?"

"Not very many."

"Have you any chance of avoiding relegation?"

"Not really."

"And you've travelled over 200 miles on a school night to watch your team?"

"Yes."

"Idiot. But you have my total respect and I would like to buy you a beer."

"Well, thank you very much."

All of this had worked well as we were staying overnight - we had a great time, and even managed to come away with what had seemed, before the game, an unlikely point.

Back at Ebbsfleet, I ordered another round of drinks and we reminisced about the Port Vale game.

Howard showed us his lucky bobble hat and recounted the story that he was given it in January 1979 in time for him to wear to the FA Cup 5th round replay against Shrewsbury. This was slightly before my time supporting the Shots but I am well versed in the story, where John Dungworth scored in the 89th minute to put the Shots 2-1 ahead, only for Shrewsbury to lob Glen Johnson a minute later to take the game to a replay. We lost the replay 3-1 after extra time, having been 1-0 up for most of the game.

Howard didn't want to talk about the game, but he was very keen to share the story of his hat with us, and while most of us would admit to having some lucky superstitions, wearing the same 'lucky hat' for nearly 40 years – without washing it – will, I'm sure take some beating.

After a while, the Shots fans at the next table started laughing in our direction. It took us a few moments to wonder why. Then we noticed a plaque in our corner of the pub right above Howards head, which read 'bullshit corner.' Slightly harsh, I thought, but based on the conversations that we had been having, not altogether unfair.

Suitably refreshed, we made our way to the ground and took our places on the terraces. A few minutes before kick-off, Terry arrived. Terry has been a good friend of mine for many years, and we used to be very close. The last time I saw Terry was at Bill's funeral at the end of last year so this was a slightly bittersweet meeting, but we do try and make a particular effort to keep in touch and football matches are a wonderful way of doing so. It was lovely to see him again. These days he lives in Erith or Belvedere or some other part of East London/North Kent. I'm not entirely sure exactly where as it all looks the same to me, but it is very close to Ebbsfleet.

Being a local, Terry didn't need to refer to a Sat Nav or read a map as, obviously, he knew where he was going. I received a text from him saying he was lost, and I advised him to head for Ebbsfleet International Railway Station (Car Park C) from where we knew it was only a short walk.

Terry just knew that Ebbsfleet was in the wrong direction and had chosen to head for Gravesend and/or Northfleet instead. The consequence of this local knowledge was that it took Terry two and a half hours to drive about five miles and he missed the pre-match beer and bullshit. But he did arrive in time to take his place on the terraces to see the teams come out, and to applaud our players. Ebbsfleet was, before the game, one of only two teams in our league who were unbeaten for the season, and we knew it would be a tough game – particularly given how depleted our squad was.

But, as you always hope with a team prepared by Sir Gary, we came out fighting, trying to take the game to Ebbsfleet. This tactic worked, with our taking the lead through James Rowe after quarter of an hour. This woke Ebbsfleet up, and for the remainder of the half they came onto us very strongly. We felt that we had done particularly well (and, it has to be said, been particularly lucky) to reach half-time without conceding, and the Ebbsfleet pressure continued in the second half.

A second goal for the Shots from Scott Rendell helped ease our anxiety and we managed to retain this lead until the final whistle. The Ebbsfleet pitch had been a good one which had suited our style of play and, although the weather was particularly wet and windy, we were delighted with the final score and the way the team had played. The inclement weather didn't bother us in the slightest as we squelched back to Ebbsfleet International Railway Station (Car Park C).

We were slightly troubled by the signs on the M25 as we returned, advising us that the A3 was closed, the M3 was closed, and that the M25 was going to close within a couple of miles, but much to our relief these all proved erroneous and I arrived back home at the expected time.

Bill was always quite proud of these signs. As a man who had spent much of his working life designing and building roads, road systems, pedestrian refuges, traffic lighting arrangements and car parks, he often said that these signs made a huge difference to the travelling public. We disagreed. Far too often, the signs did not contain enough information. Bill, Gary and I were heading to an away match a number of years ago, and a huge electronic sign read 'Accident ahead. Lane closed.' This sign was of no use whatsoever to humankind as it didn't tell us which lane was closed, and therefore gave us no hints as to whether we needed to be in the inside or outside lane. This was particularly irritating as we were turning off at the next junction and it gave us no clues as to whether it was before or after the junction. So, we had to make a guess, as, I'm sure many other drivers did, and it just caused more chaos than would have existed without the sign.

Gateshead versus Aldershot

Saturday 16 September 2017

I'd tried really hard to arrange a meeting at our Newcastle office, and had managed to come up with a brilliant reason to do so. Unfortunately, the people I wanted to meet weren't available on Friday, but the excuse I came up with was so compelling that they insisted that I travelled up on Thursday. Damn! I was sorely tempted to stay over until Saturday, but I was conscious that I have been out quite a bit of late, and I'd just booked tickets to a number of gigs over the next couple of months, and I didn't want to test Mrs C's patience. So instead, I busied myself with lots of useful jobs so that I'd have some credit in the bank, going into the next few games.

I texted Steve from Number 11 just before the game to say that we should have gone and, while he agreed with me, he did say it would be one heck of a long journey home if we had lost. Similar to Middlesboro, I thought, not wanting too many reminders of that journey. Given the first chapter of this book is largely about Steve from Number 11, I had thought that I should share it with him to check that he was comfortable with appearing in print. He said he was, and he added that he thought it read well. I asked him to think about who he would want to play him once I had sold the screen rights, but he seemed to be more concerned about whether the chap from number 11 was going to make it through the whole season in one piece. I did tell him that I was more concerned about the chap from number 11's wife making it through the season in one piece, particularly on the evidence of prioritising meeting the people on her NCT class from ten years ago over a home match. Steve from Number 11 replied, saying that once they had finished their extension, the patio was next on his list, and he agreed that she should be more concerned than she currently seems to be.

He had decided that Michael Douglas should be booked to play him. I'm not so sure about this, because even though Michael Douglas looks very good for his age, at 73 he is nearly twice as old as Steve from Number 11 and not quite so nondescript. I can't help wonder if Steve from Number 11 was actually looking forward to the obligatory sex scenes and had decided that these should be with Catherine Zeta Jones.

We were both agreed that Steve Buscemi was a perfect match for Gary and when I asked my wife, she couldn't decide whether Noel Edmonds, Julian Assange or Richard Branson should play me. I should be grateful, I suppose, that she said Noel Edmonds rather than Mr Blobby, but I did take this opportunity to ask her who she thought should play her. Of all the options that my wife might have come up, I wasn't expecting to hear her utter the words 'Catherine' or 'Zeta' or 'Jones'. I need to think through whether this is just one of those extraordinary coincidences. Or whether she's trying to tell me something…

I managed to listen to some of the game on the radio between jobs, and it sounded like it was fairly dull. I had to go for an eye test towards the end of the second half where I had a surprising conversation with the Woeking supporting optician who tried to convert me to Islam. I told him that I didn't need religion in my life as I had football, and he confessed that his main affiliation was to ManUre.

The conversation was not going well, and I was slightly concerned at the amount of time that he was shining his torch into my eyes. I told him I couldn't see and he tried to reassure me that my vision would return in a few minutes. Fortunately, it did, and I was able to see the text from Steve from Number 11 confirming Fabien Robert had scored, that we had won the game 1-0 and that we were sitting back on the top of the league.

As I exited the optician's, I found myself in the off licence next door. I said to Tim in the off-licence that I was having my eyes tested, and he told me that I should have gone to Specsavers as I was in the wrong shop. I exited with four pints of Moondance that had been delivered from the brewery that very morning and looked forward to celebrating our first ever win at Gateshead.

Aldershot versus Leyton Orient

Saturday 23 September 2017

It seems that Leyton Orient's favourite chant is "You're so quiet you could be Aldershot," which was potentially a jolly good reason for us to want them to be heavily beaten this weekend. According to the wise men on the Shots chat room this stemmed from a game in the 1980s where a tube strike limited the number of Shots fans travelling to the game. Or at least that is the rumour – I remember going on an official Ian Read outing to Mansfield once for a league game. There were too few fans for a bus, and we travelled together on the train to Nottingham, and then caught the bus to Mansfield, so the truth could be that we just didn't have a big away support back in those days. Either way, I fully intended to do my best to raise the volume from the Slab, and I was hoping my fellow fans will follow suit.

Mrs C and I had a very pleasant lunch with James before the game. He's settling into life at university well and although it has only been a week, it was nice to see him. I gave him my very best parental advice and told him to keep well clear of the Swindon fans on his corridor, and he promised me (again) that he won't switch his allegiance to the local plastic club.

I've been to Swindon a few times. The most memorable was in the Freight Rover Trophy in around 1984. We were two down before their goalkeeper came out of his area and rugby tackled our striker to earn himself a red card. From 2-0 down, we came back to win 3-2 much to the disgust of the locals who wanted to take their disappointment out on us visiting supporters. My friend Little Sue and I were sitting in her car waiting to exit the car park when it dawned on us that some local yobs had worked out that her car was from Aldershot and were about to try and over-turn it. I was of no use to anyone in the situation, but Sue bravely got out of the car and raised herself to her full four foot ten inches tall, before showing her shiny new Jimmy Connors metal tennis racquet to the yobs and asking them if they were brave enough to take her on. They soon scarpered and I thanked Sue for saving my life.

Mrs C has always been a big tennis fan, but she had gone down the John McEnroe route when metal framed tennis rackets first came out. I'm sure that a McEnroe racquet could be equally threatening in the right hands and I am equally sure that my wife has the right hands. The price for having lunch with her son was that she had to find her own way home from the pub as James and I had a football match to get to. We arrived in Aldershot in good time and walked towards the ground.

Rather unexpectedly, as a car passed James and I, we heard the driver shout out "Fuck you Aldershot Up The Orient." We were sufficiently alert to be able to offer synchronised gestures to the driver in a lovely moment of father and son bonding, but it did make me wonder if any punctuation had been intended, as this obviously, could make a significant difference to the intent behind the statement.

I went into the club shop before the game and saw someone I recognised. It took me a while to realise it was Barry from the Easy Riders and I had to ask him what he was doing at

Aldershot. He confessed to being an Orient fan. Oh, dear. The incident with the car had done nothing to improve my opinion of Orient fans, and we took our places on the Slab waiting for the game to start. Given how big a club Orient believe they are, their away support of a little over 500 was slightly disappointing given it's not that far away. Tranmere Rovers managed more than that, and Liverpool is quite a trek from Aldershot. We'll have to wait and see if we take more than they brought, but I suspect that we will take around 1,000, which surely means that we are twice as big a club as they are. Obviously.

For the first half an hour we were immense, playing some of the best football I can recall. We raced into a two-goal lead courtesy of Cheye Alexander and Matt McClure - both wonderfully struck goals from the edge of the penalty area. But as with all things Aldershot we struggled to maintain this dominance and Orient got back into the game with a goal in front of the East Bank which looked as if we could have done better to prevent. This brought a frantic last ten minutes to the first half and we could have conceded again except for Jake Cole producing a wonder save after an Orient shot bounced off the woodwork.

We endured a very tense second half which would have been more bearable had Jim Kellerman been able to direct his header from Cheye's cross into the net rather than just over the top. At 3-1, I would have fancied us to get the three points, but as it happened, Orient kept on coming, and eventually got an equaliser. It's hard to say it wasn't deserved, but a point is a point, and the East Bank was magnificent. Not much noise from the Orient contingent but, to be fair, until they scored, they didn't have very much to sing about. My favourite moment was when the Shots fans started singing "You're so quiet you could be Aldershot." I'm sure that even Orient fans would have understood the irony.

Macclesfield versus Aldershot

Saturday 30 September 2017

Mrs C had bought tickets for us to go to see Boudicca at the Globe on the South Bank in London today which meant that I couldn't travel to Macclesfield. I have a few friends in Cheshire, and this fixture always strikes me as a good one to go to, to visit them and keep in touch. But it was time to spend a day out in London with my wife, and I was hugely looking forward to it. It did occur to me though, that given it was an afternoon performance, it would be taking place at the same time as the match, and I knew she would frown upon me checking my phone every two or three minutes.

We had to rush to the Globe, thanks to the inability of South West Trains to maintain a regular service over the weekend, or to communicate to potential passengers that a journey which would normally take around 35 minutes from Guildford was going to take closer to 80 minutes. With time to kill sitting on a stationary train, I noticed on Twitter that the Eastleigh versus Chester game had been called off less than two hours before kick-off. I really felt for the Chester fans who had reached the south of Hampshire before finding this out. Given the millions of pounds that Eastleigh have spent sacking managers and recruiting players on big contracts, it's not too much to expect that they had spent some on their pitch. If there was any justice, Eastleigh would be given a huge fine, much of which would be given to the Chester fans who had a wasted day and Chester would be awarded the three points. Sadly, this is unlikely to happen, but it doesn't do anything to make fans of other clubs warm to Eastleigh.

After running from Waterloo along the South Bank, we missed the first ten minutes of the play, but we were comforted with the knowledge that it wasn't going to be called off. We raced up to our seats on the very top floor of the Globe, and I immediately shuddered as I saw the sheer forty-foot drop that was in front of us. I tried to mask my fear but it was no good. I had to ask the other people sitting on our bench to swap seats, so I could sit on the end and turn sideways on to avoid looking down. It was my fear of heights that put paid to my mountaineering career and stopped any thoughts I had of climbing Mount Everest. If I'm a gibbering wreck with a forty-foot drop, I'd hate to think what I would be like with a 10,000-foot mountain range falling away beneath me.

The play was utterly engrossing, although I noticed that it was just gone 3 o'clock when the first half finished, and the interval begun. I looked at my phone and much to my disappointment, I noticed that we had conceded after 23 seconds of play. Statto told us that this was the fastest goal that we had ever conceded, but that didn't help. As all Shots fans know, Albert Munday scored the fastest goal for us against Hartlepool after only six seconds in 1958 – a record that stood until recently, but even that's scant consolation, and indeed, of very little relevance. I was glued to my phone for the next 15 minutes waiting for us to equalise, as surely, we would, but I had to switch it off when the play re-started.

Statto (Pete) and I used to watch games together when we were much younger. I vividly recall one game, when we were standing on the East Bank and he pointed to Jimmy Hill standing behind the goal at the High Street End. I walked to the other end of the ground and, sure enough, it was Jimmy Hill, who politely autographed my programme. On my way back to the East Bank, I bumped into Arthur English, our club president who also very kindly signed my programme. I excitedly showed Pete both signatures when I got back, and he thought I might want to add George Wood, the then Arsenal goalkeeper, to my collection. I didn't have a clue who he was, but Pete pointed him out to me. I asked him if he was George Wood and, after nodding, he signed my programme with that name, so I had to assume Pete knew who it was. I did draw the line at asking for the signature of the next 'star' that Pete pointed out – the librarian from Bordon Library who had won the semi-final of Mastermind in the last week. I guess this is why Pete is now the official statistician and is able to comment authoritatively on the fastest goal that we've ever conceded.

The cast of Boudicca included the beautiful and wonderfully talented Gina McKee, and her performance succeeded in taking my mind off the game. The time flew by, and before I knew it, we were singing along to an unexpected finale, of "I fought the Law, and the Law won", written by the Clash, and the actors took a well-deserved and loudly cheered bow. I snuck a look at the phone to see that there had indeed been another goal, but it had been conceded rather than scored by the Shots. 2-0 down with 30 minutes to play, and I sensed from the comments on Twitter and the chat room that it was not going to be our day. Not only did we lose but we also dropped from second in the league to eighth, which shows you just how tight it is at the top. Sir Gary didn't sound very happy with his post-match comments, but, you know what? It's all okay. We had a really exciting team and a manager who wants us to play good football.

Nick Cansfield

As Shots fans, we can't ask for too much more. It was nice to see Shamir Fenelon and Will Evans get a little game time as they recovered from their injuries, and let's hope Billy-Joe Taylor and Bernard Mensah follow soon as they do give us some real attacking options.

Aldershot versus Dagenham

Tuesday 3 October 2017

I'd got a runny nose and a terrible headache. I'd been coughing and sneezing since yesterday morning, but I refused to accept or acknowledge that I had a cold, because if I did, it would mean that I wouldn't go to the football tonight. Deep down, I knew that I should have a Lemsip and take advantage of an early night, but we had Dagenham at home, and it felt like a long time since I'd been to a match. I think I might have irritated my colleagues by going into work and spreading my germs. I'm not entirely sure that any of them believed that I haven't got a cold, but a couple of others were feeling slightly unwell, so I can try and shift the blame onto them.

With Gary trying to find his way back to England from yet another holiday in France, I met Steve from Number 11 in the Vic for a pre-match beverage. We popped into the shop to collect the tickets I had ordered for Saturday's away match at Maidenhead and took our usual places on the Slab. I introduced myself and exchanged names with Dave, a regular on the Slab, who I had stood with for many years, but whose name I didn't know. I've never been very good with names and faces, and I may end up asking Dave his name again just to be sure, but I do feel the need to get better at names these days.

This stemmed from a rather embarrassing incident a number of years ago when I was in my office. The photocopier had broken down and the engineer was fixing it. He came over to my desk, noticed my Shots clock on the wall and tried to engage me in a conversation. In my defence (and this is the only defence I can come up), I was busy, and not paying attention, but after he had tried talking to me a few times and was clearly making no progress, he introduced himself to me as Alan. Unfortunately, this didn't help me very much, and he mouthed a number of choice words before telling me that I had stood next to him on the Slab for the previous 25 years. Since then, I've tried a little harder to find out what people are called.

There was a slightly weird feel about this evening. The crowd was low, and the floodlights seemed quite dim, but the players came out and the game kicked off. We didn't do anything wrong in the first half, but it was a difficult game to get into. In the absence of Bernard Mensah, Bobby-Joe Taylor and James Rowe we didn't have our customary pace, energy and excitement going forward, and we played a far more pedestrian game. If this was a deliberate tactic, it clearly worked as Dagenham were subdued during the first half and we were easily the better side. There were only two shots during this half…which probably said it all. Adam McDonnell scored to put us in front, and a brilliant turn and shot (I missed who it was) flew agonisingly over the top of the crossbar which could have doubled the lead.

The second half continued in much the same fashion, but everything changed on 60 minutes when Jakey Gallagher was shown a straight red card for a lunging challenge on one of the Dagenham players. The Union of Referees were in full force on the terrace which, with Steve from Number 11, gave us a total of four qualified referees to canvas for an opinion. The consensus was that the tackle was probably somewhere between a yellow card and a red card, so I guess we can't have too many complaints. Looking at it on video after the game, it was clearly worthy of a very, very, very, red card, if not worthy of a police caution! However, two things happened after this decision - Dagenham started to show a little more intent, and the referee stopped pretending he was neutral and declared his affiliation with the away team. Some terrible decisions followed, but the Shots could have no complaints about the Dagenham goal, scored in the 85th minute by Sam Ling.

And so, we had to suffer another disappointing result. I'm not sure whether it was because I was struggling with manflu, or not, but everything seemed quiet and subdued, with the single exception of the East Bank, who were magnificent and didn't stop singing their hearts out, encouraging the team for the full 90 minutes.

Maidenhead versus Aldershot

Saturday 7 October 2017

James had asked me to get him a ticket to the game. I was quite pleased about this as I hadn't seen him for three weeks, which is probably the longest time since his birth 19 years ago. Bizarrely, when I asked him if he would like me to buy him a decent lunch, he declined, and said he would rather go straight to the ground. Now, I know that going to the pub with your father isn't always the coolest way to go, but if your father is paying, and you're a broke student, then what's not to like? But it's okay - Steve from Number 11 and I went to the pub before we picked him from Reading.

After picking up Son number two, we headed to Maidenhead, picking up Little Sue, the Jimmy Connors fan, on the way. Little Sue and I used to sell programmes together during the eighties and travelled to many away games together at that time, including most memorably the play-off final at Wolves in 1987. This was the very first year that the play-offs had been held and no one really knew what to expect. One thing that was for certain though, no one expected little Aldershot to be playing Wolves to decide who was to be promoted to Division Three. We had lost 2-1 and 3-0 to Wolves during the season and finished nine points below them in the league.

We had played Bolton Wanderers, who had finished fourth from bottom in League Three in the first-round matches, winning 1-0 at home before getting a creditable 2-2 draw in the second leg. We beat Wolves 2-0 in the first leg and then managed to resist their pressure in the second game until David Barnes sent Shots fans into delirium with a goal in the 85th minute that ensured, that against all odds, we had won promotion. I'm not sure I remember too much of the game itself, but I do remember being hugely intimidated by the 20,000 Wolves fans that were in attendance. The car parked next to ours had a brick thrown through its windscreen, and that was the least of the poor behaviour that we witnessed.

Funnily enough, I was at Old Trafford watching an England cricket match a couple of years ago and there was someone sat in the row behind me, wearing a Wolves shirt. I looked for the first opportunity to engage him in a conversation about football, and his immediate retort was "...bloody David Barnes." 25 years later, and the memory was equally burned in his memory as it was mine, but for very different reasons.

I started supporting the Shots around 1980. Sadly, I had missed the excitement of the 1978/79 FA Cup round, and the years after this were generally lean ones. There had been the occasional moment of excitement, such as when we won 3-1 at Portsmouth in the second round of the FA Cup in December 1982 but it always seemed to be followed by a nightmare, such as when we lost 7-0 at Swindon in the very next round. We had a good run in the League Cup in 1984/85 when we beat Bournemouth and Brighton in the first two rounds to set up a game with the eventual winners, Norwich.

Don't get me wrong, we had some good games, and it was sufficient to get me addicted to watching the Shots, but success had been somewhat limited. Until 1986/87, which was to be our year. In addition to gaining promotion, we also reached a replay in the fourth round of the FA Cup, famously knocking first division Oxford United out in the Third Round – a game in which there was a pitiful crowd of less than 2,000 as the Directors had decided to increase the ticket price four-fold to try and raise as much cash as possible. In addition to this, we had a good run in the Freight Rover Trophy, reaching the Southern Area Final where we lost to Bristol City. Little Sue and I spent much of that year travelling together and became good friends. Unfortunately, we spent less time together as the years progressed, and I was looking forward to catching up with her at Maidenhead.

We made our way to the ground through hordes of police and police horses, something that I hadn't seen for quite a few years. Seemingly, the police were expecting a number of Reading fans to turn up and we later found out from Sergeant Jason that the police had found a number of trouble-makers and locked them in a pub. Good old-fashioned policing. That's the way to do it.

I'm not a big fan of Maidenhead. Their pitch was atrocious, and it must have been a very close call as to whether the ground was acceptable for Conference National football. I wasn't overly impressed with their team either. Their brand of football was very direct and their only tactic during the second half was hoofing the ball down the hill for one of their strikers to get on the end of. From their reputation, and the reputation of their manager, Alan Devonshire, I had expected more, but once again there was only one team trying to play football, and we were finding it very difficult on such an awful playing surface.

However, it was an exciting game. Shots went one up before Maidenhead equalised. We then went 2-1 up before once again conceding a sloppy goal and, after 85 minutes, Will De Havilland had his hand in the air when a Maidenhead cross came into our penalty area, and after a moment when we thought we might get away with it, the referee changed his mind and instead of pointing towards the corner flag, he pointed towards the penalty spot, and it was 3-2 to Maidenhead.

The one thing missing from our game in recent weeks has been the strength of character to come back from a losing situation. Too many times we have conceded after having been in front and found it difficult to get back on top, but to do so today with a Jim Kellerman goal in the 90th minute was very pleasing and had the Shots fans celebrating widely.

As we headed back to the car, we were slightly disappointed that once again we had not managed to gain three points which did seem to be there for the taking, but we'd had a very enjoyable afternoon and left in good spirits. Well, we were in good spirits until we got in the car to drive home. When we were younger, Little Sue used to do the driving, and I hadn't realised that she was from the same school of back street drivers as Mr Tickle. When asked for directions, the best that Little Sue offered was to 'follow', which was fine when we were on a long straight road, but slightly less helpful when we came to a T junction. Little Sue also seemed particularly intrigued by my supply of orange Sainsbury's bags that had been folded neatly in the pocket on the back of my seat, and she asked what they were as she took them out. Personally, I would have thought that it was pretty blindingly obvious what they were, and there was no need for Little Sue to get them out and make them untidy. I told Little Sue that they were Sainsbury's carrier bags, and she confessed to having one herself. We waited for a punchline to this deeply intimate piece of knowledge, but none came. Little Sue was merely sharing her ownership of a Sainsbury's carrier bag with us.

Fortunately, we managed to drop Sue off without further incident, and returned home in time for tea and an early night, all agreed that while we probably should have won the game, we had been entertained and had a jolly good day out.

Aldershot versus Torquay

Saturday 14 October 2017

Today was the FA Cup Fourth Qualifying Round and we were playing Torquay at home.

As Steve from Number 11 picked me up on his way through, his nine-year-old son, 'Get Down Ben' appeared on his bike. Steve from Number 11 asked 'Get Down Ben' if he would like to come to the football, and much to the surprise of us both, he said he would. No problems. A quick phone call to Kerry (also from number 11) to advise her of the situation and to ask her to shut the garage door, and we were on our way.

Because FA Cup matches are not included in a season ticket, we weren't tied to the Slab, and we could choose where we wanted to go in the ground. We discussed the options and their relative merits which included being able to sing more freely in the East Bank or catching up with Little Sue in the South Stand seats, but after an hour discussion, we found ourselves standing in our usual place on the Slab.

The first half was quite a nondescript affair, with only one chance from either team, and Torquay's was the better, with Jake Cole pulling off a terrific one handed save in front of us. I wish I'd had my camera with me as the angle of our view was near perfect.

The game could have gone either way and, truth be told, it felt a little more like a pre-season friendly than the first FA Cup game of the season. Torquay seemed to play a bit harder than they had a few weeks ago, and they picked up a number of slightly more deserved yellow cards.

The second half continued in a similar vein, with Jake Cole again pulling off a wonderful save low to his left to keep the scores level. As the game wore on, Steve from Number 11 was telling me that there wasn't enough happening in the game for me to be able to write a complete chapter on it, and that I would need to merge it with another game to have enough to write about.

I thought long and hard about this, before suggesting that the way to do it would be to travel to the replay away at Torquay on Tuesday night. Steve from Number 11 went quiet for a few minutes before he checked his diary, realised he was free, and began to warm to the idea. We arranged to meet near Winchester and were beginning to get excited about our unexpected night out. At this point though, Bernard Mensah, who had come on as a 60th minute substitute, made some space in the midfield and delivered a pass to Adam McDonnell who ran towards the High Street End before floating a brilliant pass on to Scott Rendell's head to score the winner.

A wonderful move, and a goal that must have made up for Scott's frustration a few minutes earlier when he just missed, but it signalled the end to our bonus Tuesday night out.

It was great to have Bernard back in the team, and his class was evident. He seemed to have so much time on the ball and could move his feet so much quicker than any other players on the pitch. This bode well for the upcoming games, starting with Tranmere the next Saturday.

However, the afternoon still provided more than enough to reflect on, including the relative merits of taking a nine-year-old to a football match. I had taken my kids from an early age, and Mickey could remember the very first game he took his son to (against Heybridge Swifts) when he was only a couple of months old. Maybe it's easier to take children to a match if they're a few months old. I wouldn't know as I had twins, and nothing was easy. I do recall Mickey regularly taking a box of toys for his kids to play with, including a tricycle that Tom used to ride on, up and down the back of the Slab. They were different times back when we were in the lower leagues and the Health and Safety rules were less stringent.

I also recall being told off by one of the stewards when I brought a football for my kids to play with on the terrace. The higher up the leagues you go, the more stringent the rules seem to be. I occasionally go to see Bognor Regis with my friend Fat Andy, and it's so much more relaxed, and so much more fun because of it.

I'm sure it all comes back to the Premiershit wanting to control how people watch football. Sorry Mr Murdoch, but it doesn't work that way, and sooner or later, the British public will realise that they've been conned, and they will want their game back.

However, back in the lower leagues, there is still a need for parents to brainwash their children into supporting their local team as it is not always a rational decision. And while it's good to see kids on the terraces, and it is vitally important for the future of the clubs, it does disrupt the game for others – and principally the parent. Steve from Number 11 spent the whole afternoon watching 'Get Down Ben' get up on to the crash barrier only to see him jump down seconds later. He demanded constant attention, (including food and drink) and would not focus on watching the game. Partly, I suspect, because it was not a particularly exciting spectacle.

During less than thrilling games, we tend to make our own entertainment, and we talk to each other. As an example, during the frequent dull moments in the Torquay game, we were discussing the grammatical accuracy of the East Bank chant "There's only two James Rowes." Tom was expressing his disappointment at the poor education within the Aldershot area which led to people not being able to recognise that it should be "There are only two James Rowes." I was at Sixth Form College many years ago with one of the current crop of teachers at Heron Wood, so I will make no further comment.

But all of this was wasted on 'Get Down Ben', who thought jumping up and down was much more fun. I am very impressed with Steve from Number 11 and the patience that he mustered. On the bright side though, we did manage to persuade 'Get Down Ben' to join in with our singing, although, having done so a couple of times, he refused to continue, citing that it was rather too embarrassing for him. A harsh judgement from a nine-year-old, but, equally a sentiment that was shared by Charlie, Andy and pretty much everyone else within audio range.

FA Cup First Round Draw

Monday 16 October

I missed the draw for the First Round of the FA Cup as I was driving home from work at the time while my phone was going mad in my pocket with various text messages. Steve from Number 11 texted 'Trip to Shrewsbury it is then.' Having looked at the calendar once I got home I replied, saying 'That's going to take some negotiation as we've got tickets for one of my wife's folky gigs in the evening.' But then I started to work it through. The game would finish shortly after 4.45, and I could be back in the car for 5.00. With a good run back, averaging 80 miles an hour - maybe two and a half hours and I could be back by 7.30. Mmmmm, I wondered...

But then Steve from Number 11 replied to say that he might struggle for permission as he was flying to India for work the next day. I suggested that he could tell his wife that the flight has been cancelled and he has to fly from Manchester the day before instead. That's easily fixed, surely. But Steve replied, saying 'It's not going to happen. Wives 1 – Husbands 0.' Isn't it always the case, I thought.

James asked if I'd seen the draw, and I asked him if he fancied going. He asked how far it was, and I didn't hear back from him after I told him it was around 200 miles each way.

I even asked Matt if he could be persuaded to join me. Matt is far more direct and far more sensible than his brother. He said "No," without needing too much time to think about it. I asked him to give it more thought, and he did, replying with another emphatic "No." I wasn't going to ask my wife if she fancied a weekend in Wales. I've tried that before and during the football season it rarely takes more than a few seconds for her to see through my plans and invite me to become a bachelor again if that's what I want.

I wondered if there was a chance that the game could be moved to Friday night which would be easier, but Steve from Number 11 and I agreed that the chances were very low. When Gary replied saying there was more chance of the Shots winning the FA Cup than him being allowed out, the realisation began to dawn on me that I might have to listen to this one on the radio.

In the Shots chat room, there were a number of comments suggesting this was not the draw that Shots fans were wanting. We would have preferred either a nice winnable home tie or an away trip to a new ground, or better still, to local opposition, such as Portsmouth. However, I'm sure it could have been worse. Although having said that, Shrewsbury were unbeaten this season, currently sitting second in League One and about 200 miles away from Hampshire, so actually, it couldn't be much worse.

There are a few links between the clubs. Players to have played for both teams include John Dungworth, Alex McGregor, Ben Herd, Jake Robinson and Marvin Morgan. Currently playing for the Shrews are Omar Beckles and Alex Rodman.

More dramatically, Shrewsbury knocked us out of the FA Cup in the Fifth Round in 1979, and more recently, they beat us in a penalty shoot-out in the Conference Play-Off final in 2004. I remember this game, which was held at Stoke, very well. We went one up in the first half, but conceded an equaliser, and lost on penalties.

Disturbed Postie summed it up quite nicely when he likened the draw to waiting all day for a blind date only to find Hilda Ogden turning up.

Aldershot versus Tranmere

Saturday 21 October 2017

The Shots were back in league action with a visit from Tranmere Rovers this afternoon. I'd nearly got over the drubbing they gave us in the first leg of the play-offs earlier in the year, but I suspected we would have to play much better than we have done of late if we wanted to win.

This day was shaping up to be a really good one. Watching the Shots against Tranmere in the afternoon, followed by a night out with my wife and our good friends Simon and Sue in the evening. Simon is one of my regular gig buddies, but he spends much of the summer working at music festivals, so I hadn't seen him for a while. Simon and I bonded a number of years ago when our boys played for Haslemere Town Football Club, starting in the Under 7s. When they were about 12, we accompanied them on a six-day trip to Germany which was part of an annual exchange that had been taking place for about 35 years. The facilities available in Soderburg were fantastic, and very comparable to some senior non-league teams here in the UK. A few parents joined the trip, and Simon and I got on well and became firm friends.

Simon used to be in the Army, and at the start of the 12-hour journey home, he said that he had often wondered how many soldiers one would need to successfully invade the Isle of Wight.

I know now that I should have asked him why he wanted to do this but, rather foolishly, I let myself get dragged slightly too enthusiastically into the conversation. Ultimately, we decided that he was asking the wrong question, and the right question is to ask how many navvies it would take (yes, navvies, not navy's).

We suspected that somewhere in the Ministry of Defence Headquarters there would be plans already in place for the military to re-take more obvious candidates for invasion, such as Jersey, as there is relatively recent evidence to suggest that Jersey is an attractive option. There is less evidence to suggest that anyone would ever want to invade the Isle of Wight, and therefore we would have considerably more time to enjoy ourselves before anyone came to evict us.

After much discussion, we decided that we would buy HMS Ark Royal (it was up for sale at the time), and then pull the plug out of the bottom in the middle of Portsmouth harbour, thereby effectively neutralising any threat from the Navy. We thought about the Air Force and decided that the purchase of a few stingers would prevent any aeroplanes from landing. So, the main threat seemed to come from hovercrafts, and our obvious solution was to build a giant DIY store where the hovercraft landing zone is, and then we'd be safe.

When I reflect on this conversation six or seven years later, I wonder why we hadn't thought of some of the risks posed by helicopters or from an airborne assault. Obviously, Simon had this well thought through, but I can't remember what it was or why.

After our navvies had finished building the DIY store, we would get them to work on building a giant structure that we would cunningly disguise as a telecommunications tower (and we could continue this disguise by attaching a little Vodaphone logo to it). When the authorities came to evict us, we would blow the tower, and walk across the length of it to make our escape into France. Clearly, we had every angle covered, and nothing could go wrong. Could it?

Back in the real world, Steve from Number 11 picked me up and we headed to the Vic for a pre-match beer. Suitably refreshed, we strolled down to the ground and took our places on the Slab. At five minutes to three the sounds of Alive and Kicking by Simple Minds played loudly through the speakers of the tannoy, and we waited for the players to come out of the tunnel. It was lovely to see Midlands Bill back on the terraces, recovered from his tendon problems, and we agreed that the Shots would need to be in fine form against Tranmere, who, although they were not doing quite so well this season, still had some very good players such as Andy Cook, James Norwood and Steve McNulty.

The first half was a fairly quiet affair, with Tranmere scoring from probably the only opportunity of the game. From where we were standing, we couldn't see much, but Jake Cole seemed to be appealing for something. Fans in the chat room after the game suggested that Jake was impeded by a couple of Tranmere players obstructing him, and a Tranmere fan posted on their forum that he was surprised that the goal was given. Bernard Mensah had a good shot just before half-time which proved the Shots were still in the game and, although many standing on the Slab started to cheer, the ball had clearly flown into the side netting. The eyesight of the older fan (as most Slabbers are) can obviously sometimes deceive.

The second half was much different though. The Shots came out with intent and immediately took the game to Tranmere who defended deeper and deeper against the danger in red attacking them. Disappointingly for a team with aspirations for promotion, they started wasting time from the beginning of the second half, and it was no surprise when their goal-keeper received a yellow card in the 70th minute.

As the Shots domination increased – we had 14 corners in the second half - so did the poor behaviour from the Tranmere players. Once again, much to our frustration, the referee seemed to either miss or ignore a lot of it, and surprisingly, in my opinion, Tranmere finished the game with 11 men still on the pitch.

As the Shots became more dominant, Tranmere's determination to try and hold onto their winning margin ultimately became their undoing. As they defended deeper and deeper with their striker James Norwood being dragged back onto the edge of their penalty area, the Shots had two-thirds of the pitch to themselves in order to mount their attacks. Adam McDonnell, Cheye Alexander, Jim Kellerman and Fabien Robert all had good shots blocked by the Tranmere defence, but it was a mistake from that pantomime villain, McNulty, that led to the Shots equalising in the 80th minute a moment after a beautiful rainbow appeared over the East Bank. McNulty mis-judged his header trying to clear a cross from James Rowe which fell to Fabien Robert who rifled in a shot past the Tranmere goal-keeper.

From then on, it was all Shots pressure. Jim Kellerman had another good attempt saved, after what was probably the best move of the game, with some nice one touch passing among two or three of our attackers.

But it was the Tranmere time-wasting that led to six minutes of injury time, and it served them right when Jim Kellerman swept in a beautiful cross in the 95th minute and Scott Rendell brushed it into the goal for a very late winner. We've been on the end of last

121

minute goals before, and it is hugely disappointing. But to score one so late when the opposition had been time-wasting and trying to prevent a game of football taking place was very sweet. Steve from Number 11 and I couldn't stop ourselves from grinning inanely at each other on the drive home, and occasionally bursting into laughter.

Tranmere fans admitted on their forum that the best team won, and that Aldershot were ten times better as an attacking side.

I have to admit that McNulty has been a good player. I first came across him when he was playing for Luton. He's pretty hard to miss, mind you, but I remember googling him, and Google completed the sentence with Steve McNulty 'fat.' At the time he was aged about 29. He played really well and looked to have the capability to play or to have played at a higher level. But his terrific positional awareness and experience is beginning to be let down by his lack of pace, and like many defenders, he sometimes seems to resort to dubious means to prevent strikers doing their job.

This reminded me of a similar incident involving Lincoln City's Matt Rhead at the end of last season when, after five seconds, he deliberately elbowed Will Evans in the face, and the referee completely ignored it.

It's not good enough, and probably explains why referees consistently score between five and seven out of ten in the Non-League Paper. I guess if they were any better they would be officiating at a higher level in the same way that the footballers would be, but it is so frustrating when as fans you can see incidents that involve cheating or bullying, and players get away with it. McNulty was on a yellow card when he put his arms around Scott Rendell, picked him up and threw him onto the ground. I understand (because the Union of Referees that stand on the Slab told me) that this wasn't card-able as the ball was not in play, but surely that type of behaviour is not within the laws of football.

The three points against Tranmere were very welcome, as was the display of character that saw us win after having been 1-0 down for most of the game. But these pale into insignificance compared to the sheer joy of beating a team who were relying on gamesmanship to stop us playing football.

Aldershot versus Sutton United

Tuesday 24 October 2017

Another mid-week game, and another evening that Gary had double booked himself. He told me that he was going to the theatre to watch some play with Natalie Dormer in it. I'm not a huge theatre goer, but I have booked next Wednesday off work for my wife and I to spend the day and evening at the Chichester Festival Theatre, watching all three plays which comprise the Norman Conquests. At this stage, I am not convinced about watching all three plays back to back, but it seemed like a good idea when we booked the tickets.

Gary (who used to work in the theatre) tells me that he once watched House and Garden (by the same writer) where all three plays are performed in real time, with the actors moving from one set to another. That sounded really intriguing, but also slightly hairy for the actors. It would also make the show last a little less than the six and a half that we are booked in for, but nonetheless, I was very much looking forward to it.

I have to admit to not having heard of Natalie Dormer, but Gary said that she appeared in Game of Thrones. I'm not sure about Game of Thrones. We're halfway through the second series, but it's still not capturing my imagination. Everyone tells me to keep going with it, but how much of my life do I want to invest before I get some payback? This was the same with Breaking Bad. I watched the first three or four episodes, but it didn't draw me into it. Unlike Vikings, however, which seemed to take over my life for several weeks as my wife and I binge-watched it, hungrily eating up every episode. Brilliant television.

Steve from Number 11 and I met in the Vic, and enjoyed catching up over a pre-match beer, before we headed for the ground. Steve from Number 11 told me that 'Get Down Ben' had said that he had wanted to come, but that he had told him in no uncertain terms that he wasn't welcome until his voice had broken.

I've not been a big fan of Sutton in the past. The two games against them last season weren't particularly brilliant, and I didn't think too much of their tactics or style. I also remember visiting back in 1987 when we embarrassingly lost 3-0 in the Cup. I'm told that I shouldn't dislike every team that have ever beaten the Shots, and while losing might not be the best reason for disliking a team, when it is unexpected it's not a completely irrational one.

Neither is my dislike of their strip. I can live with the light turmeric colour, but I really don't understand why they would put a strip of milk chocolate down the middle. Makes it look very odd, and I'm not sure I like it that much. Turmeric and chocolate together? You tell me...

And so, we cheered our beloved Shots on. We conceded a goal fairly early on when Jake Cole made a rare mistake. He seemed to come out to attack a cross but was far too hesitant and ended up a couple of feet short, allowing the Sutton player to get a clean head to the ball, striking a bullet header, reminiscent of Tim Sills, into the goal.

This caused Charlie to start moaning and, much to our surprise, he called our defender Will Evans a donkey. I say, much to our surprise, because most Slabbers think quite highly of Will. His role is to be the hard man at the back, and he does this very well. He sometimes overplays the diagonal pass and it can go astray, but the partnership of Will and Callum Reynolds is a really good one, and I'm not sure too many Shots fans would want to break it up.

Paul McNamara in his 2014 book entitled 'The More We Win the Better It Will Be', which described a year with Eastleigh Football Club during the 2013/14 season, described Will thus:

"It is far too early to make a comparison in playing style between Will and Steven Gerrard in the match reports I file, but I'm happy to place on record here, the way he exudes complete authority over whichever part of the pitch he bestrides is eerily reminiscent of the Liverpudlian." So, the clues can now be pieced together – the diagonal pass is obviously a throw-back to his days at Eastleigh when he played in midfield and was told that he played like Steven Gerrard.

We didn't have too long to wait before Shamir ran down the right wing towards the East Bank. The Sutton defender slipped, allowing Shamir to get a low cross to Bernard Mensah's feet and Bernard didn't disappoint. One all.

But Sutton looked hungry, wanting the three points. They attacked and soon scored a second when one of their strikers created space for himself and unleashed an unstoppable strike on goal.

We knew that Charlie had called Will a donkey out of frustration but over the previous few minutes he had obviously been thinking. He proudly declared that he had re-considered and decided that Will was more of a mule than a donkey. We weren't entirely sure of the difference, but the Union of Referees, keen to prove their higher standard of education, jumped in and advised us that the mule is a cross-breed. But the bigger question that was asked by Andy was whether mules have big ears. Charlie confidently asserted that they did, and we returned to the game in time to see the Shots awarded a penalty in front of the East Bank. My fellow Slabbers immediately cheered, and I had to ask them why. I was told that being awarded a penalty was good news, but I had to beg to differ. Unfortunately, I've seen us miss far too many penalties to get excited about them. Only a few years ago we had a run of about eight misses in a row, but these days we just don't seem to be awarded many.

However, Scot Rendell confidently addressed the ball, hesitated half-way through his run up, sending the keeper the wrong way as he stroked it into the left-hand corner of the goal. Two all, and half-time about to be called.

I read a Twitter post at half-time which said that at Hartlepool the tannoy had made an announcement asking one of the supporters to return home as his wife had been locked out of the house. This has to be one of life's great moral dilemmas. I'd like to think that I would do the right thing and return home to let my despairing wife in, but in my heart I'm not entirely sure that I would. It would take me 45 minutes to walk to the car park and get home, and probably the same amount of time to get back again, so my act of kindness would mean that I would miss the game. Gary claims he just makes sure his wife has her own key.

I did come to my wife's rescue once. We were living in Kent, and I was at work, interviewing people for a job. Between interviews my colleague passed me a message saying my distressed wife had called and asked if I could call her rather urgently. I asked the interviewee if they wouldn't mind waiting for a moment while I made the call. Apparently, she had gone home during her lunch-break, entered the kitchen and turned the hot tap on. At this point a blackbird hopped out of the cupboard and she had screamed, turned around, and slammed the door behind her. She then ran to the phone, desperate that I returned home as soon as possible to let the blackbird out of the house. I'm not sure that I possess the necessary skills for this type of assignment but obviously, being an alpha male, I had to pretend I had. So, I dashed home, closed my eyes as I entered the sauna that the kitchen had become with the hot tap running for 30 minutes and opened the window. Fortunately, the bird was as keen to escape as we were for it to do so and I dashed back to work, and my interview, leaving my wife to clean up a terrible mess of regurgitated cherries or something similar. So, I hope I would answer the call, but if I'm perfectly honest, I'm not entirely certain…

During the half-time break, we had another intellectual conversation as we tried to recall all of the films starring Clint Eastwood and donkeys. Someone thought that Clint starred with Sister Mary, who apparently had a mule or two, but, to be honest, the conversation soon dried up.

The second half started and while the Shots seemed OK for the first few minutes, Sutton soon started to assert themselves and control the game. This continued for pretty much the whole of the second half when it felt that we were the away team, trying to keep the waves of attackers at bay. Sutton had three or four very good efforts when they could very easily have scored. After one of their attacks, Will picked up the ball from our penalty area and started a run which took him to the middle of the Sutton half. As he laid the ball off to second half substitute, Shaun Okojie, we heard Charlie shout out, "Will Evans, you are the most beautiful donkey I have ever seen." But sadly, Shaun was running in the wrong direction and it came to nothing.

Charlie was in particularly big trouble for shouting out that he wanted a free kick at one point. The Union of Referees started to explain – very rationally – that a free kick wasn't deserved, but Charlie just said that he didn't really care whether it was deserved or not, he was just asking for a free kick. He said that Sutton had had a few and he felt that it was about time we had one.

Football is a passionate game, and fans are passionate for their team. We will shout and scream, and it doesn't matter whether a particular rule – sorry, a particular 'law' – has been transgressed, we just want to shout our support for our team. And given many of us aren't allowed to shout and sing at work or at home, it has to be at football.

The second half was a long, tense period of football. Ultimately, we held on for the draw, and we were so much more pleased about this than Sutton. The Shots rode their luck, but heads stayed high and huge congratulations must go to the team. This was most definitely a point won as Sutton totally destroyed us in the second half.

And my opinion of them has changed. Unlike Tranmere, a supposedly big club with aspirations of promotion who came and played for a draw, Sutton came to win three points and they were easily the best team I'd seen this season. How unfortunate that because of their plastic pitch they will be denied promotion. This is a tough call for their fans too but as they are another hobby club, I'm not going to lose too much sleep over it.

Barrow versus Aldershot

Saturday 28 October 2017

Mrs C wanted some time to herself at the weekend so I suggested that I would go to Barrow. It seems this wasn't what she had in mind. She thought that I would want to have the day to myself after I'd done the washing, the cleaning, the supermarket run and cooked the tea. Silly me. I had asked her whether she would like a weekend in the Lake District when the fixtures came out at the beginning of last season but she saw through the offer far too quickly and declined. Andy went to the game and said that although the Shots lost 1-0, we had played well and that it had been a good game.

I had struggled to reconcile this with the Barrow team that had come to Aldershot later in the season. They were pretty disgraceful and while they had two players sent off, it could easily have been considerably more.

I was shocked when I read a pre-season article that their manager wanted to "...bring in some nasty and horrible players..." before the season started. The article quoted him as saying '...we're lacking a kind of mind-set that has a little bit of nastiness and horribleness.'

Based on the game last season, I think they have more than enough of that and they may well be better off looking for players who are interested in playing football.

After a very pleasant dog walk with my wife, I completed my jobs which additionally included taking Matt to view a new car, helping him buy the car and sorting out the insurance for his new car, and Mrs C and I headed to Petworth Park with our cameras, for the annual deer rut as it was a nice day. There was quite a bit of bellowing going on (mostly the stags) with very little rutting, but we did spend a little time watching and photographing some deer sex, which always makes me feel slightly uncomfortable.

I'm still not entirely sure whether erect deer penises should be photographed and whether it is socially acceptable to post them on a Flickr account or not. But more to the point, it took me away from the radio and the commentary of the game. We got back home in time to listen to the last 15 minutes when Rob and Dr Jim Royle told me that it was not one of the better Shots performances as we went down to a tame 3-1 defeat.

I might have been tempted to go. I've not been to the Barrow ground before, and my family originally hailed from the Furness peninsular, albeit many hundreds of years ago. I love the Abbey, the coastal road around the peninsular, and the warm welcome that I have always received. I have been there many times and feel a real affinity for the area. But it *is* a very long way to go.

So, we were fairly poor today and Callum said so in his post-match interview. But nobody died – we lost a game of football. We had a week to get it together again before we are playing Shrewsbury in the Cup. And guess what? They lost today as well.

I read a very bizarre article which said that the Salford City goal-keeper had been sent off for urinating into his net as they won 2-1 at Bradford Park Avenue. The mind boggles…

Bordon Shot said in the Chat Room that he thought it was a bad day at the office. Bordon Shot had a poor game of golf today and his solution was to have a beer and an early night, and to wake up feeling better in the morning. I'm playing golf tomorrow, so I'd better get some beer ready for the inevitable.

It's important that we put this behind us and focus on the game at Shrewsbury next week. Sir Gary knows what he's doing, so let's not get too worried about it, eh?

Shrewsbury versus Aldershot FA Cup 1st Round

Saturday 4 November 2017

It felt like ages since I'd been to a football match. After doing my
Saturday morning chores (walking the dogs, cleaning out the
fridge, cooking Matt and his friend, Dan who had stayed
overnight, bacon sandwiches) I headed to the local supermarket
to re-stock. I was thinking that I should have gone to
Shrewsbury, but it was too late to change the decision, and I had
agreed to take James back to Reading in the afternoon.

As I stood at the meat aisle, trying to decide what we were going
to have for Sunday lunch, Steve (and Kerry) from Number 11
appeared, and we stopped for a chat. The first thing Steve from
Number 11 said was that we should have been sitting in a pub in
Shrewsbury waiting to go to the game. We looked at each other
before simultaneously turning around and telling 'Get Down Ben'
to get down from the trolley that he was climbing, and sullenly,
we went our separate ways. I headed to the meat section while he
went to the travel section to get an adaptor which was suitable for
Indian sockets.

Typically, when we were ready to take James back to Reading, it
was bang on 3 o'clock, so we had to try and find a way of
listening to Radio Shropshire in the car.

James managed to get this working through his phone, and we settled down to cheer the Shots to a famous victory. Sadly, it didn't turn out that way, and rather than the sneaky little win that we were optimistically hoping for, we were well beaten, eventually losing to the League One leaders 5-0. There were only one set of supporters that we could hear in the background and full respect to the 420 Shots fans who travelled for singing throughout the game, even when it seemed pretty grim going.

Huge congratulations to Maidstone, Boring Wood and Oxford City who all defeated league opposition in Cheltenham, Blackpool and Colchester respectively. This is why lower league fans love the FA Cup so much, but you can't expect to win every game against higher opposition, and today we didn't come close to doing so. I have to record my commiserations for poor old Ebbsfleet who, having been leading Doncaster 2-0, ended up losing 6-2. I know the feeling.

My wife thought that I was glad that I hadn't travelled to the game, but I'm not so sure. I still think it was one of the must go-to games, and it definitely felt more exciting than next week's match when we look forward to hosting AFC Fylde.

In case you were wondering, I bought a couple of small Welsh lamb joints to roast for Sunday. They were particularly tasty, and worked well with some homemade mint sauce, roast potatoes, roast parsnips, some veg and one or two Yorkshire puddings on the side. Yum.

Aldershot versus AFC Fylde

Saturday 11 November 2017

With Steve from Number 11 in transit on the way back from India, and Gary not allowed out to play, I made my own way to the Recreation Ground for today's match, after a very pleasant morning spent doing a bit of Christmas shopping with Mrs C. I really hate Christmas shopping, but I think she's worked out that the best way to do it is to get there early and provide me with a cooked breakfast before starting in the shops as it generally puts me in a better mood.

I was listening to Rob Worrall on the radio on the drive in to Aldershot and he was predicting a 2-2 score-line on the basis that our defence is vulnerable. He's got a point, but I did wonder if he was being slightly ambitious in thinking that we were going to score two goals, as we have only scored one in the last two games. And I was even more nervous when I saw that neither Matt McClure nor Scott Rendell our recognised strikers were in the starting eleven.

Fortunately, Charlie and Andy appeared, despite the promise of a wet and windy afternoon.

Being a military town (or more like an ex-military town now), Remembrance Day in Aldershot is always treated very respectfully, and today was no different. A short prayer from the Shots' Chaplain in front of a number of people from the forces was followed by a note perfect rendition of the Last Post, and an impeccably observed two-minute silence. The East Bank had a large red banner simply saying, 'Lest We Forget', and during the two minutes silence, hundreds of fans standing on the East Bank held large red poppies high, and the view from the Slab was wonderful. Full marks to the organisers for such a wonderful display. I do like it when the club makes an effort on Remembrance Day, and I love the way the fans get involved and elevate it to something very special. It helps us to remember that we're only there to watch a football match and, ultimately, the only reason we are able to stand on the terraces to watch our game is because of the sacrifice that so many people made over the last 100 years.

This was the first game that we had ever played against Fylde. They're a fairly new team, formed in 1988, and they won promotion to the Conference National League last year, having finished as champions of Conference North. They obviously have some significant money behind them and therefore a number of good players in the team, including Jack Muldoon who was part of Lincoln City's all conquering team from last year.

Depending upon which rumours you listen to, Jake Cole was either injured or being rested ahead of being sold and it doesn't look as though Sir Gary has too much confidence in our reserve goalkeeper Mark Smith as he has brought a new goalkeeper in on loan from Reading.

It must be tough life for a second-choice goalkeeper. You spend your time waiting for the first choice to get injured or dropped, and then you are immediately under pressure to deliver with little match practice. Mark had a couple of games last season, but he didn't seem to inspire the same level of confidence with his defence. I think it was Callum Reynolds who appeared somewhat nervous about passing the ball back to Mark towards the end of the FA Trophy game against East Thurrock which led to them scoring near the end of the game.

Mark had played at Shrewsbury the previous week and had reportedly done okay. Although the team had conceded five goals, they seemed to have been more to defensive frailties than goal-keeping errors.

Shots started reasonably well while Fylde got away with a few over-the-top tackles, a few pushes and an attempted wrestling move in the penalty area that had us howling at the referee. Fortunately, the Union of Referees was absent today, so Charlie and I were able to shout as much abuse at the officials as we wanted.

Bernard Mensah had a one-on-one with the Fylde goal-keeper but, ultimately, we had to wait until the twentieth minute before James Rowe sent a lovely cross in to the box which Shamir Fenelon managed to head loopingly into the top of the goal for the Shots to go ahead. Rather surprisingly, Fylde didn't up their pace and continued to slow the game down and waste time.

1-0 to the Shots at half-time and we were feeling reasonably happy.

Unfortunately, the second half wasn't quite as good. Fylde scored an equaliser – very much against the run of play. A hoof from their defence to Danny Rowe whose 50 goals last season will testify to the fact that he knows how to score, and he showed Bernard how to make the most of one-on-one situations.

Fylde had another break soon after, but the linesman flagged as soon as the ball entered our half and after a consultation the referee sent a Fylde player off, presumably for the assault on one of our players.

The Shots started to assert themselves against the ten men, but out of nowhere, Manny Oyeleke, who had only been on the pitch for ten minutes, was sent off. From the Slab it looked like a hard but fair challenge and we were genuinely surprised that the red card was shown. The Fylde player was rolling around on the floor looking like he had been shot. The poor fellow quickly jumped up as soon as the red card had been shown. The referee should have booked the Fylde player for gamesmanship or cheating or something. Poor, in my opinion. Having seen the slow-motion replay, some said that the red card was valid for Manny but, equally, there was a sizeable view that it was not. I guess you win some and lose others. Unfortunately, this season, we do seem to lose more than our fair share!

As the game progressed, the Shots came on stronger and we were rewarded with a goal from Will Evans in the 86th minute. We had won a free-kick from another dirty tackle and it was a lovely feeling to see the ball go into the net. To be fair Will had not been having one of his better games. Too many passes went astray including one comic moment where he kicked the ball all the way along the halfway line from the other side of the pitch and straight out of play.

Out of frustration, Charlie shouted out loudly, "You're a pantomime team," and, to our amusement, Andy very quickly managed to shout back, "Oh no, we're not."

I was not impressed with Fylde. Far too much shirt pulling, holding our players, and overly aggressive tackles, and it seems that many other Shots fans were of the same opinion. If they want to go wrestling, they should do so, but we paid our money to watch football.

I thought Lewis Ward, our new goal-keeper on-loan from Reading, performed well. He did have some work to do, but he looked calm, composed and assured right from the beginning of the match when he rose high to steer a good looking cross away from danger. While I understand that he had actually met his new team mates before the game, apparently, he hadn't been to the Rec before and had to ask for directions to the dressing room when he arrived.

We certainly had our entertainment from the game, although not in the way that we would have wanted. While I wasn't particularly impressed with Fylde, if I'm honest, I wasn't totally impressed with the Shots either. Admittedly we had a number of players playing in unusual positions, including our winger, Shamir Fenelon playing the lone striker role, and central defender, Callum Reynolds playing at left back. But we should have been able to put the game to bed more easily and much earlier, but for whatever reason we weren't able to do so, and we nearly paid the price when Fylde scored, and we had to start from scratch. With Fylde closing us down quickly, we overused our goalkeeper as a sweeper and played ourselves into trouble on too many occasions when going for safety first might have been a more sensible option.

It was interesting to read James Rowe (the Assistant Manager) tweet that 'We thoroughly deserved the win by sticking to our principles.' I'm torn – I agree with the principles, and really want to see my team trying to keep possession and play the ball from the back with slick passing and quick movement, but we do need to be realistic. We're in Division 5, and while I really like the team that Sir Gary has built, we do not have a team full of global superstars like Ronaldo or Messi, and from time to time we do need to have a second option when the opposition are parking the bus and we are finding it difficult to break them down.

Nonetheless, it was a good game and the team did well and showed real character to hold out for the three points. As I headed to the Hogs Back Brewery for some light refreshment for Matt and I to have with our take-away curry, I reflected that it was a very enjoyable one and, against the odds, we managed to stay dry.

Hartlepool versus Aldershot

Saturday 18 November 2017

This was never going to be on the short list of away matches to get to this season and I considerately offered my wife the opportunity to spend the day with me. Apparently, this was an offer that she was able to resist, and she made plans to go out for the day without me.

With a steady light drizzle throughout the day, I couldn't be bothered to go and find another match to watch so I filled my morning with a round of jobs including dog walking, visiting the vet, shopping, washing and ironing – all those little things that your average house-trained alpha male does. I completed the jobs with half an hour to go to kick-off and thought I would surprise my wife by baking her a cake. Rick Stein came up trumps with his recipe for a German Apple Cake which I am sure will elevate me to hero status for a while. I have been elevated to hero status before, but I have noticed that this generally only lasts for about 20 minutes before it is rescinded for one reason or another. I reflected that it would take me considerably longer to make the cake and felt slightly nervous that she might think that cake baking was going to be a far better use of my time on a Saturday afternoon than going to football.

Hartlepool is one of the grounds that I've not been to before. It's not the only ground I've not been to. Compared to many Shots fans I feel like a complete beginner as I have 'only' been to about 100 grounds, many of which are non-league, so I still have a fair few to tick off the 92 grounds in the football league.

Hartlepool is famous as the town where, during the Napoleonic Wars, a monkey was mistaken for a French spy and hanged. Apparently, a French ship was wrecked off the coast of an old fishing village in that part of the country and the only survivor was the ship's mascot, a monkey which, subsequently, was washed ashore. The people of Hartlepool had never seen a monkey before – nor, for that matter, had they ever set eyes on a Frenchman. Mistaking its chattering for the language of the enemy, they convicted the monkey of being a French spy and hanged the animal on the beach. The townsfolk became known as the "monkey hangers", and Hangus the Monkey is the club mascot. Maybe even more bizarre is the fact that Hangus the Monkey has been elected as mayor of Hartlepool, not once, but three times. I'm not entirely sure what this tells us about Hartlepool and its citizens but I'm sure it tells us something.

The commentary from Rob Worrall on BBC Radio Surrey was excellent as always, but even he seemed to struggle to make the first half of the match sound interesting. But just before half-time, seemingly out of nowhere, James Rowe set up Bernard Mensah to head powerfully into the net, leaving their keeper with no chance of keeping it out. 1-0 on the stroke of half-time was brilliant news.

The second half started with a burst of excitement as Bernard Mensah nodded the ball for Adam McDonnell who had what sounded like a great shot which just went wide. A few minutes later, Nicky Deverdics had an effort for Hartlepool which went just over the crossbar. The Shots' goal had seemed to have given Hartlepool an incentive to come out strongly and I settled down to enjoy a nervy second half.

The Victoria Ground in Hartlepool has stands that are very close to the pitch, and with around 3,700 home fans, Rob was describing a very feisty atmosphere within the ground. We needed to hope that the Shots players kept their discipline and didn't let themselves get embroiled in anything which would lead to an unnecessary booking or sending off.

There was a lot of Hartlepool possession in the second half but fortunately the Shots defence held firm. We so nearly had a second goal when Will Evans put the ball in the back of the net but unfortunately the referee disallowed it. Bernard Mensah had to go off injured but any concerns about whether this would take away our creativity were eased when the Shots broke forward and James Rowe set up Jim Kellerman who calmly clipped a confident finish over the advancing Hartlepool keeper in the 85th minute to ease my nerves. Watching the Shots live is pretty tense but watching it on the radio is so much harder.

Well done Shots for an unbelievable result. And well done to the 187 fans who made the very long journey to the North East. I'm sure they all had an excellent and lively journey back.

Wow, I was exhausted. I was very ready for a nice cup of tea and a slice of German Apple Cake.

Bromley versus Aldershot

Tuesday 21 November 2017

Due to a stomach upset, and a requirement not to venture too far from essential facilities, I decided against travelling to Bromley for tonight's match. I work on the South Coast, so it would involve a reasonably long journey, and I didn't feel up for it.

From about 7.00pm I was reading tweets saying that there had been a power cut at Bromley, and at 7.30pm saw the message that the game had been called off. Fortunately, this doesn't happen too often, and I guess most fans would be glad that they had only travelled the relatively short distance to Bromley and that it hadn't happened somewhere further afield. Like Hartlepool. It did appear though that Bromley had a similar problem the previous night and I'm sure people would have expected that it would have been fixed, rather than re-occurring 24 hours later when a game was due to be played. While it was pleasing to read that most Shots fans who had travelled seemed to be very understanding, I sincerely hope the Shots fans who were calling Bromley 'tin-pot' for the problem, had their tongues firmly in their cheeks.

We had a similar problem at the Rec a few years ago when we were playing the Thames Estuary Galacticos (Southend) in a league game. We were 2-0 down at half-time and suffered a floodlight failure. We won the replayed match (much to the irritation of Southend) but what sticks out most were the 600 visiting Southend fans who brought torches with them and shone them throughout the game. I thought this was football humour at its very best.

At Aldershot there was a very clear tannoy announcement at the time the game was called off as to what fans should do in order to get a refund if they were unable to make the re-arranged game, but it appears that this information was missing at Bromley.

There were slightly happier memories when I read the tweet from the Aldershot Attic, who reminded us that the Shots beat Brighton and Hove Albion in front of 4,675 fans to reach the 3rd round of the League Cup on this day back in the 1984/85 season. At this time the first two rounds were held over two legs and I remember Bill and I travelling to the first game at Brighton in Terry's Triumph Herald. Sadly, Terry's Triumph Herald couldn't do more than 50 miles an hour and even that was when it was travelling down-hill with the wind behind it. It was a long trip there but an even longer trip back after we had lost 3-1. But in the second leg the Shots did well, winning 2-0 to force extra time during which we scored a third in order to progress. We drew Norwich in the third round and Bill and I went to Carrow Road to watch us gain a very creditable 0-0 draw. We had high hopes of causing an upset in the replay, but severe fog ruined the game. Bizarrely the game was allowed to be played, but apart from seeing the odd player ghosting past, I didn't see anything – and as a programme seller, I was able to sit right on the touchline by the centre circle in front of the South Stand seats. The newspapers said we lost 4-0, but no one who was there could prove it and 9,973 fans is probably the biggest crowd I haven't seen at the Recreation Ground. Such a shame that what could have been such a big game for the team proved to be such a let-down.

Aldershot versus Wrexham

25 November 2017

Wrexham are top of the league and I was expecting today's match to be a tough one. However, the stories over the last few days have been about 'too big for this league' Orient's search for a new manager. They sacked the last one when they were hovering just above the relegation zone and the bookmakers seem to have Sir Gary Waddock as one of the front runners with the odds having shortened to 2/1. '80FC' said on the chat room that he believes an approach has already been made, but we have to hope that Sir Gary is sufficiently settled at Aldershot to want to stay. Allegedly there was an approach made last season by a League One or Two club which Sir Gary turned down. Maybe that was from Orient as well. A good performance from both the team and the crowd would hopefully reassure Sir Gary that he is at the right place and enable him to keep his focus on the job in hand. I know that when I have been approached by head-hunters it is always quite unsettling, even if I have no intention of moving from my current employment.

James decided that he would like to come to the game and asked if I could pick him up. I suggested that he could get the train to Guildford, an arrangement which has worked well in previous weeks, but he thought that this would be difficult with the bags of laundry that he wanted to bring with him and so I set off to Aldershot…via Reading. The traffic was busy, and we missed the first five minutes of the game, but James was giving me a running commentary as we hurried towards the ground, and seemed a bit too happy that he hadn't had to wait around for the game to start.

We missed an Aldershot corner but fortunately not much more. Wrexham were playing in a rather fetching outfit of yellow shirts and red shorts that some felt were reminiscent of Baywatch, but it was Aldershot who impressed with the ball and we scored twice in the first half. The first goal was put away by Bernard Mensah and the second was credited to Shamir Fenelon although Kappadeano's video showed that Adam McDonnell's fierce shot from 25 yards out which cannoned off the crossbar had bounced over the line before Shamir, reacting more quickly than the Wrexham goalkeeper, poached the goal. As neither the referee nor linesman were in a position to confirm Adam's shot had crossed the line, it was critical that Shamir had pounced, but Adam's shot will go down as one of the really brilliant goals scored at the Rec.

Shamir could have scored a second when he had a good opportunity at the High Street End but shot wide and on another day, the Wrexham player Mark Carrington might have been shown a red card for a rash tackle on Bernard Mensah when he was through on goal. I had thought that Bernard was possibly off-side, so we'll not complain too much.

Aldershot were immense throughout the game as everything seemed to come together. Other than when used as a sweeper, our goalkeeper had nothing to do. Wrexham had one chance in front of the East Bank, but their striker shot wide with what seemed like an open goal. Our defence were strong and played well as a unit, but it was the midfield players who totally dominated the game and I hope that James Rowe, Bernard Mensah and Fabien Robert all took a moment to reflect on a peerless performance against the league leaders who they made to look very poor.

What was particularly pleasing was hearing comments from some of the Wrexham fans, who were overheard saying things like "No one had done to Wrexham what Aldershot had done today"; "Aldershot's attacking play was absolutely magnificent"; "Aldershot are probably the best attacking team in the league" and "Aldershot were like a formation of Red Arrows." Equally complimentary, but taking a little while longer to digest, was the comment comparing our attack to a monkey throwing their poo around a zoo. A somewhat bizarre comparison, suggesting that our strikers were coming at the Wrexham defence from all angles, and that there was no way of avoiding being hit by us today. Maybe my choice of the word 'digest' should be reviewed in the next edition of this book.

Given that Wrexham are still doing so much better than they have in previous years and were top of the league going into the game, I found it fascinating to read this written by someone called 'Bowler' on the Wrexham chat room: 'Let's get this right this is a poor side playing some of the worst football in the 50 years I've been watching. It's dreadful. Good luck, the defeat today is one of many that will follow, we won't be in play offs this standard of football is not acceptable I am now giving my season ticket away, who wants it. Glad to be rid of it."

I think Mr Bowler needs to find a little perspective! Wrexham were no worse than many of the teams that I've seen so far this season, and maybe one or two have looked better, but it's a very open league and anyone who is capable of putting a run of results together will have a good chance of being somewhere near the top. And as for being top of the league half way through the season…I'm sure Orient fans would bite their hands off.

Bromley versus Aldershot Part 2

Tuesday 28 November 2017

I was presented with a little bit of a dilemma. James was going to meet some of his friends at Exeter and asked if I would like to take him there. After sensing my initial reticence, he reminded me that we are playing away at Torquay and it could potentially be a good excuse for us to go to the game. Permission was subsequently sought and granted, and we were excited at our visit to the English Riviera, which I understood was particularly pleasant at the time of year.

Having received a pass for Saturday, I feared it would be poor form to put in an application for permission to travel to Bromley for our re-arranged fixture so soon – particularly after having had a couple of boy's nights out in the last week or so, going to a couple of gigs with my friends from work.

As it happened I'd had some meetings which didn't finish until 6.45 so the decision was pretty much taken out of my hands. I settled down to listen to another game on the radio. Apparently listening to the Shots game on the radio wasn't what my wife had in mind for the evening and a compromise was reached with me listening through headphones while she watched Made in Chelsea. I couldn't think of anything worse but as the French would say, vive la diversité …

This is quite a big game for the Shots. A win would put us top of the league and a draw or defeat would keep us in sixth place. There were very few clear-cut opportunities during the first half. Bromley had a chance and a potential appeal for a penalty, but it was Bernard Mensah who my living room alight with a beautiful strike on the half hour mark to put us one up.

It sounded from the commentary that Bromley were going in hard with their tackles and the referee was giving little help or support to the Shots. Captain Callum Reynolds seemed to raise this with the referee and this brought the showing of two yellow cards to Shots players, including a second yellow card to Adam McDonnell for dissent. Complete agreement from Rob Shot and Nick Arnold at half-time who both felt that the referee was being inconsistent and agreed that the Shots weren't getting the rub of the green.

A tense second half loomed, and I wondered if Made in Chelsea would take my mind of the game.

Maybe for twenty seconds but only to remind me of what a load of rubbish it is. Gary admits that he has often wondered what type of person not only watches but seems to enjoy this type of 'far from reality TV'. I've not worried about this before, but having seen that my wife fits into the category of seeming to enjoy it, I admit to being slightly concerned.

With Rob and Nick counting down the minutes in the second half, Bromley's couple of efforts in the first twenty minutes were enough to have my finger nails in my mouth. But the Shots are made of strong stuff and conjured up a goal out of nowhere. Half-time substitute Scott Rendell doubled our lead following some excellent work from Matt McClure poaching the ball from one of the Bromley defenders. "Bromley do have an additional player," said Rob Shot, "But you would not know it," before confirming that there were 81 minutes gone.

"A good tackle by Mensah, and the clock is ticking down slowly," he continued, and indeed, it felt as if time was standing still. Ten minutes later Rob Shot said that there were 83 minutes left.

Desperate defending from the Shots in the last five minutes to keep Bromley out before the fourth official declared a minimum of four minutes injury time.

It's always pleasing to win a game of football and never more so than when we are playing away from home. However, to do so against a team in the top quarter of the league, playing the second half with ten men, in order to go top of the league is a wonderful feeling. I wish I'd been at the game. Our defence were superb again, playing Bromley off side time and time again and securing a third successive clean sheet on our way to a fourth consecutive victory and moving us to the top of the league. Even better, in the post-match interview, Rob Worrall asked Sir Gary whether he had anything to say to provide any reassurance to Shots fans given he was second favourite for the Orient job. Sir Gary asked Rob if he had placed a bet, adding that Rob would have been wasting his money if he had done so. This was excellent to hear. Thank you, Sir Gary!

Well done Shots. I'm very proud of you.

Torquay versus Aldershot

Saturday 2 December 2017

Missing another match when we're top of the league would not be really acceptable, so I left home at 9.30am heading for Torquay (via Reading to pick up James). We had a fairly quiet journey, with the usual arguments about what to listen to on the radio. At first it was OK as we were both happy to listen to the Ashes commentary but once that had finished we were able to start our usual argument about my choice of music versus his desire for something slightly more hip and trendy like Radio 1 or, failing that, some – or any - sports commentary. We had a listen to Barcelona versus Celta Vigo for half an hour but I really struggled to listen to a dull commentary on a game that I have no interest in. And even more so when it's not even taking place in England!

Steve from Number 11 had to attend another family event today, so he couldn't travel. I did think about telling him one of the stories that Mark had told me last time I saw him to try and encourage him to travel but, ultimately, I knew that if there was any chance of him being able to come, he would have done so. Mark had been to Norway to watch Scotland play and, as they were enjoying the hospitality of a local hostelry, a particularly drunk Scotsman came up and asked him if he could borrow Mark's phone to ring his wife. Mark obliged and overheard a conversation which went something along the lines of:

Drunk: "Hello. It's me."

Wife: "Where are you?"

Drunk: "I'm in Oslo."

Wife: "Where?"

Drunk: "Oslo. It's in Norway you stupid woman! Oh aye – I'll be back tomorrow."

It seems that the drunk Scotsman had told his wife that he was going to get the daily newspaper and obviously turned left at the crossroads and accidentally ended up in Norway, when he should have turned right to the newsagent. There's part of me that admires this spirit of adventure but I have a very visual impression of the reaction that our hero might have received when he returned home. Anyway, Steve from Number 11 is, like me, a soft southerner and we realise that we can't always do what we want to do - even though Torquay is considerably closer than Norway.

So, it was just James and I in the car, and eventually we reached a compromise which included listening to Chelsea versus Newcastle. I have very little interest in either team so took the opportunity to reflect on the beauty of the countryside as we made good progress heading west on the M4.

This isn't a route that I am overly familiar with, and I did a double take when we passed a 40-foot-high statue as we passed by Bridgewater. It seems that this sculpture is of the Willow Man, celebrating the role of willow in the ecology and craft traditions of the Somerset Levels. This is not the first Willow Man. Apparently a previous one had been burned down in an arson attack after only six months. So, a 130-foot circular moat was built around the new model as a precautionary measure. As ugly as the sculpture is I think burning it down is slightly harsh, although maybe the arsonists confused themselves with the Celtic tradition of burning a Wicker Man to celebrate the start of summer.

There is a fantastic annual Beltain event at the Butser Ancient Farm on the outskirts of Petersfield where they burn a Wicker Man, and, in fact, it was at one of these that I first met Gary. Gary and my wife had been friends for a few years when they decided to introduce Mirinda and I to each other when we went to the Wicker Man festival. Unfortunately, a West Highland Terrier had bitten someone earlier in the event and the organisers decided that they would ban dogs.

Our Westie, Basil, was suffering from piles and while he was quite placid most of the time, this ailment unsurprisingly made him a little grumpy so, once again, discretion was probably the best course of action. Gary's miniature poodles were known to eat postmen alive, so it seemed wise to ban them as well.

So, Gary and I, each thinking that an evening spent with someone else's friend would be fairly dull, agreed to sit in the beer garden of the nearest pub and look after the dogs. At least there'd be beer to console us. And bind us. Several pints of beer later, Mirinda and Mrs C returned to find us slightly drunk and at the start of a wonderful, lifelong friendship.

James and I arrived in Torquay and tried to find a pub for some pre-match refreshments following our long drive. Gary and I had driven to Torquay a couple of years ago and we'd eaten in Boots and Laces, which is a bar attached to one of the stands. While the beer had been reasonably good, the food had been disappointing, so I suggested to James that we should venture somewhere in the town so that I could report back to my wife that I had made sure that her son had filled up on a healthy meal with lots of vegetables.

The first pub we found didn't seem to do any food and the second one only had sausage rolls. James seemed reasonably content with this, possibly over-duly influenced by the large television screen and the comfortable looking seats that were available nearby. I was very happy with the Courage Best Bitter that was on offer.

Sergeant Jason appeared in the pub and when I complained loudly to the 60 people enjoying their beer about police harassment, the handcuffs came out once again. I'm not entirely sure what was going through the mind of the very young Devonian Constable who was with Sergeant Jason, but he seemed to calm down when he saw us share a beaming smile and a handshake with each other.

Suitably refreshed, but still hungry, we made our way to the ground, saying our hellos to Howard and Sara on the way in. We agreed that there was a definite need for someone to start a new thread on the chat room suggesting which pub away fans should head to and highlighting ones that serve good food and real ale. Howard's hat was still standing splendidly erect and I was sure that he hadn't succumbed to introducing it to a washing machine since we had last met at Ebbsfleet.

We made our way to the far end of the terrace where we met Andy and Roy and passed the time before the game started enjoying their company. Roy is an ex-Slabber who now prefers the comparative comforts of the North Stand. A roof over his head and a modicum of protection from the occasionally howling wind would, I thought, have made him a happier man, but it would appear that Roy has succumbed to the traits of other North Stand folk in enjoying a good moan. Even though we are top of the league Roy was complaining about all sorts of things, including Torquay's strip. Yellow shirts, blue shorts and white socks, it would appear, is Roy's least favourite colour combination. "But you only have to watch them two or three times a season, Roy," I said, "And surely it's preferable to the chocolate and turmeric colours of Sutton?" Roy agreed, saying, "I really hate Sutton's strip as well." Having got this out of his system, the game started, and for the first twenty minutes, we played brilliant football, swamping Torquay with our version of the Red Arrows. We had a couple of good chances, but Torquay were defending well, led by two former Shots, Sean McGinty and Damon Lathrope. Torquay dragged themselves back into the game, and for the last 20 minutes of the first half were arguably getting on top of us. Most impressive was the speed with which they were closing us down which, surprisingly, they managed to keep up for the remainder of the game.

Fabien Robert was having a fantastic game for the Shots. The ball seemed to be stuck to his boot with superglue as he ran rings around the Torquay defenders and it seemed only a matter of time before he created an opportunity for us to take the lead. But shortly before half-time he went for an acrobatic overhead kick and pulled a muscle during the manoeuvre. He immediately signalled to the bench and was replaced by Bobby-Joe Taylor making his first appearance for ten weeks.

The second half was slightly tighter, and the result could have gone either way. I asked Roy with twenty minutes left if he would take a draw and he replied instantly that he would, such was the dominance that Torquay were beginning to assert. The Shots had a couple of opportunities, including a free kick on the edge of the

Torquay penalty area that was closed down and Torquay had a couple of opportunities, including a free header that was sent over the bar. A side with good luck riding with it might have sneaked a win but equally, and probably more likely for Shots fans, it could have gone the other way. If I was a Torquay fan, I think I would be slightly disappointed with a point, so the Shots should accept this as a good point gained, rather than two points dropped.

Leaving the ground, we exchanged a number of "well played" and "good luck" comments with the Torquay fans walking in the other direction, which is another of the reasons why I like Torquay. Their fans are just normal people with very little of the bitterness or hostility that you seem to get from some other teams, and particularly some of the nouveau supporters of hobby clubs.

I dropped James at Exeter where he was staying with some of his friends and headed back to Hampshire. A 400-mile round trip without seeing a goal and with a sore back from seven hours in the car, but when I arrived home I settled in my armchair with a wee dram to catch up on the news and to fulfil my weekly guilty secret by looking on the Orient chat room.

Orient's new manager, Justin Edinburgh, describes them as "the biggest team in this league." I'm not so sure that I would agree with that if I was a Tranmere fan but the Orient bid for the Olympic Stadium does seem like a funny dream from a lifetime ago and I recalled the message posted earlier in the season under the title 'Joke Teams' where 'Nice Username' had posted 'Not being funny, but how are teams like Solihull and Maidstone even at this level? If we keep winning until October, the EFL should just reinstate us, it's literally embarrassing.' Well done to Solihull then for beating Orient today and redefining the definition of embarrassment.

Well done to the Shots as well, and well done to Torquay. I have every confidence on this showing that you will leave the relegation zone in the not too distant future, with Orient replacing you, and that you will end the season respectably in a mid-table position. And the final word must go to the Shots fans: 299 fans travelling to Torquay is a superb effort. Well done!

Aldershot versus Halifax

Saturday 9 December 2017

I woke up feeling very tired this morning, having had a long week. I didn't get home from work until gone 8.30 on Monday night and then had a late night on Tuesday when my wife and I went to see The Darkness at G-Live for our midweek date night. Not exactly my musical sweet spot but you can't deny that they have some good songs and Justin Hawkins is a brilliant front man. Another late night at work on Wednesday and then I went to see some of my former colleagues for a drink on Thursday night. I wasn't entirely sure I was feeling up to it, but I think it's important to keep in touch. Ruthie, Emma, Pip, Lynn, Sarah and Julie are among the loveliest people I know and it was a real privilege to have worked with them so closely for so long. I had thought it was a year or so since I last saw them but maybe it had been even longer given some of the remarks made about my hair – my least favourite of which was a comment that it is "…slightly grey in a hobo-esque way." I'm not entirely sure what Emma was trying to say, but I didn't think it was entirely complimentary.

Unfortunately, Sarah, Lynn and Pip weren't able to join us, but Pip did ask Emma to send her a picture of the four of us, at which Pip made a similar response to Emma, asking what was going on with my hair. I grabbed Emma's phone and sent a text asking the more important question, which was 'do you like it?' Pip replied with "bizarrely, I think I do." Maybe I would have preferred her not to have included the word 'bizarrely', but I have to admit to a bit of a soft spot for Pip, so I'll happily settle for her saying she likes it.

I had a really lovely evening with three beautiful women, but it did mean I was slightly later home than I had intended to be and with another late night on Friday when my wife and I went to a local pub with Simon and Sue to watch a local band that Simon likes, I started the weekend with a much-needed lie in.

Simon is an exceptionally highly skilled salesman. He runs his own company, importing fashion clothes and accessories, and tends to go to music festivals during the year selling these accessories to drunk revellers. Sadly, I don't need to be drunk to fall for Simon's sales patter and I have a collection of several of his novelty hats to prove it. Hats that he convinced me looked brilliant, including a very popular (Simon's words) Christmas Pie hat and a pair of very trendy Bert and Ernie hats. Sadly, my wife took a different view and has told me I am not allowed to see Simon unsupervised. When Simon got a new supply of elephant hats with big ears and a trunk sticking out of the front, I had to avoid him for the next few weeks, but he very kindly said he was keeping one for me.

A few years ago, Simon told me that he was holding a wake in the pub following the death of his printer. I said to my wife that I wanted to go and show my support and arrived to see Simon and another friend walking up the High Street with a cardboard coffin on their shoulders.

As it turned out, the printer was made by Canon and had come to the end of its useful life. The plan was to recognise it for its long and faithful service but, it turned out, I was the only person in a pub full of around 60 people who didn't know this and thought that it might have been the chap who did his printing for him.

So, after a relatively lazy morning, I headed to the ground picking up Martin and Gary on route. Today is a year and a day since Bill died and we thought we would get together to toast his memory. This meant that Martin was coming to the game and Gary is allowed out.

We bumped into Roy and said our hellos as we walked into the town centre, heading for the Victoria, our usual pre-match haunt much favoured by Bill. Sadly, three out of four bitters were unavailable, and I'm not sure Abbot Ale is entirely appropriate for anyone who is going to be getting into a car a couple of hours later.

So, we re-traced our steps and entered the George, which was, co-incidentally, where I had first met Bill somewhere around 1983. At the time, I regularly met a friend of mine, Mark, for lunch. Bill was working in the pub and, rather embarrassingly, remains the only person I have ever 'picked up' from a pub. How the George has changed though over the last 35 years. It now has a long bar with lots of fizzy lager for sale. I did see some pumps at the other end, and we enthusiastically raced over to see what was available. Our eyes were drawn to a label on one of the pumps advertising Doom Bar. However, when we got close, there was a much smaller sign saying, 'coming soon,' which was very disappointing. We ignored the attempted argument from the barmaid that we should enjoy a pint of John Smith's and had something from a bottle as we sat and watched the tail end of West Ham versus Chelsea.

Given the solemnity of the occasion, we had some laminated photographs of Bill with us and one was duly attached to the vacant chair at our table as we toasted his memory and shared many memories of our friend. I think Bill would have quite enjoyed the occasion except for when Sergeant Jason accidentally and unceremoniously sat on him.

After Ian had joined us we decided that we needed a decent beer and decided to head to the bar in South Stand where we were served an excellent and reasonably priced pint of TEA. It's clear that we should have a pre-match drink in the ground more often.

Steve from Bournemouth joined us. He had with him a small brass plaque that the club had kindly agreed that we could attach to the crash barrier at the top of the Slab. Steve from Bournemouth had brought some industrial strength superglue with him, the kind that requires mixing before application, and after first sanding the barrier, the plaque was successfully attached. The operation had taken about 15 minutes. Steve from Bournemouth did well to cope with the stream of advice that was being given by various people on what was straight and what wasn't. A spirit level would have been useful but was sadly forgotten.

We attached a few laminated photos of Bill, and Steve from Bournemouth tied Bill's scarf to the barrier and we spent a few moments of quiet reflection before the game started. We had agonised over what words to use, and eventually decided that we should keep it simple:

Bill Tootill
1960 – 2016
Our Friend

It says what we wanted it to say and Steve had a text from Bill's wife, Gill saying she liked it, which was good to hear.

As for the football, it was pretty poor. It felt in some ways like a pre-season friendly with neither side seeming to put in the effort required to win a game of football and neither team finding any degree of rhythm to upset the other. We were in complete control of the first half but couldn't find the passes to unlock the Halifax defence. Then, against the run of play, Lewis Ward made a mistake which let Halifax score from a fairly innocuous move just before half-time. We weren't worried as we thought that Sir Gary would change things around in the second half and we would come out with more intent, improving the quality of our passing and movement. Sadly, it wasn't to be and the game continued in much the same manner. It was one of those games where we never really got going and I'm sure Halifax would have been delighted with the three points. Maybe a draw would have been a fairer reflection on the game as neither side really did enough to win the game but, in the end, it wasn't to be our day. The highlight was most definitely Charlie joining in with the singing of "Oooh it's a corner." I'd like to think that he did so in honour of our friend Bill's memory, but I think it's probably more likely that he's losing his marbles and didn't know what he was doing.

I haven't heard anything from my friend Mike who supports Halifax since we beat them in August, but it didn't take long for him to send me an e-mail saying, 'Your boys must have been really shit today.' I wasn't quite that direct in my messages to him in August, but I guess this means I can be next time we beat them. Watch out Mike...

Nick Cansfield

East Thurrock United versus Aldershot

Saturday 16 December 2017

After last season's disappointing exits from both the FA Cup and the FA Trophy, it was a struggle to get motivated to travel to Essex today and, after last week's result, I had said to my wife that I had no further plans to go to any football before Christmas.

Steve from Number 11 rang me while we were walking the dogs in the morning and said that he wanted to go to a match and asked if I would be interested in accompanying him to watch Farnham Town versus Hanworth Villa. I said I had better decline as I had been planning a day with Mrs C. After wishing him well and hanging up, my wife said that she probably was OK with me going. I felt I needed clarification on her use of the term 'probably' before calling Steve from Number 11 back, but she confirmed I was good to go. Steve from Number 11 picked me up and we headed to Farnham in time for a beer in the club-house before entering the ground at two minutes to three.

I often find it quite difficult to watch football as a neutral spectator. I need to have something to like or dislike about one of the teams to really get into a game. We were supporting Farnham Town as it was our local team, but it was very different to watching and supporting the Shots, particularly as I have done so for so many years.

Hanworth took the lead in the first half. Just before half-time Farnham managed an equaliser. Hanworth scored a winner in the second half winning 2-1. Nonetheless, we thoroughly enjoyed the afternoon and, if I'm honest, we probably enjoyed the absence of the stress that comes with standing on the terraces watching the Shots. Not all supporters could say the same, and we were very surprised when spectators had to separate two fans about to come to blows with each other. Extraordinary behaviour from a pair of Octogenarians at a local game of football in front of no more than 50 fans! There was a lot of shouting and pushing for about 20 minutes and in one way it was quite nice to have something to distract from the whining of the Hanworth players, a number of whom should have been told to keep quiet by the Referee.

I was asking Steve for updates on the Shots game throughout the afternoon and it made for depressing reading. 1-0 down at half-time became 2-0 down, and then 3-0 and, unbelievably, 4-0 before the referee spared us further embarrassment by blowing the final whistle. There was a poor crowd in Essex of only 252 which suggested many other Shots fans struggled to raise the enthusiasm to travel but it was the post-match interview that seemed to imply that there is some cause for concern as Sir Gary suggested that the Board were not supporting him signing new players. "The squad is very thin and, subsequently, we were only able to name three substitutes today. It's hard to see how we will continue to do well without a little investment". Of greater concern though is that it seems that Sir Gary is not particularly happy at the moment. Let's hope that this is just as a result of today's result and that there is no other underlying reason which may make him feel that it's time for him to move on. It's not, Sir Gary!

Some of our fans on the chat room need to remember the journey that we have been on and just how tough life has been over the last few years before complaining about two consecutive defeats. Yes, they were poor results, and yes, we would have hoped that we would have been more competitive, but I wouldn't swap our position with anyone in our league. Sir Gary is, without question, the right man for our club, and we are, without question, the right club for this man.

Guiseley versus Aldershot

Saturday 23 December 2017

Chris Arthur has just left the club. Chris hadn't had a game for a while, and I'm not sure what match time evidence there was to suggest that he wasn't up to the job. I liked Chris. He was a big, strong player who could deliver a quick cross into the box when he was coming forward up the wing – something that generally Shots players aren't too good at. It was also confirmed that Adam McDonnell had been recalled by Ipswich. Adam will be sorely missed as he has played a big part in the success we've had this season, often just by quietly getting on with his job, without any fanfare or without grabbing the headlines.

Hopefully Sir Gary will pull a rabbit out of the hat like he did last year with Kundai Benyu, but we'll have to see. From what I've seen so far this season we could probably do with another left back (so that Callum could move back into central defence) and another striking option. Although we are near the top of the goals scored column, we haven't scored in the last three games and our top scorer, Shamir Fenelon, has only mustered five so far this season.

I was half tempted to travel to Guiseley to show my support to the team but unfortunately, I had arranged for my family to come for Christmas lunch on Christmas Eve and shopping and culinary preparations needed to be made. I remembered that I had also promised my wife that I wouldn't go to any more matches before Christmas and I had already reneged on that by visiting Farnham Town the previous weekend.

So, it was another afternoon in front of the radio listening to the commentary. With my family coming over for a Christmas dinner, there were quite a lot of jobs to be done, and I switched the radio commentary on after about ten minutes, just in time to hear Guiseley score from a free kick on the edge of the penalty area. 1-0 to Guiseley and a long afternoon beckoning.

Rob does a fantastic job making the football worth listening to even when the Shots are playing badly, as indeed they seemed to be today, and I have to give a huge thanks to the efforts that he, as a fan, puts in to travelling to every away game doing what must be quite a difficult job. Your efforts are much appreciated, thank you, Rob.

It certainly was a long afternoon. I spent time alternating between the kitchen preparing food for the next day and coming into the living room in order to catch up with the commentary. I've realised that my wife and I cooking in a fairly small kitchen at the same time is a recipe for disaster. Twice I washed up the scales only to find that she had re-used them before I got a chance. But no matter, the veg was prepared and the breadcrumbs were ready for the bread sauce. I was going to prepare the Baked Alaska shortly afterwards but had to leave the lemon meringue pies until the morning as there was no room in the fridge.

But further evidence was provided that one must never leave a football match before the final whistle regardless of the score or how badly your team is playing, as Matt McClure pounced on a loose ball one yard out in order to secure an equaliser for the Shots in the 95th minute. Interestingly, no other team in the play-off places could manage a victory and so we moved up to sixth place in the league.

It is always nice to secure a victory late in the game. Well done Shots, indeed. Bring on the turkey, and let's see what happens on Boxing Day.

Aldershot versus Woeking

Tuesday 26 December 2017

We had a particularly splendid Christmas Day this year. It was a very quiet affair, where the four of us spent the day in our pyjamas and didn't leave the house. We had intended to take the dogs for a walk, but the weather wasn't overly enticing, and so we hunkered down and opened our presents. Matt was offered the opportunity to choose the first film and so we cracked open the 36 pints of 'Halfway to Heaven' that we had ordered from the beautiful people at the wonderful Langham's brewery and settled down to watch the first Die Hard movie. There was a brief argument about whether this met the description of a 'Christmas movie', but Matt was adamant that because it had snow, and was set in the run up to Christmas, it clearly met the criteria. We had a huge fry up for brunch, and generally spent a very lazy day enjoying each other's company, sadly an all too infrequent event in our busy lives.

My expectations about being able to go to the Boxing Day match had been set many years ago, and I had been resigned to sneakily listening to it on Twitter, but James came to my rescue by insisting that he wanted to go. His lovely mother said that if he wanted to go then he could, and I was lucky enough to be allowed to drive him there.

So, in preparation, we rose early to take the dogs to the common for their walk and then headed towards the Weald and Downland Museum in Singleton to see what was going on. We both love this museum and try to show our support with an annual visit. One item I hadn't noticed before was a 'Container Wagon'. This was recently donated to the Museum from the Reynolds Furniture Store in Bognor Regis and dates back to the turn of the twentieth century. The sign attached to it says that 'It is a flat-bed wagon with a removable container which was used by the company to transport furniture, initially horse-powered, but later adapted to be towed by tractor.' It went on to offer a useful insight into the argument that Bill and Gary had been having all those years ago by saying that '...the principle of container transport is still extremely common today and allows goods to be moved from one mode of transport to another (from wagon to train for example) without the need to unpack everything.' So, there we have it – evidence that both Gary and Bill were wrong. Containerisation started 120 years ago!

Meanwhile, at the football, parking in the multi-storey was easy, and we walked to the ground.

James was rather surprised at the crowds queuing outside the turnstiles when we reached the ground. A few of the turnstiles were closed which probably didn't help, but there was a very healthy crowd of over 4,000 souls braving the weather forecast to watch the game. South Stand seating had been sold out by 2.30 but, as always, particularly when it is pouring with rain, there is always room on the Slab. The rain started pretty much bang on 3.00 and, despite a few moments of respite, it continued for the remainder of the game.

Both teams started brightly, and the first 15 minutes were evenly fought. Bernard Mensah tried a shot in front of the East Bank from 25 yards out and, although we didn't have the best view from the Slab, we hadn't expected to see the ball balloon out in the general direction of the corner flag in the North Stand corner. But clearly Bernard (generally considered to be the most intelligent man in football) had fooled not only the 11 players from Woeking, but also the 4,000 fans in the crowd, as Bobby-Joe Taylor raced on to it, and passed it into the six-yard box for Shamir Fenelon to put the Shots in front.

Our jubilant celebrations didn't last long however as Woeking took control from the re-start and, within two minutes, had torn our defence apart with a lovely move and a lovely finish from Inih Effiong. Shortly after came the moment that could have changed the direction of the game when another Woeking attack saw them hit the crossbar when a goal looked on the cards. I messaged Steve from Number 11 at this point that it was going to be a long afternoon and, had Woeking scored, the game would have been different. But we rode this pressure and we rode our luck and we dragged ourselves back into the game.

An effort from Bernard went high over the bar and when Jake Gallagher was fouled on the edge of the penalty box, the Shots had a free-kick. Nathan Baxter, the Woeking goal-keeper pulled off the first of a number of extraordinary saves from a superb Bobby Joe Taylor free-kick. The Shots had another great chance when Bobby-Joe crossed the ball and Baxter could only push it into Jake's direction, but it bounced off his knee onto a Woeking defender and into Baxter's arms. Then came a moment of brilliance which would have graced any football pitch in the world. Bobby-Joe passed the ball to Scott Rendell who lobbed the ball over the Woeking defenders for Shamir to run on to. Shamir took a couple of touches to gain control and unleashed a perfect shot that gave Baxter absolutely no chance.

2-1 to the Shots and we were on fire. Baxter had to pull off another couple of saves before half-time, and the Woeking fans had a brief moment of false hope when they thought they had scored but the linesman's flag was high and fluttering in the wind and rain, long before the ball hit the back of the net.

The Shots started the second half with the same level of commitment with which they had ended the first. Apart from a couple of moments when we put ourselves under needless pressure from poorly aimed passes, we looked in control. Bobby-Joe took a corner in front of the Slab and Bernard headed it back into the box from the far post. The ball fell to Manny Oyeleke on the edge of the penalty area, and he smashed the ball into the top of the net to make it 3-1 to the Shots

The Shots continued to dominate, winning more corners and forcing more good saves from Baxter including a good effort from Bernard Mensah which was deflected just wide of the goal.

As one of the Woeking players was receiving treatment, Jake Gallagher came off the pitch to have a chat with some of the Shots fans, who asked him if we could get another goal to let us breathe more easily. Jake was agreeing that another goal would be good, but before he could offer any further insight, the referee shouted at him to get back on to the pitch. Two good efforts from Matt McClure before the referee blew the whistle for a final 3-1 score-line.

I think if I had been a Woeking fan I might have been slightly disgruntled that the Shots seemed to win every 50/50 decision from the referee. I wasn't close enough to call all of them but from what I've seen this season from other referees, I wouldn't have been surprised to have seen a penalty given to Woeking and at least two yellow cards to each side.

But the referee seemed consistent and very content to let the game flow, which made for a really enjoyable afternoon. Maybe less so, if one came from Woeking, but they limited the damage to three goals when it could have been more. Fine performances from a number of Shots players, but Bobby-Joe Taylor, Bernard Mensah, Shamir Fenelon, Scott Rendell, Jake Gallagher and Cheye Alexander all particularly stood out for me.

I think I would still have had Nathan Baxter as the man of the match and, apart from New Year's Day, when I hope Woeking get thrashed, I hope they have a successful remainder of the season. While they are our most local club, the rivalry is generally friendly, and good natured.

Aldershot versus Maidstone

Saturday 30 December 2017

We had been invited to a BBQ at Steve from Number 11's last night. It seemed a slightly odd choice of meal given the temperature had only just risen above zero but who am I to argue. I enjoy cooking, but I find doing anything on a BBQ quite difficult and, given the choice, I would prefer to cook in a kitchen using a proper cooker. We had dug out our brightest Hawaiian shirts and with cans of Lilt and cartons of Um Bongo to accompany some beer and wine, we made our way up to the far end of the close.

Steve and I had a wonderful evening talking about the Shots and our hopes and aspirations for the forthcoming games, the remainder of the season and beyond, and agreed that the future looked so much rosier all the time that Sir Gary remains in charge. I sincerely hope that Sir Gary feels the same way about the club and us fans as we do about him and that he is happy to see out the remainder of his career with us. Steve from Number 11 is of the opinion that he may be tempted if a bigger club comes after him but there comes a time in your life where the ambition to be promoted to a bigger job or a bigger club is tempered by the ambition to focus on doing a really good job in an environment where you feel comfortable and appreciated. I guess time will tell. I'm more hopeful that Sir Gary will stay with the Shots, and we backed our respective views with a bet of a pint of beer.

I mentioned to Steve from number 11 that James and I had briefly thought about trying to get as many live games of football into a day or a weekend as possible. With kick-off times being moved, we felt it should be possible to do two, if not three, games in a single day. Having noticed that the Maidstone game had been brought forward to a 12.30 kick off, I looked at the local fixtures and asked if either of them fancied trying to get to Fleet Town for 3.00. Sadly, neither of them were particularly keen, but we jumped into Steve from Number 11's car and headed to Aldershot for what would have undoubtedly been the highlight of the day.

I do have to say the 12.30 kick off felt decidedly odd. We went straight to the ground and headed for the South Stand bar. I've been very impressed the times I've been there in the last year or two as there is generally a barrel or two of real ale on the counter, and it has always been in excellent condition. Today we were treated to some Old Golden Hen, but Steve from Number 11 had a rather pathetic pint of fizz. I know that real ale is an acquired taste but persevere my friend, and you will be rewarded. Last night Steve from Number 11 was drinking a revolting Australian lager that has to be one of the most awful drinks that has ever been invented. I think I need to help Steve from Number 11 discover the delights of real ale. It can become my new year's resolution. I'm sure our wives would be hugely supportive of this. More likely, they will be completely disinterested.

No Sergeant Jason to handcuff me today but it was great to see our very first captain after we reformed in 1992, Dave Osgood, having a quiet drink in the bar. Dave is the nephew of the late ex-Chelsea and England striker Peter Osgood and played 152 games for the Shots between 1992 and 1997. According to Pete Stanford, he is ninth in the appearance list and tenth in the goal-scorers list. He always led by example and was a firm favourite with the fans. What a team we had in those first years with Steve Stairs, Mark Butler, Dave Osgood, Andy Nunn, Keith Baker, Tony Calvert, Steve Harris, Shaun May and so on. It was a real joy to watch after the struggles of the previous few years.

We couldn't help but notice a rather odd looking individual standing at the bar. He had a trilby, dark sunglasses, a handlebar moustache and a leather trench-coat. We noticed a certain similarity with Ron Jeremy. Certainly, it was someone who, in an attempt to disguise themselves, was creating some attention. Maybe we were wrong. Maybe it was a member of the SAS who was undercover and trying to go for a double-bluff. Either way, he looked very out of place in the South Stand bar.

With our Captain, Callum Reynolds not in the side today, the last thing we wanted was to lose Will Evans to injury within the first three minutes, but Jim Kellerman smashed a clearance from our penalty area that hit Will right in the face, and he had to be substituted. The game got off to a relatively slow start with very little to report in the first twenty minutes. This isn't unusual as both teams try and work each other out. Besides a Jim Kellerman free kick on the edge of the box that went just wide, the only excitement in the first half was an extraordinary moment where the ball came very slowly across the six yard line and Shamir managed to knock it back but it evaded everyone and went just wide – even though the ball was not travelling any faster than it would in a slow motion replay. Bernard Mensah seemed to be particularly targeted by Maidstone and was hacked down on a number of occasions, with the referee not offering him any protection.

As the half-time whistle went, we felt that we were shading the game and that it would only be a matter of time before we found a second gear and managed to assert ourselves.

And at the beginning of the second half our confidence seemed to have been well placed as Shamir very nearly managed to pounce on the ball after a sharp shot from Cheye. But it wasn't to be and, shortly after, Aaron Collins scored for Maidstone after our goal-keeper came out towards the edge of the penalty area and just couldn't manage to nudge the ball out of harm's way. This was the obvious cue for Maidstone to slow the game down, but we were beginning to think that we were getting back into the game when Maidstone made a succession of rash tackles, resulting in two yellow cards for nasty assaults on Bernard and Jim.

James Rowe had a good shot after a lovely run by Bernard in the middle of the second half but, unfortunately, this was about it, and the second half belonged to Maidstone. A rebound off the post that crawled across the goal-line, a shot that hit the back of the net before being ruled off-side and two outstanding saves from Lewis Ward in the Aldershot goal managed to retain a degree of respectability to the score-line, but the truth was that Maidstone seemed to want it more than us. Just as we were thinking that it wasn't going to be our game, Bobby-Joe Taylor crossed the ball and Jim Kellerman flicked his header into the Maidstone net for our equaliser. I'm not sure if it was deserved or not but scoring in the 93rd minute was sweet revenge for the away game at Maidstone earlier in the season when we were comfortably winning and Maidstone levelled in the 95th minute.

They say that the sign of a good team is winning when they are not playing well. Maybe, but I would much rather see slightly more assured performances!

Woeking versus Aldershot

Monday 1 January 2018

Steve from Number 11's family wanted to go to Woeking for the game which meant two things. Firstly, we couldn't travel together as I needed to pick up Gary and his sister Denise and, secondly, it meant that we couldn't watch together as he would need to head to the seats. Gary and I caught up with him briefly before the game (after we'd queued for the customary 20 minutes to enter the ground) and made our way to the far end. It seems that Steve from Number 11's kids maybe weren't looking forward to it quite as much as Mum and Dad were as they were clutching their computer games. Hopefully this would mean they wouldn't be causing their parents too many difficulties.

We also bumped into Howard, who offered us a prediction that Kundai Benyu would be coming back to Aldershot on loan for the rest of the season before being transferred from Celtic to MK Dons. We thought this was a bold prophecy and it would be a tremendous boost if it were to happen. We weren't confident enough to contact Reuters though, just in case this might scupper the deal.

Denise is over from Australia visiting Gary and Mirinda. She hails from Queensland which I suspect has a slightly milder climate than this part of Hampshire/Surrey at this time of the year. She said that she was familiar with football, having watched her son play at school, and told us that she had gone to Anfield once. We told her that the game was likely to be slightly different from a Premiershit game, but she was excitedly looking forward to it.

Woeking had clearly decided that they needed to show more steel against us in this game and some of their tackling in the first half was decidedly questionable. The assault on Jake Gallagher after five minutes saw the referee play an initial advantage but not take any action against the perpetrator. The Woeking number four, Joey Jones, tackled Jim Kellerman from behind after about a quarter of an hour when he was just breaking through the Woeking defence and we were surprised when the referee only brandished a yellow card. On another day we felt it might have been red. Poor Jim was to have a tough afternoon as he was pushed over again a few minutes later, something which the referee seemed to be quite happy when it was the Woeking players doing the pushing but, as we saw later in the game, when a Woeking player was to fall to the ground after the slightest bodily contact, he was more than happy to give them a free kick.

Woeking picked up another yellow card before the Shots created a wonderful effort, with Scott Rendell passing the ball through to Cheye Alexander. All the travelling Shots fans shouted as one "Shoot!", and Cheye delivered a fabulous shot towards the top left corner of the goal which Baxter did well to get his fingers to and deflect over the bar for a corner.

More fouls then followed with Jake being pulled over once again, but Scott had his revenge with a brilliant header that had the terraces screaming with delight on the half hour mark as the Shots went 1-0 up. The Shots had what felt like a good chance to increase the score after 40 minutes when two or three players had chances to get a shot in as the ball bounced around the Woeking penalty area, but it just wasn't going in, and Woeking immediately counter-attacked. As Inih Effiong attacked the Aldershot goal, Lewis Ward came out to meet him. Unfortunately, though Inih got around Lewis and we were fortunate that George Fowler was standing on the goal-line and able to head the ball clear. Lewis Ward redeemed himself with a good save a few minutes later, and as the half drew to a close, Effiong was finally booked for a foul on Will Evans.

Woeking came out of the blocks quickly in the second half and, within two minutes, Kane Ferdinand had scored an equaliser. The Shots didn't give up, gradually forcing themselves back into the game. Some of our passing was still a little below par, but with Cheye and Jake both unwell before the game, we put in a pretty good performance.

Manny went in for two tackles in quick succession, the first of which looked perfectly acceptable. The second looked as if it might get the referee reaching for his cards. Fortunately, the player who went down first rolled around for many minutes and Manny managed to get away with it.

The referee continued his inconsistency and gave a free kick to Woeking for a foul by Jim on Joey Jones. The truth was that Jim barely touched Jones and he seemed to take a bit of a dive. Fortunately, the referee missed a handball by Lewis when he once again went on a walkabout which evened things up. Woeking had two good chances to go ahead but our defence managed to stop the first and the shot from the rebound went over the bar.

Chances continued to come for the Shots, the best of which was when substitute Matt McClure flicked a wicked cross into the box, forcing Baxter to push the ball over the penalty area with his finger-tips. The game ebbed and flowed, continually going from one penalty area to the other. It seemed to be heading for a draw. After scoring, Woeking seemed to have moved to a 7–2–1 formation, booting the ball over the top of the midfield to Effiong whenever they got a chance and it was tough breaking down their dogged defence. But in the 90th minute, Jakey sent a through ball to Scott who made no mistake in securing the three points for us. To our amusement, the Woeking tannoy announcer said the goal had been scored by Scott 'Rundle', whoever he is.

The second half of the game had been difficult to concentrate on due to the poor stewarding in the away terrace. People buying seats had been told that they could seat anywhere rather than on the seat with the number that was printed on their tickets. They were soon full and families who had bought tickets were unable to sit together, and an elderly fan who had specifically bought a seat at the bottom of the stand as he was unable to walk up the stairs due to a lack of hand-rails, was unable to take his seat at all.

The away crowd was given as 1,085 but the terrace was considerably busier than it had been in the last couple of years. Someone posted that he had had a lengthy conversation with one of the Woeking steward supervisors at the end of the game. He wrote 'The terrace is certified for 940 and we were given 200 seats, down from the 450 we've had the last two years. He confirmed they received 500 too many tickets and there were 200 left on the turnstiles, meaning there was about 1450 Shots fans in there. He said the official number would always be announced at or below the allowable capacity or they would be in trouble.' So, there were potentially an additional 300 fans on the away terrace. No wonder it was feeling snug. Interestingly, the tickets for this year were exactly the same as those used for the last two years. My ticket for last year was number 10107 and my ticket for this year was 07903. Apart from the number, they are identical. , Howard said that the ticket he was given this year for the seating area had 1 January 2017 printed on it so altogether it wasn't a huge surprise that there may have been more fans than the terrace was designed to hold.

During the second half, the end of the terrace where we were attacking was becoming even more crowded and the stewards didn't seem to know what to do. Fans had to stand on the safety zone between the terrace and the advertising hoardings as there wasn't enough room on the terrace. There are only a limited number of gaps where fans can get behind the safety barriers, which made it difficult to get behind them.

As it was, around 35 Surrey Police Officers strode forcefully up the terrace and promptly stood right in front of the fans which, with the 15 stewards, caused a significantly greater obstruction than the similar number of fans who were quietly watching the game. After half an hour and several tannoy announcements, the fans were duly moved along the terrace. Well, some were. Most still stood exactly where they were, which meant that our view was still more restricted with the police involvement than it would have been without. I couldn't help but wonder why they were standing there doing absolutely nothing. It looked as if the stewards were asking for their help but that the police were refusing to give it.

When the goal was scored the advertising hoardings attached to the far end of the terrace gave way, leaving a number of fans falling onto the pitch and Aldershot fans reported items being thrown at them by Woeking fans. This was the third consecutive year that the same barrier had broken, which seems totally unacceptable. Given that safety certificates have to be given, surely barriers have some kind of test to make sure they do what they need to. I can understand things going wrong once but for it to happen three consecutive years just feels like incompetence. Some Woeking fans suggested that the Shots fans were deliberately trying to break the barrier which I'm not sure is true. If they were, surely they would have done so earlier in the game rather than hoping that we would score a winner in the 90th minute.

This was at the other end of the pitch to where we were standing and, incidentally, the other end of the pitch to where all the police were standing, so they all moved up to the other end of the ground while the game was delayed by 10 minutes for peace and harmony to be resumed. This meant that our view was cleared for the rest of the game. I had thought that there was still another five minutes plus maybe three minutes of time to be added on but after a couple of minutes of Woeking attacking our goal, and our defence staying strong, the referee blew his whistle and we could take a deep breath and recover from an exhilarating afternoon of football.

While we might not have set any new records for the number of fans celebrating our corners, we almost certainly hit a record for the greatest distance from one end of those singers to the other, as Steve from Number 11 joined in with Gary and me while he was sitting in the seats. Sadly, it still hadn't taken off but there is always hope.

The match was a fantastic advert for lower league football and a wonderful introduction to proper football for Denise who said that it was one of the best days of her trip to the UK. Well done to the Shots players for sticking to the task and giving us a memorable afternoon.

Woeking fans were understandably disappointed but there really was no need for one of them to head-butt one of our youngish supporters shortly after the game finished.

Gary had gone to China for a holiday a couple of years ago and bought me a tee-shirt as a present. It is very yellow, and has 'I love BJ' (for Beijing) on the front, in the same style as the Americans have popularised their 'I love New York' slogan. My wife didn't think this was going to get too much wear and had, if we were to give her the benefit of the doubt, accidentally knocked it into the waste paper bin. James thought it was dead cool, rescued it, and has hardly taken it off over the last six months. At the beginning of the season when we signed Bobby Joe, the tee-shirt suddenly had a new significance, and I thought I should ask him to autograph it for me. I'd carried it with me in my pocket to the last few games and thought it might be worthwhile taking it to Woeking as the players generally come across to the fans at the end of the game.

Caught up in the emotion of Scotty's winning goal in the 90th minute, the tee-shirt seemed to come out of my pocket and was lofted high above the crowd. Unfortunately, Bobby-Joe had headed off towards the dressing room by the time I could escape around the crash barriers leaving me to try another day, but the tee-shirt was very prominent on the photographs on both the official Twitter link to the review of the game and on the weekly e-mail that came out a few days later talking about the away game at Dover.

Unlike James, who was very excited to see his tee-shirt given so much attention, his mother wasn't keen that the tee-shirt had been liberated. It could have been worse, I guess. I could have been wearing it.

Dover versus Aldershot

Saturday 6 January 2018

It was a busy week, news wise. Chairman Shahid said that we had turned down a request from a league club to talk to Sir Gary and James Rowe and, with their support, he had turned it down. I guess that given our relative success and the wonderful football that we are playing, this is always likely to happen but it's brilliant news that Sir Gary, James and Shahid are all committed to the success of the club. Long may it continue.

It was also announced that Shaun Okojie and Kodi Lyons-Foster have both left the club, and that Lewis Ward and George Fowler have both extended their loan periods. We also brought in a much-needed left back, on loan from Colchester and a striker on loan from Portsmouth. Welcome to Lewis Kinsella and Nicke Kabamba. I hope they will both be very happy at our fantastic club and will flourish with us.

I read that Kundai Benyu is set for a loan switch to Oldham for the remainder of the season. Sorry Howard, but it looks like you called this one wrong.

There was some disappointing news that the away match at Dagenham is going to be televised and, subsequently, the kick off moved to 5.30 on a Saturday evening. This will require more careful negotiations with my wife, as it will wipe out any plans that we might have for Saturday night.

While Gary, Steve from Number 11 and I were all tempted to travel to Dover for this match, we all had to temper our enthusiasm. Having gone to the last three games, which were within a week of each other, I felt that my wife might frown on my prioritisation. I have been to Dover a couple of times, the most recent of which was when we lost 2-0 in a cup game. It was a freezing cold day and Bill, James and I had decided to travel on the official supporters' coach. Actually, there were quite a few supporters' coaches as Terry Owens had very kindly offered to pay for the away travel. A number of fans were encouraged to travel and I believe we eventually had as many as seven coaches. It was freezing cold, our performance was woeful and generally it was an all-together miserable experience. The weather forecast for today was for heavy rain and it seemed like a game to watch on the radio inside a nice warm house.

From the radio commentary the first half sounded quite even, with Dover playing very defensively and allowing us to have some possession. Unfortunately, we couldn't find a way through until just before half-time when Jim Kellerman, who is quickly becoming one of my players of the season, bundled the ball into the net to put us into the lead. Unfortunately, Dover equalised straight away and we went into the break one apiece.

The second half sounded a lot more exciting. Well, it would have done except for the twenty minutes when the commentary was lost.

Someone posted on the chat room that he thought our new signing, Kabamba, was going to be the hero and so it seemed when he got on the end of a low and hard cross half way through the second half which spilled out of the Dover goal-keeper's hands, to put the Shots 2-1 ahead. We had a few chances, but it was the customary squeaky bum time for the last ten to fifteen minutes as Dover, who were lying in fourth place before the game, came on strongly. Four minutes injury time made it feel even longer until, mercifully, the referee finally blew his whistle for a Shots victory.

Rob talked very enthusiastically of the second half of the game and Nicke Kabamba seemed to have a particularly good debut. I really wished I'd gone! But I consoled myself by looking at the league table, enjoying seeing us closing the gap on top of the table Macclesfield who only managed a draw against Solihull Moors. 51 points should also make us mathematically safe from relegation, which for most fans is always a good place to be.

Another fabulous day at the office and very well done Shots!

Bernard Mensah

Thursday 11 January

I was just leaving the office when I noticed a text from James
saying it had just been announced that Bernard had accepted a
transfer to Bristol Rovers.   My initial reaction was huge
disappointment as Bernard has been such a fantastic asset for us
over the last season and a half and is one of the few players that
can genuinely change a game.   But we must remember that the
more successful Sir Gary is in developing players, the more
chances there are of them progressing to teams in higher leagues
who are able to pay much higher wages.   This is the way it is and
we need to remind ourselves that there is much to be proud about
as the alternative would be that we don't have any players
progressing to higher leagues because no one is interested in
them, because we are not playing good football.

So, thank you, Bernard. It has been a real privilege being able to
watch you play at Aldershot. The leaving message that you posted
on Twitter sounded very sincere and I hope you look back with
terrific fondness at your time with us.

Bernard said that he '…wanted to thank everyone at Aldershot
Town! From the Gaffer and Rowey who signed me when I left
Watford and gave me an opportunity to play and show my
ability! To all the back-room staff, Russ, Steve, Sam and everyone

else who I dealt with on a day to day basis at the training ground! To the staff and volunteers who do a lot behind the scenes to make our jobs as players easier on a match day, thank you! Also, to the teammates both last season and this season. Best bunch of lads I've had a privilege to share a season with. I will miss you all!' 'Now to the fans! Who since day one welcomed me and sang my name throughout my time at the club, thank you! It was a tough decision to leave, but an opportunity in which I couldn't turn down! I really do hope the club get promoted this season! Everything is there for it to happen! Best wishes for the remainder of the season! I know I'll be seeing you sooner rather than later!!! Thanks for all the memories, Bernard Mensah x'

A slight over-enthusiasm for exclamation marks perhaps but otherwise a lovely message from a player who had totally endeared himself to the fans over the time he was with us, and will quite rightly be very fondly remembered. The news persuaded Steve from number 11 to text me saying that he thought '...this had wider implications for Sir Gary's stickability and I can almost taste that pint.' Hmmm, I thought, before asking how confident he was, and offering to increase the bet to a bottle of single malt if Sir Gary leaves before the start of next season. Steve from Number 11 has accepted the bet, so please don't go anywhere Sir Gary!

Bognor Regis Town versus Leyton Orient

Saturday 13 January 2018

With no Shots match today I got in touch with my friend Fat
Andy and joined him in heading to Nyewood Lane to watch
Bognor's FA Trophy Second Round game against Orient. I've
known Fat Andy for about ten years now. Our kids played in the
same local football and cricket teams and we used to have regular
arguments about which one of us wasn't going to be the
linesman. I should have won these arguments because I am really
bad at it. I remember one time I was doing it and the ball crossed
the line, so I held my flag up and waved it around. The referee
then asked a really difficult question, namely, which team had put
the ball into touch which had a direct influence on who was going
to take the throw in. My answer of "No idea, I didn't notice,"
was apparently not what he was expecting. Then, as the kids grew
older, fewer parents came to watch the games and eventually it
was between Fat Andy, Chris, Simon and myself as to who drew
the short straw.

Fat Andy and I also play golf together and try and get a weekend
away each year with Paul and Doris. Doris and I used to work
together, and he has the most extraordinary attention to detail.

Doris asked whether I would like to go to Wembley for the first
game after the new stadium opened a number of years ago. I

think it was a Community Shield match with ManUre playing Chelski, and the tickets were reasonably priced at around £15 each so it seemed quite appealing to tick a new ground off the list. However, we were in the upper balcony and so far away from the pitch that I should have brought my opera glasses.

There's only one train an hour at the weekends in the village where I live, and so I said to Doris that I would be on the train which left at about 10.30. Doris lives one stop further, so his train was a couple of minutes earlier. Not difficult. I had suggested that we went to the pub when we got to Waterloo for some lunch, before heading off to the game. Gary was meeting us in London and we agreed that we might head for a curry after the game if we felt like it. Now for me I thought this was a pretty good plan and it told us everything that we wanted to know for the day. It might have had a bit too much detail for Gary but, otherwise, it did the trick. Not so for Doris, however. He came armed with a printed itinerary, which was something along the lines of:

10.27	Doris catches the train to Waterloo
10.32	Nick catches the train to Waterloo
11.37	arrive London Waterloo
11.47	arrive at the Duke of Wellington for lunch
13.40	leave the Duke of Wellington
13.55	catch Jubilee Line tube from Waterloo to Baker Street
14.12	catch Metropolitan line tube to Wembley Park
14.29	arrive Wembley
14.50	arrive in seats
15.00	kick off
15.45	half-time
16.00	second half starts
16.50	game finishes (allowing for injury time)
17.00	watch trophy presentation
17.30	depart Wembley

He then repeated the itinerary in reverse.

I've been to new Wembley a few times since, and I have always been massively underwhelmed by the experience. It might help if the band was refused entry for England internationals. Sheffield Wednesday saw the light, so why not England? I don't want to watch a game of football listening to a brass band. The odd drum works well, especially when it's in the expert hands of someone like East Bank Steve (aka Elvis), but trumpets and trombones and a repetition of the same three or four songs over and over again for 90 minutes? No thank you.

England always seem to disappoint too. There's rarely any passion or excitement, either from the team or the fans, although the 2018 World Cup might signal a bit of a change. Maybe a domestic game would be more exciting, but if and when the Shots ever do get to play there, it's likely to be half empty, so I'm not so sure. When we made the final of the play-offs in our first season in the Conference back in 2004/5, it was held at Stoke. While it's obviously quite a lot further to travel, holding it in a ground with a 25,000 capacity makes a lot of sense.

Doris describes himself as a football fan and every time we meet we seem to argue. I have often asked him if he would like to come and watch a game with me, but he always whines "…why would I want to go and stand out in the cold to watch Aldershot, when I can watch ManUre from the comfort of my living room."

And so Fat Andy and I went to Bognor Regis and we met up with Fat Andy's fat friend, Fat Reggie, and his lad.

There was a crowd of 1,372 at the game though I'd have thought that Orient would have brought more fans with them. The first 10-15 minutes were quite even but then Bognor started to assert themselves and completely dominated the remainder of the first half. The game continued in a similar vein in the second half, and any neutral fans in the ground would have sworn that the green and white Rocks were the team from the higher league. Orient were poor. Their passing was not good enough and their crossing and shooting was at a level that would have embarrassed a Sunday morning pub team. But as so often happens, Bognor were reduced to ten men halfway through the second half and the game suddenly became much harder.

Orient were a big, strong, physical team, lacking in much finesse. After having been booked for a moment of stupidity in the first half when he man-handled a Bognor player onto the floor in an unnecessary off the ball incident, Joe Widdowson was shown a red card for a rash tackle and the number of players was even again.

But, from a goal-mouth scramble shortly after, Orient managed to bundle the ball through the Rocks defenders on the goal-line to go in front. The Orient fans and players thought that with eight minutes to go they had stolen the game, but they hadn't banked on Bognor's Jimmy Muitt who sent a screamer from 20 yards out into the very top right-hand corner of the net to equalise and force the game into extra-time. Sadly, Josh Koroma flighted a ball in the 117th minute to give Orient a very undeserved victory.

Stand out players from Bognor included the goal-keeper Dan Lincoln, full-back Kristian Campbell, and central defender Sami El-Abd. Stand out players from Orient were slightly harder to find. Jobi McAnuff and Macauley Bonne looked as if they had something going forward but they didn't really show us what that was. Matt Harrold was a big physical presence in the middle but so long as the Shots are on form there was nothing in this Orient team that should worry us when we play them.

I had a wonderful afternoon in great company. I like Bognor and if it was acceptable to have a second team then Bognor might be mine. But as it is not really acceptable, I'll continue to use them as an excuse to go and see my friend Fat Andy instead.

Aldershot versus Ebbsfleet

Saturday 20 January 2018

I heard on the radio that Graham Westley has been appointed as the Barnet Head Coach. Looking on the Barnet chat room, this news was met with mixed views. Actually, there aren't too many mixed views and I couldn't find anyone who was pleased with the appointment.

Keen for more insight, I thought I would ask my Barnet supporting friend Stephen what he thought. He said he "...was driving home last night chuckling at the news that 'Laughing Boy' Lambert had gone to Stoke when the next news item was that Westley was coming in to Barnet !?! Nooooooooooo!" he said, before saying that he "...turned off his phone and refused to read any emails until the next morning."

Even a Newport County fan logged on to the website to offer his sympathy, and said that he was "sorry but you are down and out. Miracles do happen so wish you the best."

I first heard of Graham when he was managing Farnborough Town. He had bought a controlling interest in the Club and appointed himself as manager. He had done quite well in his first couple of years with the club but then tried to arrange a merger with Kingstonian. He had said at the time that he was interested in buying a Football League rated ground but, unsurprisingly, the fans were in uproar and, to AFC Wimbledon's subsequent relief, the merger did not proceed. The following year was also successful as Farnborough reached the fourth round of the FA Cup and were rewarded with a home tie against Arsenal. The tie was controversially moved to Highbury, but it's hard for a Shots fan to take too dim a view of this given we did the same thing when we drew West Ham in the FA Cup in 1991. Co-incidentally, Farnborough drew West Ham the following year and switched their home tie too.

Shortly after losing 5-1 at Highbury in 2003 (a game that Bill and I went to), Graham resigned and became the manager at Stevenage. He subsequently signed seven of Farnborough's best players, leaving a number of other players on longer term contracts and large salaries that the club could not afford to pay. This started a huge decline for the club that arguably 15 years later they still do not seem to have recovered from.

Farnborough seem to have a history of appointing interesting characters as their managers. Their current manager is Spencer Day (previously known as Threthewy), who originally came to prominence with Aldershot fans back in the early 1990's when we were in terrible financial difficulties and he pronounced himself, very publicly, as our saviour. Sadly, while domestic fame came his way including an appearance on Wogan, the 19-year-old 'Property Developer' actually didn't have any money and was soon on his way to prison for fraud.

The rivalry between Barnet and Stevenage seems to stem from the time that Mr Westley was in charge of the latter and would send his teams out with a particularly combative approach in mind.

Stephen the Barnet fan did agree that "…things are so bad at the Hive right now that something radical needs to be done," and he acknowledged that it's just possible that Graham Westley will save Barnet from relegation. But he quickly followed this up adding that "…one thing's for sure - it won't be pretty." Stephen is still planning on going to the game on Saturday albeit with his fingers firmly crossed.

For some reason it feels like a long time since I've watched the Shots. Maybe that's because my last game was away at Woeking nearly three weeks ago. As a consequence, I had a degree of excitement over and above that which I would normally expect to have for the visit of Ebbsfleet. I'm not entirely certain whether James actually wanted to go to the game or whether he was just in need of someone to do his laundry, but either way I collected him from Reading and we made our way to the ground.

We rushed into the South Stand bar to meet Steve from Number 11 who had already bought two rounds of drinks. This might have been because we were running late but, very politely, he said that he had arrived early. The excitement of going to a game after three weeks clearly wasn't confined to just me. We only had time for a quick catch up before we had to leave the warmth of the bar to head onto the cold and slightly damp terrace.

The first half was relatively quiet, the only excitement being a fabulous save by Lewis Ward, getting down low to palm the ball past the post and out of play, and a Bobby-Joe Taylor effort for the Shots that deflected inches wide for a corner.

It was nice to see Midlands Bill on the terrace again. I hadn't seen him for a while. He always joins in with our chants with more enthusiasm and energy than anyone else as if the chant was his own. Always nice to see some passion shown from the older supporters.

During half-time I finally got around to asking Charlie why he stood on the Slab. I had to explain why I was asking the question, so I said that the only reason I stood on the Slab was because I wanted to stand with my friend Bill.

Bill and I stood on the Slab for many years and, in fact, sometime in the 1980s, we decided to form a 6 a-side football team which we called the South Stand Wanderers and we entered a league in Farnborough. We weren't that good, to be honest. We lost the first game 42-1 but I wasn't playing. So, it wasn't my fault. I featured in goal for the next match (even 30 years ago I was too lazy to run around for long) and we did considerably better, losing only 28-0.

We did show some signs of improvement and at one stage we even got ourselves promoted to a higher league. It was nice at Bill's funeral to see Martin and Pal and some of the other people who had played regularly for the Wanderers which had kept on going until only about four or five years ago. Bill had told me that the only reason he stood on the Slab was because he wanted to have a chat and catch up with Charlie. So, the reason why I got cold and wet so often was down to Charlie. Charlie took a moment to reflect on this before admitting that he didn't have a clue why he stood on the Slab.

Charlie said he used to come with his father and his older brother and his father used to go into the North Stand, his brother into the East Bank, and Charlie therefore decided to go onto the Slab! This gives a whole new meaning to a family going to the football match together. Charlie also admitted to having sung back in his youth but I'm not sure I believe him. I had once offered him £20 to join in with our corner chant but he had declined. Maybe now he's retired his financial circumstances might be different, and he could be tempted. One to try on another day, maybe.

The Shots started the second half with a bit more intent and Bobby-Joe delivered a wonderful cross that just flew over the bar onto the top of the netting. The action moved to the High Street End with Ebbsfleet's Coulson chasing a ball down the touchline with Will Evans. The ball came off Will but the referee, Mr Peter Gibbons, made the first of several curious decisions, awarding a throw to the Shots. Mr Coulson was clearly disappointed with this decision and showed it by making the most extraordinary guttural grunt which lasted several seconds. I know footballers are generally not thought of being overly intelligent but most of the time they are capable of forming words and generally the words are found somewhere within the Oxford English Dictionary.

Ebbsfleet continued to threaten and man of the match, Lewis Ward, made another wonderful save when Ebbsfleet broke through our defence with their striker having only Lewis to beat. There was a burst of excitement when Bobby-Joe attempted a shot which ballooned onto the roof of the East Bank and we readied ourselves to cheer when it eventually dropped back to the ground.

After an hour the Shots were awarded a free kick 20 yards out after a blatant foul by one of the Ebbsfleet defenders. Bobby-Joe struck the ball beautifully, well-directed to the right-hand corner of the net but the Ebbsfleet wall did its job and one of the defenders headed the ball into touch, bizarrely, for a goal kick. The Ebbsfleet goal-keeper has probably the longest kick I can recall seeing and the goal-kick was punted into our penalty area after one bounce, where Coulson just shot wide.

This was beginning to become end to end stuff, and either side could take the three points. Jim Kellerman had a good effort that just went wide, and then Bobby-Joe ran the length of the pitch with the ball. Unfortunately, he couldn't make anything happen where it mattered most.

The officials missed what seemed to be a very obvious off-side run from one of the Ebbsfleet players that could have proved costly as our defenders failed to get a meaningful tackle in to recover possession.

In the last ten minutes the Shots upped their game and started to put the Ebbsfleet goal under considerable pressure. James Rowe delivered a stunning pass to Matt McClure who cut right through the Ebbsfleet defence and delivered a beautiful cross across the goal line. Unfortunately, no one could get a boot on to the end of it. We had another shot that was deflected behind for a goal-kick and the Ebbsfleet goal-keeper was awarded a yellow card for his ridiculous time-wasting. There was just time for Matt McClure to hit a thunderous shot that went inches wide before the referee blew his whistle.

As we walked out the ground the discussion was whether we had gained a point or dropped two. Before the game I was optimistic of three points, but we weren't quite at our best. We had lost a bit of momentum, not having played for two weeks, but Sir Gary seemed quite upbeat in his post-match interview, pleased with having gained a point while not playing particularly well.

Leyton Orient versus Aldershot

Saturday 27 January 2018

I visited Brisbane Road in September 1983 for a League Cup match. I can't remember much about the game but Graham Brookland said we drew 3-3 and I wouldn't like to disagree with him.

Graham Brookland said in his book, 'To Make a Dream Survive', that '…after the match we were walking up Leyton High Road heading for the tube. All of a sudden, we were set upon by the locals and it became nasty. I pegged it up the road and survived any problems, but my friend Duncan believed it best to carry on walking to try and convince the locals that he was one of them. They weren't convinced, and he got a pounding.'

I wish I had followed Graham's approach back then. I remember waiting to get on the official supporters' club coach after the game when some Orient fans came running through and one of them punched me in the face. This was a cowardly attack on a very young me who was looking the other way and minding his own business and I think I've been quite justified in disliking them ever since.

Nevertheless, I awoke on Saturday morning, hugely excited. London games always seem to spark an extra level of interest and there is the added benefit of having to use public transport which affords an opportunity for a couple of drinks at lunchtime on the way to the ground. Steve from Number 11 and I were travelling together, and he texted me to say that he was going to have to go for a run first to try and calm his excitement. I knew how he felt but I'm not sure that running would do me any good and I'm not entirely sure if I did go for a run whether I would have recovered in time.

It had been an exciting week for the Shots, hearing that George Fowler and Adam McDonnell had both signed permanent contracts with us and that we'd signed Josh McQuoid from Luton. Stephen from Barnet said that he's followed Josh's career with interest, and noted that "…he isn't very big, he isn't very quick, and he doesn't score very many goals." I replied that we had considerably more faith in our GW than he did in his GW, and I sense there was a degree of envy involved.

Getting to Waterloo provided no problems as the train was punctual and empty enough for us to find seats next to each other. We talked through the options for getting a drink which included the Old Fire Station, the Hole in the Wall or the Wellington, but Steve from Number 11 said that he hadn't been to the Kings Arms in Roupell Street, so we headed there. This is one of the best London pubs that I've been to. It's considerably busier on a weekday evening when the working day is over, but it's relatively quiet at the weekends and we found a table with a couple of other Shots fans sharing the bar.

This is where the first of Steve from Number 11's misjudgements of the day occurred. At 1.30pm I asked him if he fancied another beer. Steve from Number 11 replied with a question, asking whether we should be starting to head to the ground. We discussed whether the away end was going to be sold out; both agreed that this was clearly not going to be the case and, sensing his indecision and the lack of urgency shown by the other Shots fans in the pub, I went to the bar.

We left at about 1.45pm and Steve from Number 11 quickly showed another error of judgement when he left me to navigate our way on the tube. I had looked at the tube map a few days earlier and realised that the quickest way was to take the Waterloo and City Line to Bank and then change to the Central line which would take us to Leyton in four stops. Sadly, after a couple of pints, I confused the Central Line with the Circle Line, and I led us north to Embankment. In my defence, Circle and Central do sound slightly similar in that they both begin with 'C' and they both have two syllables. If only someone had the foresight to colour code the different tube lines so that all I had to remember was the colour red. It would have been so much easier.

Steve from Number 11 responded well to my little error and, assuredly took control of the situation quickly getting us from Embankment to Bank Station. Unfortunately, and much to our irritation, Bank Station was closed for the weekend. Neither of us had thought to check this and we hadn't seen any sign at Waterloo to confirm this was the case. Steve from Number 11 was conscious that time was running away from us and pulled out his phone, saying he would solve our particular problem by ordering an Uber. I asked why we didn't just hail a black cab but Steve from Number 11, who is a bit more familiar with the capabilities of his mobile phone that I am, assured me that this would be quick.

The Uber driver soon texted Steve from Number 11 to advise us that he would 'be with us in eight minutes in his 3 series BMW.' I wanted to say to Steve from Number 11 that I didn't like BMW's, but I sensed this wasn't the right moment as Steve from Number

11 seemed a little tense. Eight minutes would eat into our time, so we hailed a black cab and Steve from Number 11 cancelled the Uber. The Uber driver texted back to acknowledge that he had been stood down, but this didn't stop Steve from Number 11 being charged £5 as a cancellation fee.

Meanwhile we were stuck in traffic, heading very slowly to the ground. We talked to the driver who said he was a Chelsea fan as a boy but that his father-in-law was a big Charlton fan, and this had become his team. He said he didn't know anything about Leyton Orient and I'm not sure if he knew too much about Aldershot either. This was, apparently, his first ever fare to Brisbane Road and we asked him to step on it. Steve from Number 11's next error of judgement was to admit to the Cabbie that we had tried to order an Uber first. The Cabbie's approach changed from that moment and he told Steve from Number 11 that it "...served him f***ing right if we're late," before adding that "I never trusted you from the moment that you got in my Cab. Your eyes are too close together."

Harsh feedback, I thought, and I tried to tell Steve from Number 11 some stories from happier days to keep his mind off the ticking clock. We eventually arrived at the ground a few minutes past kick off. I'm not sure whether the Cabbie had deliberately taken us on a longer circuit as a protest against Ubers but by this time Steve from Number 11 had deleted the Uber app from his phone in a stroppy response to being charged £5.

This paled into insignificance compared to the £30 that the Cabbie charged us. I paid, and we exited the Cab and started running towards the ground. Obviously, Steve from Number 11 has a slight advantage over me when it comes to running but I did my best to stumble after him. We passed Sergeant Jason outside the ground who took evasive action as I tried to knock his cap off as he asked us if we knew that we were already one nil down. Not the start we were hoping for but at least we hadn't had to watch it. We made it into the ground and looked around trying to find somewhere to sit. There wasn't anywhere. The away section of the ground looked completely full and we later learned that over 1,200 Shots fans had made the trip. We shuffled along a part of the terracing and stood, ready to cheer on our team.

The first half looked fairly even with both teams making mistakes and neither team able to capitalise on them. The condition of the pitch was seriously poor, and it was going to be difficult for us to rely on our usual slick passing game. But out of nowhere, in the 44th minute, a through ball found Shamir who controlled it, advanced on the Orient goal-keeper, and scored. We held on until half-time with a renewed sense of optimism.

'RedDwarf' posted on the Orient chat room that 'You're so loud you sound like Aldershot has a bit of a hollow ring to it now. A lot of Aldershot fans here and they're easily out-singing us.' And indeed, we did. The noise and the passion from the fans was truly sensational.

Orient is a slightly weird ground with blocks of flats having been built in each of the four corners. It may well be a good place to watch the game for nothing but I'm sure that the residents could do without numerous football fans singing "We can see you washing up," at them.

Unbelievably, at the start of the second half, Adam McDonnell took a free-kick which hit the cross bar and bounced vertically down. Any arguments about whether it had crossed the line or not were redundant as Will Evans responded quickly to head the ball into the net and put the Shots 2-1 up. The game continued to ebb and flow with chances being available to both sides, but it was Orient who seized the initiative with a shot drilled home from a corner mid-way through the second half.

We've seen a number of teams at the Rec this season who, when level with 15 minutes to play, will start to waste time and run down the clock, but not this Shots team. They kept going and were rewarded with a splendid goal from Adam McDonnell in the 76th minute. Sir Gary has obviously made a wonderful signing during the week and the Shots fans were, once again, in raptures.

We shut up shop and tried to retain possession and keep Orient out of the remainder of the game and other than an effort from Dan Holman that was blasted high over the crossbar in injury time at the end of the game, we did this successfully to hold on to the lead and secure the three points. After the final whistle had been blown the Shots players came to applaud the Shots fans and to receive our thanks and praise for their performance. Sir Gary and James came over afterwards and you could see how much this win meant to them. Their body language was relaxed, and you could see that they are close to each other and work well together.

Days like this make me a very proud fan.

And so, we headed back to Leyton tube station, Steve from Number 11 assertively said that we were going to take the Central Line to Tottenham Court Road before switching to the Bakerloo line to get to Waterloo. I didn't mind. I'm quite happy being led, and we took the opportunity to chat to a very demoralised Orient fan. He said that the Shots had brought the biggest and loudest away following to Brisbane Road for many years and, while wishing us well, you could tell that he feared for Orient's future as they seemed set on a journey that could take them into Conference South.

We told him not to worry about relegation as you can always get promoted again afterwards and that the most important thing was whether you were enjoying your football. He said that he wasn't but that he had confidence in the recent appointment of Justin Edinburgh and hoped that things would get better.

This chap was a much better advert for Orient fans than the thug I had met on my previous visit and reminded me that while every team has a small minority of idiots, most fans were just like us, making the most of the good times, because there are far more lean times. We sat and talked with East Bankers, Ken and Graham, as we headed towards Guildford and reflected on one of the best away trips that we could remember since West Ham.

Aldershot versus Gateshead

Saturday 3 February 2018

Gateshead are still in the FA Trophy so today's game had been postponed. While that's a shame, it could open up an opportunity to go and watch Bognor Regis play against Truro, or potentially, a quite exciting tie between Farnborough and Hereford, but with my well-honed degree of 'interpersonal awareness', I suspect it actually means that I can spend a bonus day with my wife which will hopefully give me something in the bag for when I tell her that the Dagenham game next week has been moved to a 5.30 pm kick off.

There had been quite a lot of media stories over the last couple of days to add to the well documented financial troubles at Hartlepool and Chester. Macclesfield players made an announcement that they hadn't received their salaries for January and Dagenham had announced that their benefactor was trying to sell the club as he wasn't happy with some flags that some of the Dagenham supporters had put up at away games. This is bad news for fans of both clubs, but it might explain why they have not kept up their early season form over the last couple of weeks. Dagenham seem to have been through the mill a bit, narrowly avoiding Glenn Tamplin buying the club before he switched his attentions to Billericay.

My Dagenham supporting friend Mark had said that he was is convinced that Dagenham have tried to buy their way out of the league through paying unsustainable wages and confirmed that the final straw which seemed to have annoyed Glyn Hopkin was flags that supporters put around the ground which said "Trump's Daggers", "The Soviet Union of Dagenham" and "North Korean Daggers". Apparently, Mr Hopkin thought these were inappropriate and might hurt his business interests. I love the idea of a Pyongyang branch of the Dagenham Supporters Club. Maybe this would be similar to the active branch of the Shots Supporters Club in Oslo, but maybe with a little more edge.

It seems that Mr Hopkin had previously stated his displeasure over a confederate flag that had been taken to some away games and had been picked up by BT Sport TV cameras. He had said that it had racist undertones which were inappropriate for a family club like Dagenham (or indeed any club). Given the turmoil at the club this week one of the Daggers fans on their chat room did suggest that they could replace all of the flags with ones simply saying, 'Everything for Sale'. I wonder whether, with hindsight, they would take Mr Tamplin now. There are numerous comments on their chat room but, on balance, they seem happier that Glyn Hopkin bought them than Glenn Tamplin. I think this possibly says more about Glenn Tamplin than it does about Glyn Hopkin.

Two players were lost with Kevin Lokko ending his loan spell and returning to Satanage and Joe White moving across with him. Allegedly, this was because money was outstanding from Kevin's loan spell with Dagenham and Joe went in lieu. The official announcement also stated that they will need to lose further players. Indeed, the following 48 hours saw Morgan Ferrier head to Boring Wood, Sam Ling return to Orient and club captain, Scott Doe, depart for Whitehawk.

I half-jokingly asked my Daggers supporting friend Mark if he thought they would finish above Orient. While I had thought this was a gentle tease Mark thought there was a real chance that they could finish below Orient this season.

'IanC' posted a message that summed up how they were feeling: "… need to get our family and fun club back. Only have those who care and have cared about our wonderful little club down the years, when the place was buzzing." This resonates with me as a Shots fan. Sir Gary has been instrumental in getting a buzz back into the Shots and the fan unity has returned. All lower league football fans have blind faith but the extra ingredient which is necessary is a little hope.

One of the Daggers season ticket holders asked whether times had ever been this bad for Dagenham before. 'RampantDuke' offered a wonderfully concise history lesson, writing "It's cyclical with Dagenham. First we ran out of money in 1992 and had to merge with Redbridge Ferrets, then we went to pieces under Graham Carr, spunked the money and went down to the Ryman with no team left, then we came back under Ted and Garry Hill, then we gave GH too much cash which he spent on rubbish players and we ran out of money again, then we got John Still back who took us all the way to League One and all the way back down again (with a bit of help from Wayne B along the way) and then we ran out of cash (again) and then we got some cash from Tamplin/Hopkin which we duly spunked again and now we have no cash. It will take a few years and possibly another relegation, but I guess the boom bust cycle means we will eventually come back again". He concluded by saying "Daggers are like global bankers but without the glamour and free lunches".

Dagenham versus Aldershot

Saturday 10 February 2018

I've visited Dagenham a number of times over the years and have mixed memories. The train journey always seems to take an intolerable length of time though when Gary and I go and we tend to break the journey up with numerous stop-offs to refresh and rehydrate ourselves. Sometimes this is okay and doesn't impact on anyone else but unfortunately it occasionally has caused unintentional offence. On one occasion, Gary and I had rather too much to drink. The plan had been that Gary's wife, Mirinda, was going to pick us up from the railway station after which we would collect a Chinese take-away before heading to our house to catch up with my wife for the evening. A simple plan and I would have thought it would be difficult for it to go too wrong. However ... Gary and I rang the Chinese take-away from the train and made our order. It was slightly random as we had no menu to work from, but we recounted the names of all of our favourite dishes. I have to admit that we were slightly surprised as we picked up four very full carrier bags to feed just the four of us and sheepishly handed over the best part of £80.

Normally when we have a Chinese take-away I will put a number of heat resistant mats on our dining table. I take the cardboard lids off the trays and place the trays on the heat-resistant mats which are on the dining table. I suspect I'm not alone in this and the majority of people would do something similar. To be honest, it works quite well, and means that people can help themselves to a selection of those dishes that catch their interest. Unfortunately, on this occasion I decided to get four of the largest dinner plates available and, for some inexplicable reason I proceeded to heap the contents from each tray onto each of the dinner plates, building a veritable Vesuvian mountain of mess with a generous helping of a sticky sweet and sour molten sauce running down from the erupting crater.

This revolting mess didn't hamper Gary and I. We were very hungry after our exertions during the day and we ravenously got stuck in to our dinner. Suitably replete, I poured us a glass of Laphroag each and, within a minute, we were fast asleep, curled up on each other's shoulders on the settee while our wives looked on in exasperation.

I have no excuses and I would like to publicly offer my profuse apologies. To my long-suffering wife and to the lovely Mirinda, I am really very sorry.

So, with rain pouring out of the sky, and Gary and Steve from Number 11 otherwise occupied, I hatched a plan to take my wife out to dinner (at a pub that would be showing the game). Planning ahead I rang our local 'sports bar'. It prides itself on having about 18 huge TV screens simultaneously showing every sport and non-sport event being broadcast and, to my huge disappointment, they said they were not going to have the game on.

Now I realise that it clashed with England playing Wales at rugby, but I would have thought that they might have devoted one of their screens to a team within their own county who were playing that night. The last time I went to this sports bar was to watch the Cup Final between Southampton and ManUre. I have a bit of a soft spot for the Saints given they are my wife's team. When she was younger she was a regular attendee at the Dell and when we were courting we had numerous battles, as I tried to take her to exciting places such as Chertsey and Basingrad. A number of times, her argument of "...or we could go and watch Southampton versus Liverpool..." won through and I have been to a large number of Saints games over the years.

We had watched the Cup Final with our friend Doris who went armed with two iPads so that he could watch on every channel at the same time and make sure he looked at all the angles. As I've said before, Doris genuinely believes that football is a TV sport and going to the pub to watch ManUre play is a bit of a treat for him. We were willing the Saints on but, bizarrely for a pub in Hampshire, we seemed to be in the minority. The cheers for ManUre were quite embarrassing. I wish people would support their local teams and stop trying to follow the crowd because of the brand or the marketing. Doing what everyone else is doing does not make you cool. It makes you a dull, unimaginative idiot.

Sorry. Where was I? Oh yes, the sports bar refused to show the game, so I had a bit of a dilemma to solve. James came to my rescue by ringing to say that all his friends had gone home from University for the week and he therefore wanted to come back. His mother suggested he could take the train, but the lazy individual hasn't done any washing over the last six weeks so had an awful lot of luggage to bring with him. Genius – I offered to go and collect him knowing that we could pop into the ground on the way back to watch the game with like-minded fans.

And so, we watched the game with around 80 other fans in the EBB lounge. We missed our first goal, which Jim Kellerman scored after four minutes. When we arrived it seemed pretty tense, with Dagenham trying hard and looking as if they had a goal or two in them. They had lots of possession but lacked bite in the last third of the pitch. It wasn't a brilliant game, but Scott Rendell managed to score in the second half to calm our nerves. We then played a strong defensive game to win 2-0. It was, in many ways, the perfect away performance. Score an early goal to force the opposition to come at you and catch them on the break to score a second goal and secure the points. Far from the one-sided game that might have been, Dagenham played well, and their fans, on the chat room anyway, seemed relatively happy with the performance.

We had a good time in the bar. It was a happy atmosphere and the staff looked after us well. Watching your team win on live TV. What could be better? Actually, lots could be better. There was none of the anticipation that you get from travelling to the game and I dug out the article that Steve Hill wrote for the Non-League Paper a few weeks earlier.

Steve is a Chester fan, who has recently written a book called 'The Card: Every Match, Every Mile' and wrote that "…away matches were less about the hardship of travelling to the game…" and more about "…the journey, the camaraderie, and a couple of pre-match 'nerve-calmers' as a requisite for any match." After watching a game on TV, Steve said "Once it was over, I turned it off and got on with my life, feeling almost nothing. Tellingly, it provided some insight into the experience of the vast majority of Premier league fans, a fast food version of supporting a club. Without spending four hours in the car, stewing on the result, it may well not have happened, all over in the flick of a switch."

Such an insightful comment and, as James and I arrived at home, I felt decidedly unsatisfied and wished I had been one of the 470 Shots fans who had made the journey. Well done to all, I'm very proud of you, and sorry I wasn't there with you.

Aldershot versus Macclesfield

Saturday 17 February 2018

The week has not been a good one. Sadly, my father passed away yesterday. He had been ill for a while, but we went out to dinner with him on Thursday night, when he seemed in pretty good form. After a good night's sleep, he woke up, breakfasted on coffee and crumpets and his heart gave up shortly after he got dressed.

He was telling me on Thursday that he had been to the Opera a couple of days earlier and although there were a couple of good songs, he thought there was a little too much 'operatic singing' for his liking. I told him that his daughter-in-law and I had nearly gone to a show earlier in the week but unfortunately the lead singer had been unwell, and the show had been cancelled. My father expressed his surprise that there wasn't an understudy waiting in the wings for this eventuality at which point I'm afraid to say, I did laugh a little too loudly. I was visualising a gig where the announcer came on the stage to say, "Ladies and Gentlemen, unfortunately Dave Vanian (of punk band the Damned) is feeling unwell, and will not be able to take to the stage tonight, but don't worry as Steve from Number 11 is here in his place."

I think my Dad might have spent too much time in amateur dramatics and the theatre to see how this might not work quite so effectively.

My Dad didn't understand football. He didn't understand the joys of standing on the terraces living through the highs and lows of a game. He quite enjoyed rugby but not beyond being an armchair fan if it was on television. I did take him to the Rec once. It must have been around 1981 or 1982 and, because my brother and little sister came with us, he insisted on our sitting down. At the time I was an enthusiastic regular in the East Bank and the front rows of the South Stand seats were a poor substitute. Fortunately, this was just a one-off appearance and none of them have since returned.

My father was quite a character and made a huge impact on everyone he came into contact with. I love you Dad, and I am really going to miss you.

It really felt like a very long time since I'd seen a game of football and an even longer time since I'd been to the Rec. (Watching last week on the television doesn't count and, even a week later, the experience left me completely unsatisfied.) But the league leaders were in town and although they would likely only bring a handful of fans (officially it was 39 last season but my friend Phil crept onto the Slab so we'll call it 40) it was still an exciting prospect and I was looking forward to it.

Steve from Number 11 and I headed into the ground slightly earlier than normal in order to ensure we had time for a couple of leisurely pints before the game and this meant that we were able to park in Parsons Barrack. We walked up to the Vic and immediately realised that the crowd was bigger than normal. The pub was heaving with people who I assumed were there to go and

217

watch the Shots rather than having hit the pub in order to watch Sheffield Wednesday play out a goal-less draw against Swansea.

The beer wasn't great and there were a few odd characters in the pub. We're used to odd characters but some of the clientele enjoying a pre-match beer were more odd than usual and one in particular smelled as if he hadn't washed or changed his underwear for many, many months. It was pretty obvious that he had recently had a bit of an accident, and we wished that he had wanted to talk to someone else. We didn't mind who, but just wished that it wasn't us who were stuck with the rather gross smell.

We headed down to the ground slightly earlier than normal and were immediately taken aback by the number of people queuing to get in. I can't recall the last time I saw so many people outside the Rec trying to get in. We joined Roy and pushed our way into the queue for the South Stand.

It was good to catch up with Roy again. I took the opportunity to ask him why he had moved from the Slab to the North Stand. I tentatively asked whether it was due to our singing, or whether it was so he could moan with a bit more abandon. He said it wasn't either of these reasons and that he had moved as a protest against the club not allowing home fans to move from one end of the ground to the other at half-time but allowing away fans to do so. Roy said that he was delighted to spend time with opposition fans before and after the game but during the game he wanted to spend his time with his own kind. I know what he means. I always have mixed views when there is no segregation in place. I enjoy talking to away fans, but I don't like hearing them singing in my face when they score. Roy went on to say that because we won promotion the year he first moved to the North Stand superstition dictates that he needs to stay there forever more.

Andy subsequently pointed out the flaw in Roy's logic. We were relegated five years after the promotion so clearly it hasn't always been a lucky move.

After waiting patiently for twenty minutes, we were about ten people from the front when it was announced that the South Stand, including the Slab, was sold out and no more tickets were going to be issued. After being turned away from the South Stand we begged some fans to let us jump into their queue. We said that we had done our fair share of queuing and they kindly took pity on us. Well, they took pity on Steve from Number 11. As I have a season ticket, I found an empty turnstile and sailed through. Steve eventually managed to sneak onto the Slab, hiding his East Bank ticket stub and all was well with the world.

I thought of my Dad during the minute's applause for Shots fan Steve Wilding who died outside the ground at the last home match. My Dad was nearly 80 and had had a good innings. Steve was in his thirties and left three young children without a father. I also thought of my good friend Bill and ruminated on how cruel life (and death) can sometimes be. Proof once again that football is only a game and, ultimately, not really that important.

The Shots were once again slow in starting and after only three minutes, one of the defenders had us shouting from the other end of the ground when he let the ball bounce over his head rather than trying to close it down quickly. This immediately put pressure on Will Evans who conceded a penalty and received a straight red card. From the Slab we didn't have a good view of what happened but judging from the lack of reaction from our players they must have thought it was the right decision. It wasn't the right decision for the 4,000 Shots fans in the ground because, while goalie Lewis Ward went the right way, the shot just edged beyond his hand. After three minutes we were playing the league leaders, one nil down and reduced to ten men. It was effectively game over when it had only just begun.

What football fans want more than anything, is consistency. If Will's tackle was worthy of a red card and the referee was happy to give a red card in the third minute of the game, why did Lincoln's Matt Rhead not get one for elbowing Will Evans in the face after five seconds in the home game last season? Similarly, why did the Macclesfield player Durrell not get cautioned or sent off (or even spoken to) for a terrible tackle on Callum Reynolds in front of the South Stand a few minutes later?

The Shots re-grouped with Bobby-Joe Taylor being replaced by Manny Oyeleke after 15 minutes and we managed to stabilise the situation. While not a big team (with the exception of Blissett), Macclesfield knew all the tricks in the book, closing us down quickly and refusing to let us settle on the ball. Some of the tackling was over the top and, extraordinarily, during the first half, some nasty tackles by Durrell and Hancox went unpunished. Macclesfield having a player sent off looked to be our best chance of getting something out of the game and when the referee talked to Hancox we began to get excited. He was only shown a yellow card and our excitement died.

At the beginning of the second half the Shots came out brightly and we nearly had a chance for an equaliser when their goal-keeper flapped at a cross, but no one could get on the end of it.

Macclesfield came right back at us and, after Callum Reynolds tried to lob the ball over one of their strikers' heads, Macclesfield got the ball, attacked and scored. 2-0 down after 49 minutes, to two needless mistakes. The Shots looked down and out. Playing pretty football from the back might suit the global greats but we do need to learn when a good, old-fashioned hoof to clear our lines is a safer option.

Durrell continued to be the pantomime villain when he went down under a light tackle as if he had been shot but he was soon handed his comeuppance with a booking for time-wasting when he took about ten seconds to take a throw-in. Even to me, who desperately wanted him to be sent off, this felt harsh, but we hoped that it set the precedent for the rest of the game.

Macclesfield had a corner a few minutes later, and the ball went right through a crowd of about 15 players standing near the penalty spot. This felt like a let off. But the crowd soon had an opportunity to go wild. A Macclesfield player hand-balled in their penalty area and the Shots received a penalty, clinically dispatched by Scott Rendell. From that moment onwards, the game was full of end-to-end action as the Shots tried hard to equalise, leaving gaps open for Macclesfield to exploit.

In the 67th minute, another mistake from Callum let Macclesfield in but Manny was there to clear off the line. A few minutes later Lewis made a good save from a close-range effort and my man of the match, Scott Rendell, made a brilliant block to keep Macclesfield from increasing their lead.

The Rec booed as one when Durrell was substituted on 81 minutes. The Shots had a couple of good efforts that were just off target and there was a wonderful ball to Robert right at the death that he was just unable to control, leaving the Shots defeated despite a valiant effort.

A huge crowd of 4,358, including a disappointing 215 from Macclesfield had a thoroughly entertaining afternoon. It was somewhat spoilt by the early sending off and penalty, but the

Shots showed a lot of bottle and did well to get back into the game.

I had a lovely text from my colleague Jude towards the end of the game saying she was sorry for my loss. My immediate reaction was to think that we hadn't lost, and we still had ten minutes to rescue a draw, but it only took a few seconds for me to be dragged back to the reality of the situation and realise that she wasn't talking about the game.

Aldershot versus Bromley

20 February 2018

After a poor result on Saturday, a good come back was the order of the day. Gary, Steve from Number 11 and I met up in an altogether quieter and more fragrant Vic for a bite to eat before the game.

It was good to catch up with Gary as I hadn't seen him since New Year's Day, and we caught up on the gossip. Actually, there hadn't been much gossip, but we still managed to natter away like the three old women on Last of the Summer Wine.

Neither Gary, nor Steve from Number 11 could remember what was arguably the funniest thread on the Shots chat room, from probably about ten years ago. Alex had recently moved jobs and was asking Shots fans for some ideas for office pranks to play on a Cambridge fan who he was sitting next to.

I might have some previous form in this direction having once caught my colleague Mike with some purple ink from a stamp pad on the ear-piece of his phone a long time ago. When my wife and I worked together, I kidnapped her cuddly squashed hedgehog and sent a ransom demand, but possibly the funniest moment was when I Sellotaped the black pips on her phone down. This meant that she could only answer the phone through the loud speaker which she found particularly embarrassing in our open plan office. Even funnier was listening to her ring the IT help-desk to see if they could tell her why it wasn't working properly.

Alex had had some fun with some fairly low-level stuff, such as Sellotape over the laser of his mouse and was after some more suggestions.

So, I read with interest the multiple pages of wonderful opportunities for starting a revengeful war in an office.

'Stonehenge Shot' thought disconnecting his ear piece from his phone would be a good start, quickly followed by reversing the right and left click settings on his mouse. 'Anon E Mouse' was going for the jugular by suggesting that Alex loosened the wheels of his office chair. 'Shots in Sussex' was after inflicting more pain with a drawing pin under the arm rest of the chair.

Then the techy brigade got in on the action and 'Andy Chillman' suggested that Control-Alt-Down would make his screen appear upside down and then described how you could take a photograph of his screen and hide everything so that the mouse wouldn't appear on the screen.

'Lightwater Shot' had a brilliant idea by using the 'AutoCorrect Options' in MS Word. He suggested taking a relatively common word for which the computer would automatically change into 'Cambridge United are crap and will never get promoted back into the league.'

Mr Chillman (who clearly had too much time to think about these stunts) offered another suggestion where you could program Word so that clicking a simple letter on the keyboard would cause the document to close without saving it.

I think the best of all of the suggestions came from 'Simmotino' who suggested getting about 20 plastic cups; filling them to the brim with water and stapling them together on his desk. I think you need to let this idea float around your mind for a few seconds to realise just how brilliant it is. Pure genius. I thought I might steal this idea and play it on one of my colleagues. I thought I should mention it to their Head of Department who thought it was a fabulous idea. Sadly, when I mentioned it to their immediate Line Manager, she didn't understand why it might be funny, and sadly, the joke had to be shelved.

We also talked about my father and we talked about Bill. I suddenly asked if either Gary or Steve from Number 11 had ever given any thought to travelling to an away game by canal. Time for another strange look in my direction but the question seemed to make sense when I told the story of when Bill and I drove to an away game at Luton a few years ago and Bill started musing about the possible options for getting to Luton from where he lived in Farnborough via canal. Bill suggested that it would be pretty easy to get onto the Basingstoke Canal in Farnborough and he seemed to know that this connected to the River Wey which you could join close to the M25 near West Byfleet.

The River Wey would then connect you to the River Thames north of Weybridge, which in turn would lead you to the Grand Union Canal, North of Richmond. This was some kind of T junction and Bill was insistent that one would need to turn left rather than right. Bill said he could get us to Hemel Hempstead, only about ten miles away from Luton.

Bill seemed rather proud of himself but what he didn't say was how long this journey would take. I reckon if you could average 4 miles an hour, the canal journey would be at least 18 hours. I don't know if there are any rules about using canal boats during the hours of darkness. I'm not sure I've seen any canal boats with headlights but then again, I've not specifically looked for this feature when I have been in the vicinity of a canal.

I think Bill also failed to recognise that there were some 35 locks that we would need to negotiate and if we said 30 minutes per lock, this will add another 17 or 18 hours to the journey. 36 hours would probably therefore take us three days, travelling 12 hours a day, and we'd still have three hours walking when we arrived at Hemel Hempstead.

I didn't need much time to reflect and realise that given driving would take about 75 minutes and parking was relatively easily available in Luton, this seemed a far more preferable option. However, looking at our remaining fixtures, Chester was right on a canal so, if we chose the right starting point (which isn't Farnborough), I reckon it would be quite a cool way to get to a game. Maybe this could be an even better idea for that difficult second book.

And so, we made our way to the Rec. There were no queues outside and therefore no problem taking our places on the Slab. It was nice to see Charlie and Andy again and a whole bunch of hellos were exchanged whilst we eagerly waited for the game to start.

A chap walked up to me and, referring to me by my name, asked me how I was. I replied that I was well and tried to work out whether I should know him. After about 15 minutes, curiosity got the better of me and I asked him what his name was. It turned out it was Steve from Number 11's friend Adie, who I had met at the Torquay match right at the beginning of the season. Adie clearly has a much better memory for faces than I have but it would have helped me had he gone and said hello to his friend Steve from Number 11 rather than chatting to me first.

After eight minutes I thought we had scored. I'm not very good at following the play at the best of times and when Fabien Robert put the ball in the back of net, I started to cheer – all by myself. Everyone else noticed that he went up with his hand and were not surprised when the referee showed him a yellow card, but I was left wondering what had happened.

The Shots were sloppy and made far too many mistakes. It was a poor pass in the middle of the pitch that let Bromley launch an attack on our goal and Wolfenden, the Bromley number 23, had coincidentally scored after 23 minutes.

Manny was our most effective player and picked up a booking a few minutes later for a rash tackle. This seemed like a potentially fair booking but the referee unfairly penalised Callum when he made a perfectly good tackle in front of the South Stand a little while later. We had our only real opportunity of the half when a shot fell to McQuoid, but it was blocked, and we were lucky not to concede another before half-time following another silly error.

In the second half Bromley seemed to come out quicker than the Shots but the momentum changed when Sir Gary introduced Shamir Fenelon, Scott Rendell and Bobby-Joe Taylor. The Shots got back into the game.

Though good chances were being created, we were unable to put them away.

The comedy moment of the game was when a Bromley striker had run past Callum Reynolds, normally one of our most assured players, who didn't really seem to know what to do about it.

From the Slab it looked as if he tried to hack him down about three or four times, but he was too slow and kept missing. His subsequent shot was well blocked and, fortunately the Shots were still in the game.

After 68 minutes McDonnell had a shot that went just wide and, shortly afterwards, Bobby-Joe delivered a pass that looked as if it might just have grazed the crossbar before bouncing out towards the corner flag.

Bromley was not a particularly impressive team. They had a game plan and parked 11 players in their defence, trying to catch us on the break. They were time-wasting for much of the second half and it was no surprise when Denis was booked for kicking the ball out of play after the whistle had blown.

Cheye had a thunderous shot saved by the Bromley goal-keeper but it was in the 92nd minute that our man of the match, Manny, picked up on a loose ball and smashed it into the net for an equaliser.

There was still time for the Shots to win the game but James Rowe, having been nominated as the match sponsors man of the match blazed high over the bar with the goal-keeper way out of the goal area.

So, we had to make do with a point. Macclesfield extended their lead at the top to six points but miraculously, we are still in third place.

Our next game was at Wrexham which would be a difficult place to get a result and, after two poor results, maybe we were aiming for the play-offs rather than the automatic promotion spot.

Wrexham versus Aldershot

Saturday 24 February 2018

I did ask my wife if she fancied coming to Wrexham with me and she gave me a curt response. She wasn't entirely sure where Wrexham was, thinking that it might be in the North East. I tried to reassure her that it was nowhere near as far to go as that. When she forced its location out of me, she delivered an equally curt response. Oh well, you can't win them all. But it's possible that my attendance over the last couple of games had jinxed us, so if I didn't go to the game, we might return to winning ways. Or at least that's the logic I used to console myself as I contemplated other things to do on a Saturday afternoon.

Mrs C and I took a drive down to Arundel in the morning to see if we could get lucky in sighting and photographing a kingfisher. We got lucky on both counts and will be back soon to have another go. It took her about a nanosecond to wonder why I was spelling Arundel 'W R E X H A M' in the sat nav. One of us laughed while the other tittered in desperation. I said we had time to get there as there was only 235 miles to go but it seemed that visiting Wales wasn't high on her list of things to do this weekend.

We got back at 3pm, just in time to listen to the commentary. Sadly, there was only Radio Wales to listen to and there were real problems with our woeful broadband trying to get enough signal to listen to it. The commentary kept on cutting out with the broadband telling me that I didn't have enough bandwidth for the radio to play. However, during the moments when I did have enough, I was hearing the commentators tell me that the Shots were all over Wrexham and Wrexham were really poor. So, it was a huge shock to read on the chat room that we had conceded during the next moment when the broadband couldn't cope. But the commentators said that we looked dangerous and had an imminent goal in us and the only sound I could hear in the background were Shots fans cheering them on. As I started to type 'Come on Shots,' Shamir scored an equaliser with three minutes to go to half-time.

In the second half, we seemed to continue to be all over Wrexham but, again, the commentary disappeared and when it came back we had again conceded and were losing 2-1. By now, I was getting in a seriously bad mood. Not only was I not at the game but I couldn't listen to it because the internet coverage was so poor.

Unsurprisingly the commentary soon disappeared again but, surprisingly, when I looked on the chat room we had scored an equaliser. The commentary returned and was a couple of minutes behind the play, so I could enjoy listening to the goal. Actually, the commentary was slightly more than a couple of minutes behind the play and, in my world, Aldershot scored the equaliser 12 minutes after it was scored in the real world. James Rowe took a corner and, after a little flick on, it went straight into the net.

So now I had a dilemma. I noticed that there had been another two pages of updates on the chat room since I last looked, 12 minutes ago. Should I look on the chat room and see what the final score was, or should I carry on listening to the commentary and find out in 12 minutes time? I opted for the latter, so I hid my phone and anything else that might spoil my next few minutes and listened positively as the commentators told me that the Shots were the better team and that they felt there was another goal left in the game.

My heart sank when I heard the crowd roar as Wrexham had a good effort, but Jake Cole managed to keep it out of the goal with his legs. Lewis Kinsella had a shot that was deflected for a corner and the 249 Shots fans in the background were loud and proud (although I couldn't hear any chant of "Oooh it's a corner!").

Wrexham cleared the corner at the second chance, but they broke from a second corner and Callum Reynolds managed to clear the danger. It was an open ending to the game and good end to end stuff. Another good save from Jake Cole but it was difficult listening to the emotion of the commentator the wrong way round.

A bold move by Sir Gary, seven minutes later, when he replaced our central defender, Will Evans, with a striker, Matt McClure. And immediately Wrexham had a shot deflected into the side netting and a corner. Jake punched the ball out and Wrexham won a free kick 30 yards out.

The wall did its job and, with five minutes to play, Quigley was unmarked and had a brilliant chance for his hat-trick, but fortunately pulled it wide. It sounded as if Wrexham were dominant and the Shots were just about hanging on. Four minutes of extra time to go. Time for Scott Rendell to get into the Wrexham penalty area and have a shot which was saved and time for Wrexham to have a free kick from 40 yards out which was headed out by the same Scott Rendell. From the corner, Wrexham had another good effort which was just steered over the crossbar, and the referee put me out of my misery with my clock showing 17:06.

Tranmere and Macclesfield both scored late goals to win their games, so the point meant we are losing ground on them. Two points from a possible nine is not championship form but we were playing three of the sides with aspirations of their seasons extending beyond the end of April and we showed good bottle in coming from behind twice during the game.

But again, sad news clouds everything else, as I heard that ex-Shots player, Damon Lathrope had broken his leg rather badly, playing for Woeking against Boring Wood. I wish him a speedy and full recovery.

Aldershot versus Hartlepool

Saturday 3 March 2018

Boy, what a week. Big snow on Thursday and Friday left me snowed in and unable to go to work. This reminded me very much of the game against Northampton a few years ago. This was the last of three games that Danny Hylton was banned for and was the game immediately before we went to Middlesbrough for the fourth round League Cup match.

Danny was a firm favourite at Aldershot and, indeed, seems to be at the clubs he has subsequently played for including Luton, where he is currently the top scorer in League Two this year.

Gary and I were sitting in the Vic when the snow started at about 5.30 and, by the time we were ready to head to the ground, we were convinced that the game was going to be called off and we would not be able to get home. But we underestimated just how much Danny wanted to play at Middlesbrough and he joined the groundsmen in helping to clear the snow from the edges of the playing surface, before Groundsman Andy Nunn went over the lines with a rather fetching red paint. I still have no idea how the game was allowed to be played. The crowd was, unsurprisingly poor and it was difficult to play any decent football. And we lost 2-0. Not ideal preparation for the big match but at least we weren't snowed in at the Recreation Ground.

The Slab was closed on that day too and Steve Gibbs confirmed on Thursday that it would also be closed this Saturday. In his announcement, he said that it would be closed due to Health and Safety – and the comfort of the fans. Now then, Steve. us Old Age Slabbers are made of stern stuff and the words 'comfort' and 'Slab' rarely feature in the same sentence. The snow is fine; it's the driving horizontal rain and cold that we find harder to deal with! As we started thinking about where to stand, the message came through that the game was being postponed until Tuesday. Probably a very sensible move given the distance Hartlepool have to travel - and it meant that Gary could now make the game.

Sadly, it also meant that I was going to have to miss badminton again next Tuesday night – a New Year resolution that we had made a couple of months ago. We went shopping over the weekend to Chav World to buy some new rackets and a pair of trainers for me but, sadly, I had a particularly nasty repeat of my arthritic attack which had me hobbling into the store. Not a great advert for anything remotely sporting and it meant I couldn't try any trainers on as getting into a shoe was far too painful. My wife prefers to call my arthritis 'gout,' but I find that I get more sympathy when I describe it as arthritis. I have gout on the list of attributes I have inherited from my Dad. And possibly Gary.

Aldershot versus Hartlepool

Tuesday 6 March 2018

The weather forecast for Tuesday night was much more tolerable than last Saturday and we hoped that the Slab would be open for business. But as it turned out this was the least of my problems. My 'arthritis' had steadily got worse and, by early afternoon, even I had worked out that I couldn't go to the game. As my good friend and gout mentor, Gary counselled me, "Gout and football just don't mix well together."

Fortunately, the pain remained high, so I wasn't in that terrible position where you make a decision and then start having doubts soon after. Steve from Number 11 still went but I resigned myself to listening to Rob Worrell and Lewis Ward commentating on the game while I sat at home feeling sorry for myself.

It sounded as if the Shots got off to a good start and they were duly rewarded with a Scott Rendell goal after 15 minutes. I thought it would be a solid professional display and that, having secured the early advantage, we would wait for Hartlepool to create some more space as they looked for an equaliser which we could exploit with our pace and endeavour.

However, it sounded as if after scoring we lost some of our tempo and stopped closing Hartlepool down as quickly as we were at the beginning of the game. This gave them some hope that they might get back into it. Hartlepool made a forced substitution in the first half bringing on Blair Adams, who put in a strong performance. Just before half-time he unleashed an unstoppable shot to level the score and I'm sure the Shots went in to the dressing room the more disappointed team.

My foot was really hurting so I decided to have a bath during the half time break. 15 minutes isn't quite long enough for a bath and, sadly, I didn't feel any better having given my offending extremity a nice warm soaking. I came down to see four texts from Steve from Number 11:

- We're better since the break
- We got away with one – We handled the ball in our area
- BJ is on now. All will be fine
- Goal – Manny!

As I picked up the commentary in the second half I was excited to hear a shout out from Rob for the Norwegian Shots Supporters' Club. I hadn't heard anything from them for a while and had been feeling slightly disappointed that their support had dwindled or maybe died.

It sounded as if the second half was very similar to the first with the Shots unable to take the game to Hartlepool and ease the supporters' nerves with another goal. Bobby-Joe seemed to be making an impact and made a couple of lovely runs which unfortunately came to nothing. Hopefully he will get back into the starting 11 soon which will give him more game time.

As the game moved into the last ten minutes, it was clear that it was going to be another squeaky bum finale. Steve from Number 11 texted to say that he was convinced we were about to concede. I told him to keep the faith and fortune smiled on us as we secured a valuable three points. With Sutton also winning, this win moved us above Tranmere into third position and pulled us back to just the five points behind Macclesfield, although they had a game in hand.

I was unable to toast our victory as my wife has banned me from drinking. She believes there is a link between alcohol and gout. I'm not so sure. I believe it is more likely to be a result of the diet I've been on since the New Year. Surely no one believes alcohol can cause gout. Isn't that just an old wives' tale?

Sywell FC v Leatherhead FC

Tuesday 6 March 2018

I was sitting at the dining table with my foot resting on a cushion on one of the other chairs and I took the opportunity to put off working – or more accurately, pretending to work - for a little longer by catching up on Twitter. One tweet in particular caught my attention. It was posted by Sywell Football Club who are based in Northamptonshire (@SywellFC). Or at least I assume they are based in Northamptonshire – the village of Sywell is in Northamptonshire, but unfortunately the club doesn't seem to have a website. The tweet simply said 'Tonight's attendance was 7. Thank you for your continued support.' As I looked back through their Twitter feed I managed to put off working for a little bit longer. There is an official post that reminds supporters that '…this Saturday's match against Enfield Town has been moved from 3.00 pm to 4.00 pm due to a timetable clash with a dog walking competition.'

The Tenches' Manager, Tony Pyke seemed to be quite open with the club's followers in keeping them up to date with news such as: 'Of course, Freddie Stokes will be a huge loss. It's not often a player is able to bag himself three goals in one season.' A second tweet gave even more information 'Obviously Freddie felt that football is not his desired career and we all respect and support his decision to pursue his dream of joining the country choir. Everyone at the club wishes him the best of luck for the future.'

But it was the tweet confirming the size of the crowd that got me intrigued, and I had to delve deeper into the conversation. Sywell tweeted that Leatherhead had brought one fan, but that the rest of the crowd was their own support.

A number of followers offered their praise to the folk who had attended, with comments such as "Those 7 fans are true football supporters the game could be doing with more of them tbh"

There was some interesting discussion about the Leatherhead fan which started with "Fair play to the Leatherhead one! #topsupporter". But this received a response suggesting that "He probably lives around the corner" and "Probably doesn't even support Leatherhead" to which it was surmised that he must be a "Glory supporter" and "Bet he wasn't supporting them before the money." The Twitter feed continued to praise the "The magnificent seven" and noted that the "Atmosphere must have been rocking".

Someone had noticed that the tweet asking for re-tweets for nominating the man of the match had received seven replies tweeted. Someone else quickly noted that "Every one of those fans got involved, which is 100% fan engagement."

It was suggested that the Sywell support was comparable with Reading and the thread was distracted about the number of plastic fans that Reading had when they briefly thought they were better than they are and I was struck by the irony of Nathan Butterworth, a Spurs fan who professes to only watching Champions League football on the TV who had to ask what a plastic fan was.

I kept reading and laughing, but I was amazed by the number of tweeters in the thread of over 250 who hadn't seemed to have worked out that they weren't actually a real team. I admit it took me a moment, but there seemed to be a huge number of people out there who believed it was for real.

But it was Jim Pesh who made the best post. He wondered "How many people who've RT'd this have been to a live football match this season?" And I think that probably sums it up quite nicely. This is a parody account that has somehow generated excitement and interest about what a football match *might* be like..

Well let me assure you, there's loads of matches that are exactly like this every week. Head away from your television set and go and find yourself one to watch. Football is not a TV sport, and you never know, you might even enjoy watching it.

AFC Fylde versus Aldershot

Saturday 10 March 2018

This was the designated 'Tour of Duty' game for this season. Shots fan Tony Roberts originally came up with the idea and this is the tenth year that it has taken place. The idea is very simple and based on the military heritage of the town. Tony said that they "…wanted to pick an obscure away game that we would not usually expect to take that many fans to and try to surprise the locals with the numbers we took and the noise we made."

We've certainly done that over the years. Last year's trip to Solihull Moors, for instance, included an astonishing 725 Shots fans in a crowd of 1,248. Unfortunately, Fylde is quite a lot further away than Solihull and I'm not sure I could cope with that much time in a car. Have I mentioned that my foot really hurts? A big well done to all the fans who made the trip though – I'm sure they had a wonderful time.

Mrs C, while refusing to don a previous year's Christmas present of a nurse's uniform, did volunteer to head to the pharmacy to pick up some more drugs. She asked me whether I had a preference. I replied that I needed the strongest ones they would allow me to take with the anti-inflammatory pills the doctor had prescribed.

A quick Google search suggested that I should avoid Aspirin, Diclofenac and Ibuprofen but I was welcome to fill my boots with Paracetamol, Codeine or Morphine. Now, being a true alpha male (when she allows me to), I have a high pain threshold. I felt morphine would probably be the best option, but my wife came back from the pharmacy armed with a huge bag of 'DrSalts finest fragrance free Himalayan Bath Salts'. Not quite what I had in mind unfortunately, and having given them a go, I still think morphine might have done a better job.

We had booked to spend the afternoon taking photographs of little harvest mice at this photographic studio near Ringwood, so I wasn't able to listen to the radio commentary. At five minutes past three I received a text from James, saying '1-1 after 5 minutes!' I had to look at what had happened. Fylde had scored first, but McQuoid had then equalised a couple of minutes later. Well, this was clearly good news. The Shots had scored the equaliser which obviously meant that we were in the ascendency. 'Obviously' might not have been the right term to use as further goals from Fylde in the 9th, 17th and 19th minutes made it 4-1 very early in the game and it was effectively game over before the 5th goal went in on the stroke of half-time.

Shots fans are generally quite optimistic, and the half-time chat-room chatter was trying to remember whether we had come back from 5-1 down before now. 'Headley Shot' could remember us coming back from 3-0 down at half-time to beat Plymouth 4-3, but 'Fuggletim' could trump him in the memory stakes from the Billy Minter Trophy game in around 1993 when we came back from 4-0 down with twenty minutes to go to win 5-4. Sadly, all this conversation managed to do was pass 15 minutes until the second half. And after twenty minutes of the second half we were losing 7-1 even though Fylde had been reduced to ten men. Fortunately, we didn't concede any more but, even so, 7-1 is a pretty crushing defeat – our heaviest since we lost at Chester 8-2, funnily enough on this day a couple of years ago.

We're playing Chester away next week, but I'm confident that Sir Gary will turn it around and steady the ship.

I'm really pleased that I had been fully occupied for the afternoon so that I didn't have to listen to it on the radio. I do, however, have over 1,000 very cute pictures to edit though.

In other news, Sywell FC conceded in the 97th minute of their game to lose 3-2 at home to Enfield which must put the Tench in relegation danger.

Chester versus Aldershot

Saturday 17 March 2018

I was talking to Phil at work a little while ago, and he mentioned that Sports Relief was on March 17th. Phil has come up with a couple of charitable ideas in the past. Not always particularly charitable to me, as he seems to be more concerned about supporting the charities themselves. His latest idea is that we should do a triathlon together. I'm not very good on bikes after a serious accident when I was 15 left me in a coma for three days. I find swimming very tiring - particularly when you have to turn around at the end of the pool and come back again. And, believe me, when you get to my age, running holds very limited appeal. It's safe to say that this suggestion was treated with the disdain and contempt that I felt it deserved. I did, however, offer to come and take some photographs of my colleagues in action. This kind offer he has yet to take up. I can only assume he still thinks he can persuade me to join in.

In an attempt to find something that we could do together I have come up with a plan that involves the rather exciting sport of extreme ironing. I speculated that we could find a number of fellow ironing enthusiasts and venture to a Shots match clutching our ironing boards and do our weekly ironing on the terraces during the game. In addition to raising sponsorship I felt we could charge fellow supporters to iron their shirts and raise a tidy sum.

An excellent idea, I thought, and a good opportunity to get Phil to come and watch the Shots again. He went to the away game at Eastleigh last season when we disappointingly let in a goal towards the end of the game to draw 1-1 after one of our players was sent off, so his opinion of the Shots is somewhat blinkered.

I thought I would see if I could rustle up some more interest on the Slab and while he was keen to join us, Steve from Number 11 had other plans for that weekend and Charlie wasn't familiar with such modern technology as an iron. Andy eventually put our enthusiasm out by saying that the Chester game was seating only for away fans. Clearly it is not possible to iron sitting down (though Gary claims that is actually not true) so unfortunately, we have had had to shelve the idea. Maybe one for next year then at a different ground.

Phil and I have a few days away each year. I manage a supplier who are based in Edinburgh and need to go and visit them at least once a year. In an attempt to build a good relationship with Mark, our Account Manager, who visits the Shots a couple of times a year when he's down in the south, we make our meeting on a Friday and stay over on Friday night so that we can enjoy a little culture in this lovely City. We then go and watch Mark's team on the Saturday. Mark supports Dunfermline Athletic, a team who, like the Shots, have had one or two good years interspersed with a number of years of mediocrity and worse. Football aside, the real appeal of visiting Dunfermline's East End Park is the Stephenson's bridies that are served in the food halls. I hadn't heard of these before our first visit but if you can imagine something that on the outside looks a little like a Cornish pastie but on the inside is filled with quality steak and gravy, you might have an idea. We always suggest we should have a competition to see how many anyone can eat but no one has managed more than two. They are possibly the finest football food I have ever had. Gary claims the use of the word 'possibly' is superfluous.

Phil (specialist subject: the work of Sir Archibald Leitch) and I (specialist subjects: the wives of Henry VIII and the free kicks of Darren Barnard 2004-2007) decided that we would enter a team into the television show Only Connect. We recruited our colleague Stephen (specialist subjects: the work of Douglas Adams, John Candy and Bill Murray) and decided that with our collective inability to grow a decent beard we should call ourselves 'The Pogonophobes.' Once we received the application form, we booked a meeting room to sit the entry test and, thinking we had done pretty well in our allotted 15 minutes, we awaited our summons for filming.

Initially, we were very surprised that we weren't selected but as the questions were subsequently shown on the show we soon realised why. While we were quite good on the missing vowels round, we were pretty hopeless on all the other ones. When the first show was broadcast I couldn't resist tweeting Victoria Coren Mitchell saying #luckyescape, as we would have been lucky to have got even one point.

Emotionally, this week was a tough week for me with my Dad's funeral taking place on the Wednesday. I've been to a few funerals over the last couple of years and, a while ago, I made myself a commitment that I would deliver the eulogy when it was my Dad's turn to leave us. Fortunately, my Dad had given me a significant amount of material to use. Even so, it's not easy standing and talking about a deceased parent in front of 100 or so people in such an emotional environment.

I don't really understand religion. Part of me thinks that it's a substitute for people who don't have football in their lives - and I'm lucky enough to have Sir Gary and the Mighty Shots in mine.

But my father was religious and regularly visited the abbey near Alton, so this was a fitting place to have the service. The prior and his colleagues looked after us beautifully, providing us with an extraordinarily high level of pastoral care in the difficult circumstances. The short amount of time that we spent in their company gave me a wonderful sense of comfort and I would like to take this opportunity to thank Dom Andrew and co for their support.

It's slightly strange trying to describe this and, actually I believe it's nothing to do with whether there is a God or not. It's about looking after your fellow human being and not being afraid to face into difficult situations and treating people as you would want to be treated yourself. Dom Andrew does this wonderfully and time in his company is time well spent. Sadly, I missed the opportunity to ask him to say a prayer for the Shots but as we know, that's probably not such a bad thing. Most Shots fans will remember the last time religion came to the Rec when the Dalai Lama blessed the pitch. We finished bottom of League Two and got relegated.

Sywell FC had a big week. It started off with the manager, Tony Pyke, leaving (his 'managerial contract was terminated on Monday after a string of losses and the assault of a player') and ended with him buying a majority stake in the club. Sywell FC said that 'Pyke's 97% stake does technically make him the club owner. As a result, the Powell family have stood down after 16 years of running the club. We would like to thank the Powell family for all that they have done for the club; from cutting costs by reducing playing budgets to selling the West Stand to disreputable property redevelopment firms.'

Tony Pyke stressed that there was no need for fans to panic, that there would be no changes to the way that the club operates. He then cleared out the management staff and appointed himself as the Chairman, Club Scout, Financial Director and Director of Football.

Following a 12pm kick off (due to the pitch having been double booked for a Battle of Hastings re-enactment), Tony Pyke's first game back in charge looked to be heading for a bad start as they were trailing Thurrock FC 3-0 at half-time. But Sywell are made of stern stuff and goals from Filip Stys on the 65th minute and Moses Chiwasa in the 83rd minute, set up an opportunity for James Ball to score an equaliser in the 88th.

A quick visit to the supermarket and I was in front of the radio to listen to the commentary with Lewis Chalmers joining Rob Worrell at the microphone. Lewis was one of our star players in our promotion season in 2007/2008 and it was nice to hear him talking about how well we are playing. The first half saw Aldershot dominating throughout and this continued into the second half. We had quite a few chances but weren't able to put the ball into the net until the 56th minute, when Matt McClure did so. Unfortunately, after a long wait, the assistant referee held his flag up and the goal was disallowed.

I read on Friday that Dean Keates had resigned as Wrexham manager. Thoughts of this potentially disrupting their charge for the play-offs were high as they went a goal behind against Woeking, but it didn't last, and Wrexham were soon in front. It was good news that Dover were beating Macclesfield, Boring Wood were beating Tranmere and Maidstone were beating

Sutton, but it would count for nothing if we didn't score a goal. Despite Rob's best efforts at the mic, the game sounded quite dull. Then the Shots really seemed to get going in the last ten minutes. Unfortunately, the ball just would not fall kindly for them and, despite being camped in the Chester half with six minutes of extra time, the Shots just could not break through. Chester set themselves up to avoid defeat. The Shots, without Scott Rendell and despite 11 chances to Chester's one, will be the more disappointed side. That their goal-keeper, Andy Firth, was the man of the match, sums the game up.

But as Sir Gary once said, never underestimate a point away from home, and it was a much better result than the 7-1 thrashing that we received at Fylde the week before, or the 8-2 mauling that we received at Chester two years ago. We should be pleased that we have bounced back from last week's heavy defeat and wish Sir Gary a very happy birthday.

Bognor Regis FC v Welling United

Tuesday 20 March 2018

I noticed that the Graham Westley's experiment at Barnet didn't last long and that he had been sacked after registering just two wins out of the previous 16 games. Barnet had subsequently appointed Martin 'Mad-dog' Allen. This isn't an altogether surprising choice as it is the fifth time he has been appointed as Barnet manager. He was at Barnet before leaving them last season to join Eastleigh in a move that was almost certainly going to have been motivated by the number of pound notes in his pay packet. But having been sacked by Eastleigh when he only won two of his 14 games in charge, he's now returned to Barnet. Some say that "…you should never go back," but surely the question should probably be "…how many times can you go back?"

I was driving into work on Wednesday morning and, while the radio was on, I wasn't really paying attention to it but the comment that there was "…a points failure at Aldershot" grabbed my attention. Fortunately, it turned out it was going to have a delaying effect on the trains, but it got me worried for a moment. The Shots can't afford a points failure at this time of the season.

Sadly, neither can Bogor Regis, the scene for my mid-week football fix.

I arrived at the ground and rang Fat Andy to tell him I was there. Apparently, Fat Andy had expected me to travel to his house to pick him. He had failed to appreciate that this would take me many miles out of my way and add another 75 minutes to my journey. I told him to read my earlier text very carefully. He didn't go quite as far as apologising, but he did acknowledge that I had clearly said that I would meet him at the ground.

We walked in and Fat Andy walked up to an elderly gentleman and said "Hello, Fat John." Fat John replied, telling Fat Andy to get lost. Regardless, Fat Andy asked Fat John whether his son, Fat Reggie, was coming to the game. Fat Reggie was in Bath working, so wasn't coming to the ground. We headed to the clubhouse to buy a beer, and I thought I should spend more time in their company as it made me feel quite thin.

Sadly, because the Rocks aren't doing too well this season, the crowds have dropped which in turn means they are unable to sell sufficient ale to make it worthwhile stocking any, so I had to have a Guinness. Not as good but considerably better than the fizzy stuff that Fat Andy and Steve from number 11 drink.

Bognor were playing Welling. Bill, Gary and I went to Welling a few years ago where we met Terry for the game. Bill was very excited because this was where his lovely wife Gill hailed from. I had been less excited, particularly after we went in search of a local hostelry for some pre-match refreshments. Food wasn't easy to come by and I felt slightly uncomfortable in the couple of pubs we visited.

Bill had decided that we should compile a list of famous alumni from the school that we attended (albeit several years apart).

Number one place was quite easy. It goes to Jonny Wilkinson who would be the obvious choice for any school. Thereafter it became slightly harder. Actor Julian Sands and Dambuster legend George 'Johnny' Johnson have to be in top five, although I was in a minority in suggesting Nick Pope, the government's UFO expert. Wikipedia suggests a High Court Judge, Sir Peter Coulson as well as Rupert Whitaker, a co-founder of the Terrence Higgins Trust, together with various rugby players that I have never heard of including Ugo Monye, Peter Richards, Charlie Amesbury and Ryan Wilson. I had suggested Alex from Made in Chelsea should probably be on the list, but Gary wasn't so sure that this counted as proper fame.

I reminded Bill of the time that he had told me that someone from his year called Toby was the drummer of the Norfolk band The Farmer's Boys. I went along to see the band in Guildford on this recommendation and, while I thoroughly enjoyed the gig (and subsequently found out that Napoleon had also been to the same gig while he was a student at Surrey University), I was slightly disappointed to have seen that had Toby ever been in the band, he had now been replaced by a drum machine. The only conclusive point on which we both agreed was that neither of us had made the cut, but the pointless discussion killed an hour or so, by which time we were ready to head to the ground. The ground was unimpressive and so was the crowd. The game was fairly dull, and we had lost 1-0. The burgers, though, were fantastic!

Bognor Regis are struggling this year and look as if they are heading towards relegation. In the greater scheme of things this is not a huge problem, other than the obvious embarrassment of course.

They don't appear to have spent big so hopefully won't have accrued any big debts that would threaten their financial stability. Hopefully they can rebuild next year. It's a shame that the gate was low, but I guess this could be attributable to the temperature as much as anything else. I had two pairs of socks, thermal underwear, a tee-shirt, long sleeved thicker shirt, jumper, a hoodie, a snood, a scarf, a leather jacket and a hat, and I was still freezing cold. I make no apologies for the snood though Gary is somewhat disdainful.

Welling were superb. They didn't let Bognor settle into the game, closing them down quickly and showing lots of ideas and intent when they were in possession. They comfortably won 3-1 and Bognor's goal was a very late consolation. Nonetheless, it was a good evening, and it's always good to spend time with Fat Andy.

Aldershot versus Boring Wood

Saturday 24 March 2018

There was some very exciting news during the latter part of the week when it was announced that the Shots have put in for planning permission to improve the Recreation Ground. The response was generally popular among the fans but there's always that little niggle in the back of your mind about what it is going to look and feel like.

The Recreation Ground is an old school football ground largely unchanged for many years. The ground has been the home of the Shots since they were originally formed in 1926 and the terrace on the South Stand was built soon after. Most Shots fans love the ground and the sentimental history that we associate with it. I love the fact that every stand is different and that it has been in the middle of the town centre for around 90 years.

I used to love walking through town centres and seeing football grounds rising in front of you as you turned a corner passed a series of terraced houses. Sadly, these days, so many grounds are all built from the same plans and look and feel the same. Phil is always keen to express his disappointment that Stadia architects such as Sir Archibald Leitch no longer have the influence that they did, and you wouldn't really know where you were unless you looked at the programme or team shirts. It feels like all modern grounds have been purchased from the same Ikea catalogue. Aldershot still retains its uniqueness though and we love that. Unfortunately, it is expensive to maintain an older stadium and we need to find ways to generate income on the other 13 days of the two-week cycle between games.

Football fans are funny people. Those who stand in the East Bank are concerned about retaining the soul of this 4,200 all standing terrace, with a barrel shaped roof that holds the sound of the singing and amplifies it. I once heard that the stand is a listed building due to its unusual shape. Whether it is or not, those who stand in it love it and want to keep it. People who stand or sit in the North Stand equally love their space. As do those who sit in the South Stand or those of us who stand on the Slab. Maybe it's nothing more than us being creatures of habit, but I think we're all agreed that we need to retain some of the charm of the existing ground as we improve it for a more successful future.

I love standing on the Slab, but I think that's as much to do with the other Slab dwellers and the sense of camaraderie and friendship among us and that we offer each other. If we all moved into the East Bank, we would be fine. Except it's a bit noisier and we wouldn't be able to talk so easily, and we would get really frustrated when we tried to sing" Oooh it's a corner!" and were drowned out by "Come on you Reds." But, apart from that, I'm sure we'd be fine. We'd get used to it. But it would be a change and it's human nature to be anxious about change, particularly if you are not dissatisfied with the current situation. However, I think most fans have learnt to have confidence in our chairman, Shahid Azeem. I certainly do. He put his hand in his pocket when we needed someone to, and he brought stability to the club when Kris Machala ran out of money and we were relegated from League Two and entered administration. Shahid doesn't seem to be particularly flamboyant and isn't looking for opportunities to gain personal exposure, but he does seem to have the interests of the club at heart and I'm very pleased that we have him as our chairman. I might have said it before but stability within the club is far more important than chasing short-term dreams of promotion. I think all Shots fans will (maybe begrudgingly at times) acknowledge that this is the case.

James was finishing at Uni for the Easter holidays so that meant I had to go to Aldershot via Reading again. Normally this wouldn't be a problem, but the traffic was heavy, and we only managed to get to the ground for 2.45, which meant that we only had time for one quick pint of the beautiful Golden Hen ale that was being served in the bar under the South Stand. After the beer, the first few minutes of the game were a cagey affair but Boring Wood looked the livelier of the two teams. The Shots were lucky to get away without being punished after Cheye Alexander made an uncharacteristic mistake from six yards that on another day would have seen us 1-0 down early on in the game.

Shamir Fenelon showed some beautiful skill when the ball was played through to him and he lobbed it over a defender before unleashing a volley at the Boring Wood goal. Some might say it was 'Gazza-esque' recalling that moment of magic against Scotland in 1996, but Shots fans are more likely to describe it as 'Deano-esque' after the extraordinary goal that Dean Morgan scored for us away at Cheltenham in 2010 to secure a play-off berth for us. Sadly, Shamir's effort was straight at the goal-keeper.

But a few minutes later it was Shamir's turn to feed the ball through to Jake Gallagher, who made no mistake in scoring to put the Shots one up with ten minutes played.

Will Evans mistimed a tackle on today's pantomime villain, Bruno Andrade, conceded a free-kick and gained a yellow card. The yellow card was shown after Andrade had been rolling around on the ground for long enough for the referee to be hood-winked into believing the tackle was more serious than it was. As soon as the yellow card was shown, Andrade rather predictably jumped up, ready to take the free-kick. Another referee conned by poor gamesmanship.

Charlie was on fine form with the guidance that he was providing to the players. After Lewis Ward took a goal-kick and the ball went out of play, he shouted his words of encouragement to "Keep the ball on the pitch!" It left us wondering why the manager hadn't thought of this insightful level of coaching.

A few minutes later we were wondering if the referee was up to the job. He put his whistle into his mouth and blew a tame whistle for a possibly ever so slightly late tackle by Jake before changing his mind and waving play on. A moment later he changed his mind again, blowing for a free kick.

After 20 minutes it looked as if Boring Wood were beginning to get on top and a few minutes later Danny Woodards unleashed a tremendous shot from 25 yards out that was dipping into the top left-hand corner of the goal until Lewis Ward extended himself to his full 6 feet and 6 inches to push it clear.

Callum was having a good game and we were disappointed to see the referee only show Andrade a yellow card for stabbing his elbow into Callum's face after 34 minutes. The tide had been turning and the Shots were building some pressure. Josh McQuoid had a brilliant shot saved low in the bottom right hand corner and the game stopped for half-time.

Portuguese player Bruno Andrade was one of the loan players that Dean Holdsworth had brought into Aldershot during his tenure. Bruno was one of the luckier ones who actually got to play a game while he was on loan, but it was only one game back in 2011 and, if I'm honest, I don't remember him.

There was a rumour that Club Statistician Pete Stanford was going to publish a second volume to his work, The Phoenix Has Risen. The first volume was an A-Z of all the players who had played for the Shots between 1992 when the new club was formed and our promotion to the Football League in 2008. The second volume, recording the players that Dean Holdsworth had on loan during his two-year tenure, was hotly anticipated but had to be shelved for similar reasons that the Encyclopaedia Britannica is no longer available in a book format.

Boring Wood came out strongly for the second half, but it was the referee that was the most noticeable man on the pitch. Both Callum and Shamir were the victims of hard tackles and two Boring Wood players received yellow cards. The Shots grew into the second half and began to dominate.

Matt McClure received the ball halfway through the second half in front of the North Stand and was racing down towards the goal before he was hacked down in another rough tackle. The referee bizarrely gave the free kick to Boring Wood which left Charlie wondering if the referee's father had done National Service in Aldershot and maybe held a grudge against the town.

After 74 minutes, a Shamir cross took a deflection and Matt, six feet in the air, made a beautiful and delicate contact with the ball to lob it over the goal-keeper's head and put the Shots 2-0 in front. This broke Boring Wood's spirit. That there were only 83 away fans travelling to one of their closest games shows how poor their support is. Guiseley brought nearly half as many and that involved a five-hour coach journey each way. For the Shots to beat the team in third place in the league who hadn't lost an away game since last September was very pleasing and the football was a real joy to watch. We left the ground feeling very proud of our team.

There were pictures in the programme which were artists' impressions of what the redeveloped ground might look like. I have to say I wasn't overly impressed. A two-sided terrace along the North and East Banks, similar in some ways to Stoke City's ground, albeit on a smaller scale and a new stand all the way along the South Stand. A new hotel would sit along the High Street End.

In the chat room, 'Grayshott' asked the all-important question, about whether the leaking gutters on the North Stand would be fixed but it was 'Anon Y Mouse' who said that he had been studying the plans and that he had noticed that if you get a magnifying glass and look very, very closely at the plan, the North Stand leaky gutter is going to be turned into a Championship class water feature. Mr Mouse thought that this looked very nice, and wanted to offer his congratulations to all those involved in saving that traditional part of the Rec. Steve from Number 11 and I were more disappointed that the Slab seemed to have disappeared and we started hatching our plans for a new 'SOS' campaign to 'Save Our Slab'. I was fully prepared to go through the airing cupboard to see if I could find an old bed-sheet to make our feelings known at the next home game and we were determined to start a Twitter campaign. #SaveOurSlab.

Nick Cansfield

Solihull Moors versus Aldershot

Saturday 30 March 2018

I had asked my wife whether she had any plans for the weekend, and she told me to stop trying to over-plan it. I was ambushed with a bathroom that supposedly needed decorating. Admittedly there was a little patch on the wall beside the toilet where the paint was peeling off. This was a result of two boys who, when younger, hadn't the level of accuracy that we might have hoped and as a result, I needed to paint the whole bathroom.

I was up promptly to get some washing on, empty the dishwasher, clean the fridge out, head to the hardware store and visit Sainsbury's before starting on the decorating. I was still working (and making a mess) when the game kicked off and I ended up listening to the first half in the bathroom. It sounded like a pretty dreary game which Solihull were edging by not letting us get into their penalty area. Sir Gary changed things around at half-time and we seemed more potent in the early stages of the second half. Rob Worrell and Nick Arnold were saying that both Solihull and Aldershot were playing for the win, and after Fabien Robert and Jim Kellerman were brought on to replace Jake Gallagher and Shamir Fenelon, the intensity of the game seemed to grow considerably.

The crowd was announced and among the 1,734 in attendance were 499 Shots fans. I replied that had I gone, there would have been 500 there. Looking outside at the torrential rain, my wife suggested that I should have been pleased to have had the opportunity to stay inside a nice warm dry house. We agreed to say no more about it. I'm sure there would have been more than 499 Shots fans in attendance had it not been for some terrible traffic on the roads. Sally Taylor tweeted that she was turning around as her satnav was giving her an estimated arrival time of half-time. Tranmere's game away at Dover had been called off a couple of hours before the game and news was filtering through that Sutton's game away at Maidenhead had been abandoned, with Sutton leading 3-2. I'm not sure which of the away fans would have been the most frustrated.

After 75 minutes the Shots should have had a stonewall penalty, according to Nick Arnold, after Josh McQuoid had been wiped out by the Solihull goal-keeper. Nick called for another penalty in the 94th minute when Callum Reynolds was heading into the penalty area to attack a corner and was pulled over by the Solihull defender, but neither were given, and the game finished goalless. Should we have been relieved that we got a point or disappointed that we got a point? In his summary at the end, Rob suggested that while Solihull might have had the better of the game and Lewis Ward made a few really good saves, we were very unlucky that neither of the penalty appeals were given.

To cap it all off, Macclesfield managed to score a winner in the very last minute of their game away at Woeking. How often are they doing that at the moment? This is the sign of a team with one hand on the Championship Trophy. I'm not going to complain with an away point, but it makes three points against Eastleigh on Monday important if we're going to finish in the top three.

Aldershot versus Eastleigh

Monday 2 April 2018

We'd not beaten Eastleigh since they'd been promoted into the Conference National. The games against them have often been close but, far too often the referee makes a big decision which generally goes against us.

I'm not overly keen on Eastleigh but I was interested to hear Stuart Donald recently admit that he had thought he could buy his way out of the league. After spending over £10,000,000 he has concluded that he needs to rein in spending on transfers and wages this season. Apparently, Eastleigh lost out on a couple of players a few weeks ago because their wage demands were too high, and Mr Donald has acknowledged that buying his way out of the league isn't sustainable in the long-term. I'm sure there are a lot of non-league fans who could have told him that several million pounds ago. I fear that this season will be yet another year of disappointment for the Spitfires and their alleged 2,500 supporters. Like most clubs they offer an early bird discount for fans buying season tickets. Unlike most clubs they have extended the deadline for this. The club claimed that it was due to popular demand but in the Spitfires' chat room, 'Bomber' wrote '...popular demand my arse. The expected sales are not happening...' You can't just spend millions on a football club and expect fans to flock in and to be successful.

There were a couple of articles in this week's Non-League Paper that caught my eye.

Firstly, I read an article on 1874 Northwich in the North West Counties League who have an astonishing 23 games to play over the next 30 days. These are all part-time players, the majority of whom, I suspect, will be trying to fit some kind of paid employment into the equation. I have complete respect and admiration for these players. It really is a world away from the pampered, cosseted lives of the Premiershit.

The other story that stood out was about a Tranmere fan, Richie Hellon, who walked the 274 miles from Birkenhead to watch Tranmere play at Dover last Friday, only to find the match was called off as he arrived at the ground. The walk took him six days and he was averaging about 50 miles a day for most of the walk. Richie was raising money for 4 year old Edie Molyneux who is being treated for a brain tumour in Brazil. Richie had raised over £3,000 from his walk which is a superb achievement. Huge congratulations to him.

Richie wasn't the only Tranmere fan to have reached the ground to find the game called off. Over 80 of them subsequently decided to head to Maidstone to watch them play Hartlepool instead, for their afternoon fix. These are the joys of football are totally missed by the armchair fan!

I thought about hitting the airing cupboard to look for an old sheet before leaving for Aldershot, but having looked outside at the pouring rain, I thought that this afternoon wasn't the ideal time to start our #SaveOurSlab campaign. Maybe one to save for when the weather is slightly less inclement.

It was Steve from Number 11's turn to drive, which is fine, but it does mean that he gets to choose the music and, unfortunately, our musical tastes are not aligned. I don't particularly like Country or Western music, and Steve from Number 11 seems to like both of them. Quite a lot…

And there was a traffic jam on the A3 which meant we had to listen to quite a lot of both Country and Western music as we drove to Aldershot. Had I known that this was going to be the least worst bit of the day, I would have suggested that we turned around and headed for home but sadly, I didn't know what was coming.

The game kicked off, but it was very difficult to concentrate. While it was clear to all that Eastleigh would only bring a hand-full of fans with them, the club had decided that they would be put into the seating area of the South Stand. As it happened, they brought more fans than we have away seats and, rather than taking the somewhat obvious option of opening the gate to the away end of the East Bank, they were directed to stand on the Slab.

Eastleigh had a shot saved by Lewis Ward after three minutes and the Eastleigh fans started to make themselves known a couple of minutes later when Chris Zebroski threw himself to the ground after being bettered by Josh McQuoid. I felt reassured by the presence of former players Dave Osgood and Steve Stairs. I'm sure they would be very capable of looking after me and the other Slab dwellers if anything was to kick off.

Matt McClure had a great opening in the eighth minute with a ball threaded through for him to run onto. He took a couple of touches but looked low on confidence as he tried to take it round the goal-keeper, Graham Stack, before letting himself be tripped up by Mr Stack's outstretched hand. The referee booked Matt for diving and it was abundantly clear that the afternoon was going to be an uphill struggle.

After ten minutes, Richard the security steward walked through the Slab advising us that his supervisor was not going to move the Eastleigh fans from the Slab and in an attempt to try and diffuse the situation, asked us to be nice to them. We asked him if he would be asking them to stop swearing and shouting abuse in our direction, but it was clear that he was not being given any support from his colleagues and was finding the situation as difficult as we were. We tried to keep watching the football, but it wasn't much fun. One of the reasons we stand on the Slab is for the friendly banter with other home fans. I don't want to stand with away fans but unfortunately, buying a season ticket does not allow me to freely move from one section of the ground to another; something that the stewards have generally seemed pretty quick to pick up on.

Lewis Ward made another good block and a Shots defender managed to get a head on a shot that was goal-bound to knock it over the bar for a corner. Paul McCallum went studs first into a tackle with Jim Kellerman. Jim got there first and had kicked the ball away before Mr McCallum went into him and if we needed any further evidence of the one-sided nature of the referee we got it when he gave us a free kick (there was no way he could do anything else) but didn't produce a card or even want to talk to the Eastleigh player. Shortly afterwards, Jim had a shot on target that Graham Stack managed to get his hands to but then spilled the ball. Unfortunately, no Shots player was following up. Josh McQuoid's turn next and he seemed to have all the time in the world to place the ball but just couldn't get it on target.

We had a couple of other chances, but a counter attack by Eastleigh, after Jim had a shot charged down, led to Chris Zebroski scoring after an initial block by Will Evans, and Eastleigh were one nil up.

Charlie arrived at half-time, having spent the first half with his friends in the North Bank, but half-time was spent trying to get someone in the club to sort out the situation on the Slab. Steve from Number 11 tweeted Laura Smith, the Shots' CEO, and he received a nice reply from her to say that she had spoken to the Safety Officer to ensure our concerns were dealt with.

But sadly nothing really changed and the second half was equally difficult. Whilst the club had finally opened the away end the Eastleigh fans refused to move because they were kicking towards the High Street End. The stewards obviously have no power to move people who do not want to move and, unfortunately, it's nothing to do with the police either.

So, we had a stand-off, very similar to the Woeking match on New Year's Day, where any potential enjoyment of watching a game of football was ruined by inept crowd management and a number of Eastleigh fans who should not have been in the home end and did not know how to behave themselves appropriately.

For the record, in the second half, the Shots had a good break after 56 minutes but two of our players throwing themselves into the box were unable to get onto the end of a superb cross that was crying out to be put into the net.

And then Paul McCallum scored a second for Eastleigh after 62 minutes. Some said that he shoved a Shots player as he went for the ball. I didn't see it and if I didn't see it, then obviously there was no way the referee was going to have done so.

Scott Rendell headed the ball into an Eastleigh player who nodded it out behind the goal-line. As we waited for the corner to be taken the referee awarded Eastleigh a goal-kick. It really was one of those days.

The Shots were toothless and lacklustre. We had another few efforts; notably from Shamir who went wide, Lewis Kinsella who managed to clear the East Bank roof, and Callum Reynolds who managed to head wide from only six yards out, but it was to be Eastleigh's day. In fact, they could have added to their score when Williamson was one on one with Lewis Ward, our goal-keeper managed to block the goal-bound shot with his knee.

By this time, we had ceased caring. We had left the Slab amid a barrage of taunts from some of the Eastleigh fans and watched the last ten minutes of the game in the Community Stand. We were so angry that we couldn't even be bothered to acknowledge the excitement of a corner.

I could never bring myself to leave a game before the final whistle, but this was the closest I have got. I'm sorry Shots, but I love you slightly less today than I did yesterday.

And if I didn't like Eastleigh too much before the game, the behaviour of their fans has moved them up the list of clubs I dislike. Still below Crawley of course, but catching up fast on Reading.

Aldershot versus Maidenhead

Saturday 7 April 2018

After the debacle of Monday, I'd lost a little bit of motivation for the game against Maidenhead, but a habit is a habit and I was back on the Slab this afternoon.

On Monday I bought myself a pair of the rather snazzy red and blue socks that have recently gone on sale in the Club Shop. This meant I was faced with a major decision. Buying a new item of clothing interferes with existing superstitions. Are these going to be lucky socks? Or do I stick with my existing lucky clothing that I normally wear? I think the last few games had been rather variable in quality and that's good enough for me to crack open a new pair of lucky socks. And they're on.

Voting was taking place for this year's player of the season. I found it a difficult choice as we've lacked a little consistency and while most of the players in the squad have had some really good games, earning their place in the team, I'm not sure that many have done so in every game.

My shortlist included Shamir Fenelon and Jim Kellerman who have both developed really well between last season and this. I also think that Scott Rendell, Manny Oyeleke and Jake Gallagher have been very consistent this season for us. Some players have done well but not played for the whole year, including Bobby-Joe Taylor and Lewis Ward, and I ruled them out for this reason. It was a difficult decision, but I went for Manny in the end as I think he has been that little bit more consistent and I really can't recall him having had a bad game.

Fortunately, the club had realised that the arrangements on the Slab on Monday were not acceptable and there was a nice apology in the programme. Sadly, there was also a report that Shots fans had been fighting with each other at the other end of the ground. How you would know they were all home fans rather than Eastleigh fans having just wandered up there, I'm not sure, but it's totally unnecessary.

Steve from Number 11 had decided to take his wife, Kerry, away for a romantic weekend, which included visiting Hillsborough to watch Sheffield Wednesday play. It's nice that he still thinks of small ways in which he can keep his marriage fresh and I'm sure Kerry and the boys would have a lovely time. But he admitted that he got his weekends confused and that he had meant to pick a weekend when the Shots were a long way from home. I said I would send him regular updates. I also told him not to bother sending me any as I really wasn't that interested in what the score was, just so long as they had a good time.

James had come to the game with his good friend Joe, but they decided to head to the East Bank. I wondered how much of this was down to Monday. Hopefully it wasn't, and they just wanted the more youth-friendly atmosphere provided by the East Bank.

The game started with the officials once again being the first to get noticed. The Maidenhead defender Rene Steer tackled Bobby-Joe and was awarded for his foul with a free-kick. We had a good shout for a handball in the penalty area from a corner five minutes later then on ten minutes Scott Rendell made the Maidenhead goal-keeper, Carl Pentney, pull off the first of a number of fine saves for the afternoon with a powerful header.

Maidenhead were quite strong, but they didn't seem to have too much class. They had two big strikers and a defensive mind-set, looking to hoof the ball up to their strikers whenever they got the chance. The difference in style between this and the Shots' attempt to play the ball on the deck with slick passing and movement was very evident, and while some of our passing went awry, the Shots were still in control of the game. After Jim Kellerman shot just wide, Scott Rendell scored a lovely goal from a Bobby-Joe free kick. The players had been celebrating for about 45 seconds when the referee changed his mind and disallowed the goal. No one was entirely clear as to why but when Kappadeano screened a video clip later in the evening we concluded that it must have been for Scott being off-side when he was celebrating the goal. There seemed to be no other explanation possible.

The Shots continued to dominate proceedings and Scott was having a fantastic game. Before half-time he had another couple of good headers, one of which was just over the bar and another that was saved by the keeper. Scott scored another 'goal' in the 40th minute. The ball had gone behind the 'keeper, who had managed to get a hand behind him and scoop it out of the goal. From the Slab, it looked a clear goal but, again, it was disallowed by the officials. Video evidence showed that the keeper had been a couple of feet off his line when he reached behind and that the ball possibly hadn't crossed the line.

I was thinking that I should offer an apology to the officials for accusing them of getting this particular decision wrong. Doesn't affect the other 30 or so that they did get wrong, but on this occasion, it may be that they were right. Although, having said that, I've just read Rob Worrall's tweet saying that after watching Kappadeano's highlights, he thinks there were '...two howlers from the Assistant Referee. Rens was not offside/did not touch Bobby-Joe's free-kick and it looks like the Maidenhead 'keeper hooked the ball back from over the goal line.' Who am I going to believe? Damn right. Rob Worrall, every time! My apology is withdrawn.

Maidenhead picked up a couple of yellow cards during the first half and could have had more had the officials not held our players responsible for themselves being fouled. Predictably, the half-time talk on the Slab was about the poor standard of officiating. We were discussing whether the officials were biased or incompetent. I had come to the conclusion that they were incompetent as they had given us a couple of decisions where our players had perpetrated the fouls, however one of my fellow Slabbers suggested that they had to be biased because there was no way that anyone could be as incompetent as they were. Actually, I'm sure I would be more incompetent.

The comments from the Union of Referees towards me over the years suggest that I'm not the most observant of people. I know this and most of the time it's fine so long as I wait for someone else to shout the abuse before me. If the abuse is already being shouted, then no one is going to notice me joining in. Mind you, when I start singing for a corner and it's been given as a goal-kick it's rather embarrassing. Admittedly, if it goes out for a throw in it's almost recoverable, but "Oooh it's a throw in" hasn't really taken off as a terrace chant, and is, quite frankly, VERY embarrassing.

Andy went to catch up with Roy over in the North Stand at half-time and Roy's friend John had come to the game. John lives in

Altrincham but is a regular traveller to Aldershot, and many other grounds. We asked Andy what Roy's view on 'the goal' was and Andy replied that it hadn't come up in conversation. Seemingly they were far more interested in talking about exciting places to visit. I initially thought they were sharing exciting holiday destinations but actually they were talking about the recent visit John had made to Berkhampstead for a game. I understand travelling to new grounds but to travel from Altrincham to Berkhampstead for a game of football not involving a team that you support seemed well worthy a follow up question. I asked Andy whether he had asked John the seemingly blindingly obvious question of "why?". Andy, who follows the Shots to every home and away game during the season, acknowledged this question hadn't occur to him.

The start of the second half was, as always, a welcome relief, and the Shots continued to dominate in a game that was literally moving from end to end. The East Bank were in fine form, cheering on our team but our passing and movement weren't quite as slick and accurate as they are when we are at our best.

The officials continued to want to take centre stage and gave Cheye Alexander a free-kick when he pulled a Maidenhead player over and a free-kick against Josh McQuoid when Maidenhead's number 14, Harry Pritchard, decided that he was going to fall over before he actually reached Josh – following which, and adding insult to injury, the referee incredibly showed Josh a yellow card. Fortunately, besides disallowing two goals and turning down a penalty appeal, the referee didn't get any 'big' decisions wrong.

The Shots dealt with the frustrations well and continued to take the game to Maidenhead. Lewis Ward had another outstanding save to make mid-way through the second half but apart from a five to ten-minute spell in the middle of the second half when they briefly came to life, the Shots dominated against the 12 men from Berkshire, and the only question was whether we could turn this advantage into a goal. Scott hit the post in the 83rd minute after a great cross from Cheye and just as we were beginning to worry about how much injury time would be added to the end of the game, Matt McClure, who had looked excellent since his late introduction into the game, sent in a cross that Nicke Kabamba managed to get a head onto while two feet off the ground and directed it passed Carl Pentney, who looked to get a hand to it, into the bottom corner of the goal.

'YoghurtPotts' tweeted 'And the East Bank goes mental.' I had to reply, sharing that the celebrations were fairly wild on the Slab too. For a moment I thought I saw Charlie smile and Andy certainly let out an involuntary whoop for joy.

There were three minutes of injury time left. Maidenhead won a corner but showed little energy to take it quickly. There was, however, still time for the referee to tell Lewis Ward to get a wiggle on, which seemed to irritate our mild-mannered friend Charlie, who shouted to the referee that he could "Bog off."

The final whistle went and we sighed with relief. That the Shots were the better team was not in question. We dominated the game, creating a number of chances, though it looked as if it wasn't going to be our day. Sadly, we've had a few of these of late but today the footballing gods were smiling on us and fortune favoured our brave players.

All in all, a much better experience today and, clearly, my lucky socks were an inspired purchase.

Tuesday 17 April 2018

It seemed as if every other team in the league was playing tonight except for the Shots and we could move from our current third position down to seventh if the results didn't go in our favour.

The evening started off positively with Brett Williams scoring a penalty for Torquay (at home against Fylde) and soon after Halifax scored at home against Sutton United. Things were off to a really good start for us.

Boring Wood versus Macclesfield was a difficult one as, in an ideal world, we wanted both teams to lose. However, I think the automatic promotion spot has already gone, so Macclesfield winning would keep us above Boring Wood and, after 20 minutes, Macclesfield obliged by going 1-0 up. The evening was looking very rosy. Sadly, it was never likely to stay that way. Fylde equalised against Torquay, before quickly scoring again to go 2-1 ahead. And then the really good news came through that Gateshead had scored a goal at Tranmere. Then, 20 minutes later, they went and scored another. Tranmere got one back before half-time while Ebbsfleet managed to score at home against Wrexham.

Listening to the results coming in was a roller-coaster of all of the emotions of watching the Shots crammed into a couple of hours.

Sadly, in the second half Andy Cook of Tranmere went on the rampage, adding goal after goal for Tranmere, who eventually won 4-2. Sutton got back on level terms at Halifax, but Halifax soon restored their lead. Ebbsfleet were on fire, beating Wrexham, and the evening left us in fifth place in the league.

The league was incredibly tight and there were potentially seven teams vying for the play-off positions. I'd resisted the urge to write down my predictions for each game in order to try and work out where we were going to finish because so many teams had been hugely unpredictable which would make it a bit of a waste of time.

Position	Team	Games Played	Goal Difference	Points
1	Macclesfield	43	17	85
2	Tranmere	41	29	73
3	Sutton	42	13	72
4	Fylde	43	27	71
5	Aldershot	42	14	71
6	Boreham Wood	43	14	69
7	Wrexham	43	12	69
8	Dover	42	18	67

This year the play-offs have been changed. Teams finishing between second and seventh will continue their season. The first round of matches will see the team finishing 4th playing the team that finish 7th at home and the team finishing 5th will play the 6th placed team at home. The winners will then travel to the teams that finish 2nd and 3rd, which means there is a significant advantage in trying to secure 2nd or 3rd place.

At this time, I wonder if Wrexham might be the team who miss out on the play-offs. Just the three games left but if they beat Fylde on the last day they should get there, though Fylde are in really good form, and I wouldn't bet against them.

I might have a small concern that the Shots could potentially miss out. We have to win our two home games, and if we draw away at Tranmere and Sutton, we would have 79 points.

Tranmere have home games against us, Solihull and Hartlepool, and away games at Dover and Halifax. I could see Dover and us getting a point but three wins against the other teams would put them on 84 points and second place.

Sutton are the unknown quantity, having lost their last three games. Away games at Maidenhead and Ebbsfleet would provide a return of four points, leaving Hartlepool as a safe further three points, meaning they just need a point against us in the last game of the season to finish on 80 points, one ahead of us.

I could see Fylde and Boring Wood both getting seven points out of nine and Dover's game in hand over Wrexham could see them leap-frog them into the final play-off place.

So, my conclusion is that three wins and a draw might be the requirement to finish second or third and it really could come down to the very last game of the season.

Tranmere versus Aldershot

Saturday 14 April 2018

I still felt slightly excited after last Saturday, but it didn't take much self-talk to realise that, with my wife having been away with a couple of friends for the last three days, it would be poor form for me to disappear to Tranmere the moment she got back.

Actually, I was quite looking forward to seeing her and spending some time with her again, and hopefully I could still listen to the game on the radio. After all, there's only four games to go!

It's been a bit of an expensive week. Having bought myself a season ticket for next season and two tickets for Sutton, I couldn't resist pre-ordering one of next season's shirts that were previewed this week. And then James chimed in that he wanted one, so I had to buy two. In a Twitter exchange with Shots CEO Laura Smith, she suggested that the best way to avoid my getting into trouble for buying two new shirts was to treat my wife to one as well. I must try and introduce the two of them to each other someday. It could be fun to watch. From a distance.

Today was going to be a particularly tense day. It always is when listening on the radio, but at this stage of the season, even more so. The day got off to a difficult start as I decided whether I should wear my new lucky socks or not. Part of me was thinking that maybe they would be lucky for live matches only, but the other part of me thought differently. I did ask Mrs C for an opinion but that was never going to help me solve my conundrum. So, I wore them.

I missed the first couple of minutes of the game as we had visited Thursley Common to see if Colin the Cuckoo had returned from his wintering in South Africa. We heard him but couldn't see him and had to settle with photographs of a Stonechat, a Curlew, a Buzzard and a Dartford Warbler; so not an entirely wasted trip.

While I was waiting for my computer to fire up so that I could open the commentary, the live scores and the updated tables, I noticed a tweet that said '2 – Yes!!! The perfect start #ATFC Live.' After whooping for a couple of moments, I read the tweet more carefully, and realised that 'ATFC' was referring to Alfreton Town.

The Shots were holding their own in what sounded like an entertaining first half as both teams carved out reasonable efforts which they were unable to get on target. Positively, Hartlepool managed to score at Sutton to level the scores at half-time, and Maidstone were beating Fylde 1-0. But other results weren't going our way with Boring Wood winning 2-0 against Chester and Wrexham winning 1-0 against Dagenham. At this point in time the Shots would be fifth in the league, level on points with Boring Wood and Wrexham, one point ahead of Fylde, one point behind Sutton, and two behind Tranmere. It was very tight for the play-off places.

I was feeling quite tense, so I thought I would mow the lawn during the second half, while listening to the commentary. Unfortunately, after 15 minutes of listening the commentary started to cut out. This was rather irritating and further investigation showed that the BBC needed me to sign in before I could continue listening. In order to sign in, I had to register. This process took far more than five minutes which was enough time for the commentary to change from Lewis Chalmers asserting that "The Shots are definitely on top in this second half," to Rob stating that "It's Norwood who has broken the deadlock." James Norwood went on to score another goal before the end of the game and Tranmere managed to win 2-0. Shots fans seem to agree that we were set up for a draw and for the first 70 minutes we were looking good value for it. But we can't do this again as we need to register some wins and get some points.

I think this game proved a point in the lucky socks department. Clearly not lucky for all games but I shall make sure they're washed for Tuesday night as they could be lucky home socks.

So, another frustrating afternoon for the Shots, but it wasn't as bad as it could have been. Sutton were held to a draw (I had predicted a win) and Fylde, Wrexham and Dover had all lost (I had assumed victories). This meant that Boring Wood were the only other team with aspirations of a play-off place who had won, making the maths slightly easier to work out.

Macclesfield must have done enough to be champions and Tranmere seem to be pulling away into second place.

Fylde still had a home game against Solihull and an away game at Wrexham. It was hard to see them getting more than two points from these games. Wrexham were fighting for a play-off place and Solihull were one of the form teams in the league at the time as they battle away from relegation. This would move them to 73 points.

Boring Wood had a trip to Bromley and a home game against Guiseley. I could see them picking up four points which would take them to 76, but there was an outside chance that they could win both which would take them to 78.

Wrexham had to visit Orient and host Fylde. Difficult to see more than two points here, which would take them to 72 points, potentially level with Dover who, like us, had a game in hand. I couldn't see Dover getting anything from their game against Tranmere, but even if they did win against Gateshead and Woeking, they would only have 74 points.

That left us and Sutton. Sutton had two tricky away games. While they might be able to collect all three points at Maidenhead, I thought they'd struggle at Ebbsfleet. If they secured a point, they would be on 77 points, going into the last game against the Shots.

This meant that the two home games coming up against Gateshead and Barrow were must win games for us. Win both, and we would be on 77 points, level with Sutton. The winners would finish third, securing the important bye to the semi-finals of the play-offs, which would be Boring Wood if they were successful, but equally could be Sutton!

Beat Sutton again and then we should meet Tranmere in the finals at Wembley. Of all the teams left in competition, I think Tranmere are the ones who need to get to Wembley. If the Shots were to get there, I can't imagine that we would take more than 10,000 fans. Against the less well supported sides like Fylde, Boring Wood or Dover, the ground would be empty.

It needs a well-supported team like Tranmere to ensure there is a decent attendance, but equally begs us to revisit the question about Wembley is the best choice for the play-off final. The Shots have made the final of the play-offs twice before. In their very first year we knocked Bolton Wanderers out in the first round before playing Wolves home and away in the final. We won 2-0 and 1-0 respectively. Bloody David Barnes!

The Second time was at the end of our first year in the Conference, 2003-2004, when Terry Brown led us into the play-offs. Two draws against Hereford in the first round and we managed to win the penalty shoot-out, setting up a final against Shrewsbury. As Wembley was being redeveloped (for such an extraordinary amount of money), the final was held at the Britannia Ground in Stoke. While it was a long way for Shots fans to travel, the ground was about the right size, and it looked pretty full.

Like everyone else, I want to go to Wembley to see my team play but I'm not sure about Wembley with only 20,000 fans in it. But I think I'll reserve judgement until I've seen us play there.

Nick Cansfield

Aldershot versus Gateshead

Tuesday 17 April 2018

I'd arranged to meet Gary in the Vic before the game. My gout
still hadn't completely cleared up so I had to have a soft drink. I
went to see the doctor during the week, and while she nodded
sympathetically to my assertion that I had read gout could be
caused by stress and dieting, sadly she seemed to agree with my
wife that there can be a link to alcohol consumption. The doctor
helpfully printed a sheet of information for me and I tried hard
not to become too defensive. The leaflet said that insufficient
vitamin C can cause gout. The leaflet also said sugar-sweetened
drinks that are high in fructose can cause gout, as can eating a lot
of heart, herring, sardines, yeast extracts or mussels. The doctor
didn't ask me about my consumption of these items so I'm not
sure why she would automatically assume that alcohol could be a
factor. I did ask her why she jumped to the conclusion that it
must have been alcohol and she reminded me, very calmly but
quite assertively, that she had access to my medical records.
Ah....

Visiting the pub and not having a beer is not brilliant, but then
again, not being able to get to the pub in the first place because
your gout is so painful is even worse, so I won't complain.

So, with my lucky socks on, I met Gary in the Vic for a quick catch up before the game. Among lots of other rubbish, we talked about films and actors. Gary used to be an actor and we used to enjoy our regular boys' movie nights. I asked Gary whether he remembered us watching the TV film of Andy McNab's book, Bravo Two Zero, and he did. .

I said to Gary that subsequent to this I had been to a talk by Andy as part of the Petworth literary festival a year or two ago and when I went to buy a copy of his latest book after the talk, I took the opportunity to talk to him. I had asked him whether the film was a true and accurate reflection of what actually happened during the Gulf War. McNab looked at me slightly quizzically. For those of you who aren't familiar with this volume it covers a Special Air Service (SAS) Special Forces patrol during the Gulf War, when McNab was in charge of a patrol of eight members of the SAS, dropped behind enemy lines, tasked with destroying Iraqi communication cables. Other members of the patrol, including Chris Ryan, disputed some of McNab's story, and Michael Asher and Peter Ratcliffe, both former members of the Regiment, added further question marks as to whether the story was an accurate telling of what happened.

So, when I asked him whether the film was an accurate portrayal of what took place, I feared for a moment that he might be wondering if I was suggesting he might have made it up. I took quick steps to reassure him that nothing could be further from the truth. The question I did want answering related to the part where Sean Bean went into the shower with two yellow towels and came out of the shower with one wrapped around his waist and one wrapped around his head. I can understand matching towels, but what was less obvious was a bloke coming out of the shower with a towel wrapped around his head. I have asked a number of my male friends and colleagues if they have ever wrapped a towel around their heads after a shower and 100% have looked at me rather funnily, before confessing that they had not.

Andy replied that he knew exactly the part of the film I was referencing; assured me that he had never wrapped a towel around his head and said that he would e-mail Sean Bean that evening to ask what he had been trying to do to his (McNab's) public image.

We walked to the ground, stopping off at the shop to pick up tickets for the last game of the season (away at Sutton) and we took our places on the Slab, anticipating a rather nervy game as the Shots tried to secure the three points.

Steve from Number 11 was attending a first aid training course in his attempt to re-join the Cub Scouts, but Charlie, Andy, Dave and the Union of Referees had all turned out, in what was a slightly disappointing crowd of slightly under 2,000 people. We weren't surprised at the attendance from Gateshead given it is undoubtedly a long way to come on a school night, but 26 fans is not a particularly good effort.

The Shots got off to a flying start, and it wasn't long before Lewis Kinsella delivered an in-swinging corner that the Gateshead goalkeeper, James Montgomery punched onto his post. He then, shortly after, saved a goal-bound shot from Matt McClure. The Shots were looking good and dominating the game in a manner that the fans hadn't seen of late. We had to be wary though, as after ten minutes, a Gateshead break could have changed the course of the game had Lewis Ward not been quick off his line to deny Gateshead striker Danny Johnson with a save by his feet. The ball soon came back to the other end of the ground and Shamir Fenelon delivered a lovely cross to Scott Rendell, who managed to get himself into a tangle with the feet of one of the defenders and the ball was cleared.

After 20 minutes a fine through ball was just too hard for Scott to run on to and, five minutes later, Matt had another good effort that was saved by Montgomery. The follow up shot from Callum Reynolds was blocked by a dogged defensive effort by Gateshead.

Gateshead continued to try and catch the Shots on the break. On the half-hour mark, Callum anticipated a dangerous move and cleared the ball. Then, shortly afterwards, back in the Gateshead half, the Shots hit the crossbar with the goal-keeper well beaten. More positive moves from the Shots saw more corners and balls that just would not run for us, but the reality was that James Montgomery was in superb form.

As the fourth official went to raise the board to show a minute of injury time, Jim Kellerman took a corner. Gary filmed twenty seconds of play during the entire game and it just happened to be the play from the corner which resulted in the ball going into the Gateshead net to put the Shots one up. We watched the footage several times during the half-time interval but struggled to work out what happened. The ball came across, but before it went in the net, the linesman started waving his flag and Scott Rendell started to celebrate. We found out in the match report the next day that Scott Rendell, with his back to the goal, flicked the ball with the inside of his foot before Montgomery could claw it away. But Will Evans was following up and not in the mood to take any chances as he smashed the ball into the net

One nil to the Shots at half-time, and it was as one-sided a game as we could remember. While I was looking at what was happening on Twitter, Gary looked at the other half-time scores. We were excited to see that Sutton were losing 2-0 away at

Maidenhead. I'm not sure what happened to Sutton, but this would be the fourth of their last five games that they would have lost. I guess conspiracy theorists will link this to the dangers of inadvertently getting promoted when you have a plastic pitch and whether they are deliberately trying to avoid getting into the play-offs. I guess we will find out when we visit in ten days' time. They were the best team I'd seen when they visited Aldershot earlier in the season, so it is going to be interesting.

The Shots weren't quite so dominant in the second half, but we looked in control throughout, and seemed relatively comfortable. Matt and Scott continued where they left off and both had chances that were saved by Maidenhead's man of the match, James Montgomery. Cheye was equally having a great game, and as we approached the hour mark, he had a storming run in front of the South Stand which came to an abrupt end when the Gateshead defender pulled him over and gained himself a yellow card.

Gateshead manager Steve Watson made a double substitution which appeared to have little impact on the game and the Shots dominance continued. Matt and Jim Kellerman both had speculative efforts that went over the bar and all the remaining substitutions slowed the game down with fifteen minutes left to play.

There was still time for a wonderful low hard cross by Shamir that went across the goal begging to be slotted into the net and for Manny to chip Montgomery only to see the ball bounce off the crossbar, before the final whistle was blown after four minutes of added time.

Man of the match could have been given to a number of players and it possibly should have been given collectively to the team for a wonderful performance. We thought Scott was our man of the match, closely followed by Matt, Jim and Manny. The sponsors gave the award to Will Evans. A wonderful game, played in a great spirit with a good referee. Far too often some of the northern teams tend to take a more physical approach against us and it was good to see Gateshead try and play football. My respect for them has grown as a result of this game and how they played it.

With Sutton losing, the Shots are back up to third in the league and securing that spot in the play-offs was firmly within our grasp. My lucky socks were a good purchase from the club shop after all.

As I drove home, I heard on the radio that Accrington Stanley have been promoted to League One for the first time in their history. I visited Accrington a few years ago when the company I was working for had a manufacturing site based in Huddersfield. I rang my friend Pete and asked whether I could come and visit him for a meeting. He said that that would be wonderful, and we agreed to meet on a Wednesday morning. I flew up to Manchester airport on the Tuesday afternoon to pick up a hire car to drive to the match. Mark Lawrenson was on the same flight and, having changed into my Shots shirt and jeans on the flight, I struck up a conversation as we disembarked. He was attending a slightly higher profile match than I was but he seemed very impressed that anyone would actually be prepared to fly in order to watch the Shots play at Accrington Stanley. We drew 3-3 which helped us secure a play-off spot, where we drew Carlisle in the first round. We managed a one nil victory in the home leg and were losing 2-0 until Jamie Slabber headed in an equaliser in the 95th minute. No further goals in extra time meant the tie went to a penalty shoot-out and, despite winning 3-1 at one stage, we unfortunately lost 5-4 after some poor behaviour from the

Carlisle fans who invaded the pitch before the penalties had been concluded.

Anyway. Well done, Accrington. I'm pleased for you.

Aldershot versus Barrow

Saturday 21 April 2018

I had a bit of a sleepless night which I think is due to PMT – 'Pre-Match Tension'. It's unusual that it's kicked in this early, but it's that part of the season when everything seems that little bit more important.

As we left the car park, it started to rain. Steve from Number 11 said that he had been preparing for a BBQ that he was having that evening and said that he had left the matches outside. I said I had left the washing on the line. We looked at each other and wondered what the chances were of our wives noticing that it was raining and bringing in the matches and the washing. We were both confident.

Steve from Number 11 and I arrived at the ground in good time, stopping off in the shop to put in his season ticket application and make a spur-of-the-moment decision to pre-order a new shirt. I felt quite good in that, although I have already made both purchases, I didn't have to pay £350 all over again.

We bumped into Bill from the Midlands and Heather in the South Stand bar and enjoyed their company with a pre-match drink. I was tempted by the Golden Hen and my resistance wasn't good enough to stop me ordering a pint. As this was my first pint for a while, it tasted superb.

It was fantastic to see Alan on the Slab for his first game of the season and, remembering the unfortunate photocopier moment, I thought I would introduce myself to fellow Old Age Slabbers, Tim, Greg and Mick, who I had spoken to many times but didn't know their names.

The Shots started where they left off on Tuesday night with lots of possession and lots of intent but unfortunately little to trouble the Barrow goal-keeper. Shamir had a good cross in the tenth minute, but it was that little bit too close to the Barrow goal-keeper and he was able to collect the ball comfortably.

The Shots had other chances and, as Alan stole a look at his new Garmin watch like thing, it told him that what his heart rate was, and suggested that he was highly stressed. "Have you been highly stressed before?" someone asked him, and he replied "No. Not until I wore it here."

Scott Rendell was everywhere. Trying to get on a cross to score the all-important goal one minute, then back in our area clearing our lines the next. Lewis Ward kicked the ball from a goal-kick and unfortunately it went straight out of play, which led to Charlie shouting at him to stop 'wanging' the ball.

I haven't heard this expression before, so I had to resort to Google, which offered me a number of potential translations. Firstly, 'wanging', as described by the urban dictionary, can mean high volatility in price movements – or highly unpredictable market movements. I'm not sure that this was what Charlie meant.

Wikipedia, once thought to be a somewhat unreliable source of information, informed me that welly wanging is a sport that originated in Upperthong, Holmfirth (co-incidentally the very same hamlet that my life coach and mentor, Big Al, lives in), where competitors are required to hurl a wellington boot as far as possible. I didn't think that this was relevant to the game. Neither was I convinced that the third option, suggested by Wiktionary, was of any use. According to Wiktionary, 'wanging' is the present participle of wang, and an anagram of gnaw. Sadly, it didn't offer any suggestion as to what wang actually meant so, all in all, it was a pretty useless advice, but not too far off what I had been expecting to see.

Wordnik, the final option, offered what I thought Charlie might have meant, when it gave an example of a use of the word, with 'Pardew is one of those familiar managers who believe in playing football the 'right way', which invariably involves wingers wanging the ball into the penalty area in the direction of a target man.' Armed with this knowledge, I was able to continue talking with Charlie, but he remained convinced that a 'wanger' was a long hopeful ball that goes out of play.

I guess we could use the term for whatever we want but he was right with his thinking. Too many kicks from the back go out of play. It's a huge pitch at the Rec and surely can't be that difficult to keep it in.

Our afternoon took a turn for the worse when Matt McClure picked up an injury in the 26th minute and had to be replaced by Josh McQuoid. Josh did pretty well after coming on, but Matt had been looking sharp and I did wonder if this would reduce our effectiveness in front of their goal.

Ten minutes later the referee, who I think had been having a reasonably good game, missed one of the most blatant pushes on Scott deep into the Barrow half and waved play on. I initially wondered if he was playing an advantage but, with the Union of Referees on the Slab today, I wasn't brave enough to say anything out loud. We were to have one more good move before half-time, when Will Evans made a beautiful pass to Cheye, who did well to keep the ball in play before delivering a lovely cross which Scott couldn't direct on target and eventually flew wide for a goal-kick.

The Shots weren't quite as good in the second half but were still dominating the proceedings. As the game approached the hour mark, James Rowe sent a lovely through ball for Shamir to pick up but sadly his shot flew high over the crossbar. Moments later Barrow were attacking and a cross flashed across the Shots' six-yard box, which fortunately continued with no one getting on to the end of it.

I was very impressed with the number of Barrow fans who had made the trip. 119 is a good effort considering the distance – and especially when you compare it with what was a similar number from Eastleigh which is only an hour away.

It was the Shots turn to attack and I definitely heard a song break out from the North Stand. After only 62 minutes the Barrow players' time-wasting was becoming more and more apparent. Up until then they had been okay and tried to play football but there was a distinct change in their tactics for the last half an hour as they upped the physical side of their game. Shots fans who witnessed the home game against Barrow two years previously will recall a side who should have been called to FA Headquarters to explain their appalling behaviour. Indeed, we were calling for the referee to abandon the game before any of our players ended up in hospital with life-threatening injuries, such was the nature of the tackling taking place on the pitch. On that occasion Barrow only had two players sent off but it could very easily have been more.

The referee gave a handball against Scott Rendell which even had the easy-going Charlie shouting at the referee. "Utter tosh!" he shouted and, soon after, the referee penalised one of our players for a foul that only he had seen. From the resultant free kick that should never have been given, in true Shots fashion we conceded a goal as Luke James headed in Lewis Ward's punched save. Twenty minutes to go and if Barrow had been time-wasting before the goal went in we knew it was only going to get worse.

We created a good move with Will Evans ploughing his way through the Barrow midfield and unleashing a rocket of shot that went wide. Had it been a couple of feet further away from the goal it would have taken poor Eric the photographer's head right off his shoulders.

Although he ignored the Barrow goal-keepers time-wasting, the referee did book the goal-scorer Luke James and, as the Shots tried to get back into the game, Barrow lost some of their composure and discipline.

Man of the Match, Manny Oyeleke, had a shot blocked and a good follow up shot went just wide, and in the 85th minute, the Barrow player Bradley Bauress saw red for a horrible tackle on Will Evans.

The Fourth Official held up the board showing there would be five minutes of injury time, and the Shots continued to attack. Three minutes in, and our faith was rewarded when Scott Rendell got on the end of a Manny cross to head the equaliser, secure a point for the Shots and keep alive our hopes for finishing third.

I'm not sure whether my new socks are indeed lucky or not. We rescued a draw when a defeat looked likely but, equally, would we have won had I not worn them? I've got a week to decide if they will help us against Sutton or not.

The players performed a lap of appreciation after the game before the player of the season awards were made. Well done to Manny who picked up the Supporters Player of the Year and the Players' Player of the Year. I think this was well deserved after a very strong and consistent season. As the players walked around the pitch I was finally able to grab Bobby-Joe and ask him to autograph my Chinese t-shirt that Gary had brought back for me from his visit to Beijing. I proudly showed it to my wife when I got home. She was considerably underwhelmed, but James was more excited and asked if he could have 'his' tee-shirt back again.

In the other fixtures, Solihull somehow grabbed a point away at Fylde and, although Boring Wood were twice ahead away at Bromley, they lost 3-2, with Bromley, like us, scoring the winner in injury time after the 90 minutes had been played. Wrexham lost at Orient and, somewhat surprisingly, given the difference that the form guide had shown over the last six matches, Sutton won away at Ebbsfleet.

This meant that Macclesfield were Champions and Tranmere were guaranteed second place. Sutton were third on 76 points, and we were immediately behind them on 75. Fylde and Boring Wood were both on 72 points and virtually guaranteed a play-off place, leaving Dover, Ebbsfleet, Bromley, Wrexham and Dagenham fighting it out for the final place in order to extend their season.

For the Shots, the maths were easy. If we were going to finish third, we needed to win away at Sutton the next Saturday. A draw and we might finish fourth and a defeat could mean we'd finish anywhere between fourth and potentially, eighth place. In some ways I would prefer to go to Sutton needing to win. Needing to draw might suggest an option to play more defensively. In my experience of watching the Shots, this is rarely particularly attractive to watch and rarely particularly effective, so this would mean that we needed to go out wanting to win a one-off game of football. I couldn't wait!

What is more of a shame is that Torquay have been relegated and Woeking will be if they fail to get a better result than Barrow next week. Barrow at home against already relegated Chester felt, one might think, an easier game than Woeking who were hosting Dover, and who might still hold on to a play-off place if they win. But, like us, Woeking need to go out with a positive mind-set and aim to win a one-off game of football. Good luck to them.

As a footnote, you will be pleased to hear that Kerry from number 11 had brought the matches in from the rain but possibly disappointed to hear that my very wet washing was still on the line. Somehow this was my fault for having over-loaded the washing line. But my wife hadn't even noticed that it had been raining.

Sutton versus Aldershot

Saturday 28 April 2018

Tuesday night saw some interesting results. A fine point by Barrow at Bromley meant that they were going into their final game hoping that they'd get a better result than Woeking in order to stay up. Ebbsfleet thrashed Gateshead 5-2 and were up to 5th in the league and looking good for the play-offs. But none of this was as important as Bromley now not being able to catch us, and the Shots have been guaranteed a play-off place.

If we were to lose and Ebbsfleet, Fylde and Boring Wood all won, we would drop down to seventh but if, as we hope, we win at Sutton, we would finish third and get that all-important bye through to the semi-finals.

Huge congratulations must go to Solihull for a tremendous victory at Tranmere. After 19 games of the season Solihull were bottom of the league with 11 points and looking doomed but after Tuesday's win, they were up to 15th, so well done them. This has been a tremendous effort which put our point there a few weeks ago into context.

So, after 45 games of football, it had all come down to this. Sutton United, who totally mullered us at home earlier in the season, playing on their plastic pitch, for the right to receive a bye into the semi-finals of the play-offs.

The Shots had sold out their allocation of 1,050 tickets and, while some asked for more, I'm not sure how many more we would have actually sold. The number of times we take more than 1,000 to an away match is very rare and they are generally allocated on a first come first served basis, with phone bookings accepted, so I don't think there is any reason for anyone to complain.

I have been to Sutton a few times. The first of which was the disastrous FA Cup tie in 1987 when Bill and I travelled with Steve from Bournemouth, and we lost 3-0. It hasn't been a happy ground for us, but we had high hopes that this was about to change

Adie asked if we fancied sharing a ride, so we met up somewhere between our house at number 3 and Steve at Number 11's house at number 11, and headed off, briefly stopping at Guildford train station to pick up James on the way.

The traffic as we drew closer to Sutton got heavier and the last mile or two seemed to take a disproportionate amount of time. It makes me pleased to live out in the country with little traffic, and easy parking. We parked up, co-incidentally in exactly the same space I parked in last year, and headed towards the ground.

As we walked in, there were a number of stewards frisking supporters. We laughed when James was the one of our group to have been selected for the search despite Adie's desperate pleas to the female steward. He stood with his arms out begging to be frisked, but sadly to no avail.

Despite arriving 40 minutes before kick-off, there were no programmes to be had and we made our way to the stand behind the goal.

There were a good number of Shots fans in the ground but after five minutes we decided that we would move to find somewhere else to stand. The terrace behind the goal is below ground level and does not provide a good view of the pitch. We found an area that reminded us of the Slab, towards the terrace where the Sutton supporters were standing and thought this would be better. Unlike the Slab however, there was no stepped terracing and it was just a level area, covered in two inches of water which provided us with an equally poor view of the pitch.

The team was announced with Lewis Ward in goal and Cheye, Will, Callum and Lewis Kinsella across the back. The outfield players were James Rowe, Josh McQuoid, Scott, Manny, Shamir and Jim Kellerman.

It was shame that Matt McClure was still injured as he had looked really threatening over the last couple of games.

Before the game there was a minute's applause for the former Sutton manager, Barrie Williams who had died the previous week. The Shots fans were immense as they joined in the applause and it was great to see our manager, coaching staff and substitutes who were sitting in the dugout, stand up and join in.

You would have thought that the home dugout would have done the same, but they largely ignored it and carried on regardless. Moments like this do remind me that although we occasionally have a few idiot fans, on the whole most people associated with the Shots fans are decent human beings who represent our club very well indeed.

After the game started we had an immediate glimpse of Suttons tactics when their number 23, Josh Taylor, fouled Cheye as early as the third minute. A minute later, Scott received a push in the back. And then it was Jim Kellerman's turn to be pulled back when he had the ball. The referee had given us two out of three of these fouls which we agreed was better than our normal return. Our chant of "You Dirty Northern Bastards!" was received by our fellow fans with a similar degree of enthusiasm as our corner chants normally do.

The Shots definitely created some chances. In the seventh minute James Rowe flicked a ball over the defence for Josh McQuoid but he couldn't quite pull off the finish. Sutton were pumping the ball down our right flank, giving Lewis Kinsella quite a torrid time. A couple of Sutton moves created danger but fortunately the Shots managed to escape, although when Lewis Ward took too long to off-load the ball he was quickly closed down by a Sutton striker, and we thought Sutton would go one up. But immediately at the other end Scott had one of our best chances of the afternoon cleared by a Sutton defender after the goalie had been beaten.

Steve from Number 11 went to get a round of tea and came back having scolded his arm. The tea was frighteningly hot and there was a slightly hidden lip on the shelf at the tea hut which resulted in him wounding himself. The recent first aid course that he attended has already paid for itself.

The match ebbed and flowed from one end to another. Unlike the manicured grass of the Recreation Ground, one kick on the plastic pitch and the ball would bounce nearly as high again and reach the opposite end of the ground within a nanosecond. This probably suited Sutton's direct style of route one football, but it didn't help us as we tried to play football

Halfway through the first half, Will got the ball. We weren't entirely sure if he was attempting one of his Stevie Gerard influenced masterful diagonal passes or whether he was brilliantly trying to lob the keeper. Sadly, the ball landed half way between both these options and sadly came to nothing.

Jim received a somewhat dubious yellow card for a tackle from which he came out with the ball and a moment or two later, one of the Sutton players received a booking for a crude tackle on Shamir on the edge of their penalty area. Lewis Ward made a good save, plucking the ball out of the air and out of danger during a Sutton attack and it was clear that there was only one team trying to play football, whilst the other was trying to prevent it from happening.

Josh was booked, and the referee got his can of foam out to ensure the wall was ten feet back. Humorously, rather than asking the wall to go back the six inches that it needed to, the referee squirted shaving foam where he thought it should go which resulted in it going straight over the boots of the players in the wall.

Sutton's Josh Taylor seemed anxious to make a name for himself and received a yellow card for stamping on Lewis Kinsella and with five minutes to go until half-time, Sutton had a good effort that just went over the bar from a long throw.

We had a really poor view of the game and, as we know, my ability to watch something and recall it a second or two later isn't particularly good, but when the ball seemed to hit the hand of one of the Sutton players, I couldn't stop myself from shouting out "Handball!" Sometimes in the past, vociferous shouts from the crowd have most definitely swayed decisions made by the officials, but a vociferous shout by just one person probably isn't likely to have much of an effect. But old habits die hard and it doesn't stop me from trying.

"Handball!" I shouted enthusiastically and immediately the retort from the home terrace came back "How can that be handball, you idiot?" This put-down could have come straight from the Slab's own Union of Referees, but we continued undeterred.

Moments later one of the Sutton players hoofed the ball straight at Jim and the Sutton lads appealed as one with a shout of "Handball!" I couldn't resist shouting back "How could that be handball, you idiots?" but they failed to see the irony and started trying to tell me about how the ball had hit Jim's arm. We could have launched into an interesting discussion about ball to hand or hand to ball, but given the pace of the shot, it felt so obvious that it wasn't worth the effort. And we know that I would have come off second best in this type of discussion.

At half-time we discussed the pitch. I think I'm beginning to make my mind up about plastic pitches. It was abundantly clear that the pitch suited the direct style of football played by Sutton and that it didn't do our passing game too many favours. When the ball bounced, it spun on considerably more quickly than on grass and Sutton were very quick into tackles to stop the ball getting away from them. Put together a physical side who are not shy in bullying the opposition through overly tough tackles, throw in a very direct style of football and it's easy to see why Sutton grind out results at home. This was a very different style of play to that when they visited Aldershot earlier in the season, and even if they win more than they lose, I wouldn't want to watch it every week. It was a poor advert for our league and it's no wonder the BT Sport cameras had decided not to bother turning up.

Sutton got their water sprinklers out at half-time to spray water on the plastic surface – I wondered if this was to make the ball zip around even faster, but Adie thought it might help to soften the pitch so that the players didn't hurt themselves when they fell over. Either way, when they took the sprinklers off at the end of the break there was no need for them to direct the spray over the away fans.

The second half followed a similar pattern to the first and it wasn't long before Scott was karate kicked by Nicky Bailey. The referee obviously thought that this was a legitimate part of the game and waved play on. But sadly for the Shots, a moment or too later Tommy Wright scored from a cross from Tom Bolarinwa, which our defence should have dealt better with. While the local oiks thought this was a good time to let off a smoke bomb in their home terrace, it forced the Shots into a more offensive frame of mind, and not long after, Jim had a good effort that went just wide. Finally, the referee booked Bolarinwa for a foul on James Rowe but Josh McQuoid could hardly contain his anger when the referee ignored yet another foul on him a few moments later, and shortly afterwards, Sir Gary wisely substituted him and brought on Fabien Robert.

Immediately we started showing more intent. Fabien chested the ball to the feet of Shamir, who was fouled by Kenny Davis. The Shots had a penalty and, while from where we were standing the goal looked incredibly small, Scott made it look huge as he confidently stroked the ball into the bottom left hand corner after sending the keeper the wrong way.

Time for the Sutton manager, Paul Doswell, to jump onto the pitch and start complaining about something or other. The referee told him to shut up and the game re-started.

The announcement of the attendance halfway through the second half caught Shots fans by surprise. Somehow there were two-and-a-half-times as many Sutton fans in the ground as there were Shots fans. Not from where we were standing – it looked as if there were a similar number of each, particularly when we had half of the seats allocated to our fans.

With 70 minutes gone, Will sent another 50-yard pass up the pitch which Scott did ever so well to get on to the end of but, sadly, he was never looking in control and although he managed to get a touch on it, it went wide of the goal. Sutton goal-scorer, Tommy Wright decided that he would show the rest of his team-mates that he was a hard man too and tried head-butting Will. Will is what many journalists would describe as a 'solid unit', and Wright ended up in a crumpled heap on the floor.

With twenty minutes to go it was time for Sutton to start time-wasting and, although the referee talked to a couple of their players, it got worse and the referee allowed it to continue. The Shots on the other hand were playing some good football. Callum sent a fabulous cross towards Cheye who sent a first time cross into Nicke Kabamba, but it went, agonisingly, inches wide of the goal. Josh Taylor, the Sutton number 23 then fell over and the referee awarded Sutton a free-kick. From this, Lewis Ward, who had been so secure in his handling of the ball, fumbled Bolarinwa's drive, allowing Sutton substitute, Ross Lafayette the easiest of tap-ins to score

2-1 up with ten minutes or so remaining and Sutton were determined not to let Aldershot have the ball. When they could, they wasted time, and when they couldn't, they fouled the Shots players to deliver the same outcome. Aswad Thomas pulled Cheye down from behind and we were surprised to see Cheye penalised and a free kick given to Sutton. Shortly afterwards,

Nicky Bailey went through Fabien Robert from behind which was again ignored by the referee, but he was booked a moment later for another crude tackle on Jim.

The Shots had a few more chances, with one brilliant one for Fabien. Standing near the penalty spot, the ball just needed a touch to put it into the goal, but Fabien tried to flick it over the top, and the danger was averted. Nicky Bailey committed another foul a few moments later when he pulled James Rowe to the ground, and we wondered how he was still on the pitch.

It was clear that it wasn't going to be our day and when the ball went out of play for a Shots goal-kick, we noticed the ball boy kick it away from Lewis Ward and then turn to the crowd, holding out his arms to lap up the applause for joining in the time-wasting. This just about summed up the afternoon for us.

Sutton manager, Paul Doswell, said after the game "I think Aldershot are the best footballing side in the division, and that's what we had to beat. They had more possession than us and looked better on the ball than us."

What he didn't say was "Aldershot are a much better team than us and there was no way we were going to have a chance against them playing football. We stopped them playing football, and boy, some of the Shots players are going to have some good bruises tomorrow morning to remember us by."

After applauding the Shots off the pitch, we made our way back to the car, sharing notes about everything we didn't like about Sutton. We started with the pitch, the ground, the view, the players, and ended up with the ball-boys and the sprinklers and ended up with Steve moaning about the temperature of the tea. After watching this game closely, I now have a very clear opinion on plastic pitches, and I do not like them. The ball does not bounce in the same way and, while I'm happy with an argument that it is the same for both teams, I wouldn't want to watch football played on an artificial pitch every week. It does not make for an entertaining game.

And I am going to visit the Club Shop to see if they will take my socks back, as they are clearly not the 'lucky' ones that I believed them to be.

Sadly, even though Barrow lost at home to Chester, Woeking lost at home to Dover, which meant they were relegated to Conference South. This is a real shame, and I hope they are able to sort out their off-the-field problems and come back ready to mount a challenge to return next season.

In other games, Bromley were thrashed 5-2 at Maidenhead and Fylde and Ebbsfleet could only manage draws away at Wrexham and Torquay respectively. This all meant that the Shots finished fifth in the league behind Macclesfield, Tranmere, Sutton and Boring Wood. Fylde would travel to Boring Wood on Thursday night, but before that, the Shots would entertain Ebbsfleet on Wednesday night in the first round of the play-offs.

If we win that we will travel to Tranmere on Saturday for the privilege of playing at Wembley. Adie, Steve from Number 11 and I had worked out the permutations in the car on the way back and agreed to meet for a pre-match beer on Wednesday night, and to travel together to Tranmere on Saturday, should we make it.

Adie was still wondering whether finding a local pub and spending the day in it would be a better option. I think he was thinking that the 10 hours that we would need to spend in the car could be usefully spent in the pub drowning our sorrows when the inevitable defeat happened. But football is all about hope, and I was determined that Steve from Number 11 and I would work on Adie during the week. Slightly harder was to persuade my wife that this would be a crucial journey to make.

Aldershot versus Ebbsfleet

Wednesday 2 May 2018

And so, a week after saying that it is 'extremely unlikely' that he would become part of a consortium to rescue ailing Sunderland, Eastleigh owner and multi-millionaire, Stewart Donald confirmed that he is relinquishing control of Eastleigh.

In a surprising career move, the Oxford fan says that it is with 'great sadness' that he is putting the club up for sale but acknowledges that it is the fault of the football authorities who won't allow him to 'own' two clubs at the same time. After stating that he is putting the club up for sale, Mr Donald said that he would like "...to assure the fans that I will not charge for the sale of the club."

I can see the e-bay listing in my head. Football Club for sale - asking price of £0.00. As with other clubs where a rich owner has come in and expected to buy instant success, Mr Donald has spent over £10,000,000 only to see the club plateau in the Conference National. It will be interesting to see if the ambitions of the new owner(s) are anywhere near those of the current one. Personally, I'm not sure how the conversation at home would have gone when he confessed the purchase to his wife. "Hello darling, I've given away the £10,000,000 I've thrown away at Eastleigh and bought another club. Oh, and by the way, I will be travelling to Sunderland every other weekend to go and watch the games."

I looked through our airing cupboard for an old sheet that we could use to advertise our campaign to Save the Slab but, unfortunately, I couldn't find one, and neither could Gary. Gary was looking in his airing cupboard rather than in mine. If he was looking in mine, I could have saved him the effort, because there wasn't one in there.

The other option could potentially be to spray our campaign slogan onto a wall with an aerosol paint can, but then I remembered that back in my youth I had been arrested for spraying Aldershot FC on a brick wall outside the Crimea. I hadn't actually done it, but I was in the wrong place at the wrong time and was arrested for it. As I was under 18, my mother received a phone call asking her to come and sign the necessary forms for me to be let out of my cell at Aldershot police station. I'm not sure she was expecting me to head straight back to the ground. As I recall, she said something along the lines of "Where do you think you're going?" to which I replied, "To the ground – if I hurry, I can still get there for the second half." Possibly not the expected response, and one that maybe these days with children of my own I can understand a little more than maybe I did 35 years ago. Sorry Mum.

Gary said that he didn't have any paint but he had an aerosol can of Deep Heat. I guess this is another sign of old age and, although there's probably a limit to the amount of damage that you could do with Deep Heat, we decided not to take any aerosols of any description to the game tonight. We met up with Steve from Number 11, Adie and two of Adie's friends, Tim and Dave, in the Vic for a bite to eat prior to the game. I'm not sure Dave is going to recommend the food there as the poor waitress tripped over when delivering him his fish and chips and accidentally threw it over him. When the replacement came, it was cold. I had a lasagne there a few years ago and took it back as it was burnt, only to be greeted with "What do you expect for £2.99?" My burger and chips however were good, and Gary's ham, egg and chips without the chips was significantly improved over recent versions, thanks to a well-advertised change of ham supplier. The last time Gary asked for ham, egg and chips without the chips, the waitress told his that unfortunately there wasn't any ham and there wasn't any eggs. This suddenly made his ham, eggs and chips without the chips, the ham or the eggs a particularly diet-friendly dish.

Mrs C had been out for lunch with her parents to celebrate her Mum's birthday earlier in the week and had told them about Gary's low carb diet, which doesn't allow him any potatoes and requires him to ask for ham, egg and chips without chips. When it was his turn to order his food, Uncle John had apparently asked for scampi and chips *with* the chips, which got him a rather puzzled look from the waitress who clearly had not been asked for this before.

Adie went for the altogether safer option of a kebab.

Steve from Number 11 mentioned that I was writing a book and it turned out that I was in good company. Tim had written a fabulous book on the transformation of Chelsea under Tommy Docherty called 'Diamonds, Dynamos and Devils' and Dave is in the process of finishing a book on wildlife photography. I think Steve from Number 11 may have regretted his introductions as we spent the next hour or two talking about publishing books and places to go for wildlife photography. I think he might have been hoping for a slightly different pre-match conversation, but it certainly must have beaten talking about the impact of containerisation on the outcome of the Second World War.

We had close to a full complement on the Slab for the game with only Alan missing. It was good to see Stevie from Bournemouth, who I hadn't seen for a while and everyone seemed to be in very good spirits when we realised that the Shots had taken to the field with three strikers and full of attacking intent.

We looked good from the start and it didn't take long before we had a shot on target. Unfortunately, Matt McClure shot well wide which resulted in a shout of "My eight-year-old could have done better!" from one of the regulars. The reply was immediate, as someone retorted "Well, why isn't he playing then?" Our nerves began to settle.

The referee made some howlers right from the start including missing a pulled shirt on Scott Rendell and awarding Ebbsfleet a free kick after Cheye had been pulled over.

The funniest moment of the evening was Will Evans turning on a sixpence as a rather portly Danny Kedwell came sliding in on him and Danny continued his journey, sliding on his backside along the wet grass, long after Will had turned around and started making his way up field.

Gary had observed that Danny Kedwell's shirt was a particularly snug fit, and said that he used to look like that himself. He then added, "I got a bigger shirt."

The crowd were involved in the game from the start and were truly magnificent, but they continued to be mystified by some of the decisions that were being made. In the tenth minute, there was a good shout for a handball which many thought was a much more obvious penalty than the one given to us at Sutton, but the referee ignored it.

Matt McClure, Nicke Kabamba and Scott Rendell all had chances, but none of them troubled the goal-keeper. In the 25th minute, Ebbsfleet's Jack Powell took Manny Oyeleke out with a bad challenge and rather than talking to him or booking him, the referee just helped Powell back to his feet. It certainly felt that we had another referee who was helping the other side and even the mild-mannered Charlie felt the need to shout, "Come on Ref, you keep missing blatant fouls," and a few minutes later Adam McDonnell was clattered but once again the referee chose to ignore it.

The Shots were playing some brilliant football and when we had a throw-in after 35 minutes, Bill from the Midlands confidently said that "We will profit from this." Sadly, Bill from the Midlands proved that he was no prophet as Ebbsfleet regained possession. Nicke's turn to be fouled next but the referee awarded a free kick to Ebbsfleet. When the same happened a few moments later on Scott, the East Bank were singing "You don't know what you're doing!" and I felt they had a point. There was still time for one more foul not to be given when Lewis Ward was held by one of the Ebbsfleet defenders and an Ebbsfleet player petulantly kicked the ball away after a free-kick had been awarded to the Shots before the half-time whistle was blown.

The Shots were at their best in the first half, creating loads of opportunities and completely dominating the game but as has happened more often that we would like, they couldn't turn this domination into goals. We were confident though that if we continued to play like this in the second half we would win.

The referee, having ignored several fouls in the first half against Shots players, decided that he would award Ebbsfleet a penalty shortly after the re-start. We think it was for a pull on Danny Kedwell, but it was difficult to see from the other end of the ground and there was no obvious infringement that we could see. Certainly, it was nothing worse than the fouls Ebbsfleet had been committing in the first half and getting away with. Kedwell took the penalty himself and must have wished that he had done better when a rather feeble shot was easily saved by Lewis Ward and the Shots managed to clear their lines.

Jakey, while not quite his usual combative self, went in hard for the ball and clattered an Ebbsfleet defender who was late arriving and ended up in a heap as Jake followed through. Many referees would, I'm sure, on seeing the name Gallagher on the back of his shirt, have sent him off, but for once, the decision went our way, leaving the Ebbsfleet player something to think about. Jake must have got Sir Gary worried as he replaced him with Jim Kellerman shortly afterwards.

The referee did seem to be watching a very different game of football to the 3,500 supporters in the ground. When Jack Powell kicked the ball away under his nose to prevent the Shots taking a rare free kick quickly, the supporters were up in arms, but as before, he seemed content to ignore it. But in the 71st minute came arguably the moment that changed the match. Jim Kellerman went in for what looked like an innocuous challenge, and dislocated his shoulder. After five minutes he was taken away on a stretcher to hospital. A really bad end to the season for him and it left the Shots without the midfield enforcer, a role that he, and previously Jake Gallagher, had both performed so well. As the game progressed, Ebbsfleet grew more and more into it and they won a succession of corners that turned the pressure up on the Shots. Dean Rance, the Ebbsfleet defender who had caught our eyes a number of times during the game, was finally booked towards the end of the 90 minutes by the referee for a tackle on Fabien Robert. But as the game continued, both sides seemed to grow more desperate, and the passing became sloppy.

Normal time finished goalless and we went into extra time. At the beginning of the second period of extra time, the Shots were attacking the Ebbsfleet goal and the ball came out to Lewis Kinsella who fired in from 15 yards out. The angle was narrow, but his shot went straight across the goal towards the North Stand before someone managed to get it back in the box for Nicke Kabamba to head into the net for what we felt would be a winner for the Shots. Elation followed in the home terraces as we sang "If you're all going to Tranmere clap your hands," and we started to talk about what time we would be leaving for the lunch-time kick off on Saturday.

When one of our players missed a tackle, Charlie shouted out that he was "As much use as a fart in a calendar." We weren't entirely sure that this was what Charlie had meant to say, and I did wonder if Roy Hudd would have sold more copies of his autobiography had he titled it thus, instead of the somewhat more popular term, 'Fart in a Colander'.

We returned to the football just in time to see Will take too much time clearing the ball from our goal-line and, in a heart-breaking moment, one of the Ebbsfleet players stepped in and delivered a cross for our old boy Dave Winfield to head into the corner of the goal.

Within moments, joyful thoughts of visiting Tranmere had been replaced with the stress and tension of a penalty shoot-out, and we were all feeling it. Charlie thought this would be a good moment to tell us that Roma had beaten Liverpool 4-2, but that

Liverpool had won on aggregate. We weren't interested, and Charlie was given some very clear feedback to this effect.

We took the first penalty, and Captain Callum stepped up in front of the East Bank. He smashed the ball straight down the middle into the top of the net to settle our nerves and put us ahead. Ebbsfleet scored their goal and it was all level.

James Rowe took the second penalty for the Shots and calmly placed it into the bottom right hand corner. After having been named man of the match, Lewis Ward then saved from Marvin McCoy and after Scott Rendell scored his penalty in the bottom right hand corner and Lewis made a further save from Jack Powell, we were 3-1 up and only needing to score one more to progress.

Shots fans will remember the game away at Carlisle in 2005 when we were in the same position and somehow we managed to throw the lead away. Surely history couldn't repeat itself? Lewis Kinsella shot to the right but missed the goal, Fabien Robert's shot was saved, and with Norman Wabo and Danny Kedwell both scoring for Ebbsfleet, suddenly it was 3-3 and heading into sudden death. Manny made no mistake with his penalty for the Shots and Jack Connors subsequently levelled for Ebbsfleet.

To our surprise, Lewis Ward stepped up to take the next one for the Shots and the ground went quiet when his shot bounced back off the post. Dean Rance duly scored for Ebbsfleet in the bottom right hand corner and our dreams were shattered for another year.

No negative comments from Shots fans towards the players who missed the penalties. They are always a lottery and can easily go either way. We were frustrated with the performance of the referee during the game but, actually, Ebbsfleet did come to try and play football, which was so much more than Sutton had done the week before.

While I wish them luck for next Saturday, I fear it would be a big ask for them to get a result at Tranmere. Selfishly, I hope that Tranmere win as Ebbsfleet is an easier away match for me to get to next season.

Epilogue

So that's the end of our season then. We didn't get to Wembley and we didn't win promotion.

The following evening, Boring Wood beat Fylde 2-1 in the other first round match, setting them up with a visit to Sutton on Sunday. I'm not sure from what I've seen of both these teams that either of them are worthy of a place in the League, and my hopes lie firmly with Tranmere.

Tranmere beat Ebbsfleet 4-2 after extra time in a game that Ebbsfleet had twice been in front. After Wednesday night's exertions, it would have been a tired Ebbsfleet team that took to the pitch. Dave Winfield was sent off at the end of the game, but no one seemed to want to talk about the bite marks that photographs showed were clearly visible on his arm. Tranmere then went on to play Boring Wood at Wembley after they won 3-2 at Sutton. After having a player sent off in the first minute, Tranmere held on and took the lead. Boring Wood managed an equaliser, but Tranmere won with a last gasp goal when thoughts would have been beginning to turn to a penalty shoot-out.

League sponsors, Vanarama, tweeted asking why so many fans had come disguised as red seats, but the crowd was only 16,300 which does beg the question about whether Wembley is the right venue. Not a problem for us to worry about though, as we are not going to be playing there just yet. Congratulations to Tranmere though. They were definitely one of the better teams over the course of the season, and it's a nice moment for their fans.

In League 2, I had thought Barnet were going to pull off a great escape but despite securing 13 points from their last five games, they were relegated on goal difference, meaning that they will join Chesterfield in our league next season. Coming up into the National League are moneybags Salford City and Harrogate Town from the National League North, and Braintree Town and Havant and Waterlooville from the National League South.

Sadly, we have had to say goodbye to Woeking, Torquay, Chester and Guiseley from the National League, but certainly for Woeking and Torquay this is tempered with a hope to see them again soon. I should clarify that I mean that we hope to see them again soon in the Conference National. Obviously, we do not want to meet them in Conference South!

Ultimately, I think there were a couple of areas where we came up short this season. Firstly, we didn't quite replace Kundai, Bernard and Idris. While the replacements are, in my opinion, equally skilful, what these three had was the ability to hunt as a pack. They seemed to break as one and cause chaos as they ran at opposition defenders. This season, the breaks tended to have been led by individuals and, as such, were more easily defended against, and we have run into more dead ends with fewer options to create that final ball which was going to lead to goals. It's amazing to think that we are one of the higher scoring teams in the league, yet our highest goal-scorers have only just about reached double figures.

Secondly, while we received lots of plaudits for being the best footballing side in the league – and this is important to Shots fans as we want to be entertained – we didn't know how to deal with the more aggressive teams. I think the same was true last season but when we're up against the more physical teams such as Sutton and Tranmere, we seem to surrender too easily. I don't know what the answer is but can't help thinking that running at their less mobile and less skilful defenders would lead to more fouls and therefore more free-kicks and yellow cards which would then push the momentum back to us. We need to be a bit more street-wise in order to deal with those thugs who somehow manage to con referees and get away with stuff that we never seem to, and which we don't seem to know how to deal with. I would hate to watch the dull football that many teams in our league dish up but unfortunately you can't deny that that the overly physical, route one game does bring success for some teams. We need to learn how to combat this.

The moment upon which the season seemed to turn was at home against Macclesfield where the referee sent Will Evans off in the first few minutes and awarded Macclesfield a penalty. While the ten men played well, it was too much of an uphill battle. Macclesfield won and went on to win the league. Our form left us and for the remainder of the season we dropped to the middle of the form table. To be Champions, you need some luck along the way, and it was firmly with Macclesfield that day. I can't recall opposition players being sent off at the beginning of a game against us – even when Matt Rhead of Lincoln elbowed Will in the face within five seconds of the game starting at the end of last season which was the least controversial decision that I could recall.

What was very noticeable this season though is the very fine line that separates victories from defeats. Of course, there are one-sided games where the victor has never been in doubt but, equally, there have been many games where it really could have gone either way. Some we won, some we lost, but over the course of the season, I think it probably balanced out fairly evenly.

What has also been noticeable this season has been the poor quality of the referees. There has been a consistent lack of protection against our players from some of the bullies that other teams have and we need to develop tactics to deal with them so that they don't come out on top.

I managed to get to take in 34 games during the season. Hard to say which was my best game, but the away games at Orient, Woeking and Ebbsfleet together with the home game against Tranmere would all be very strong contenders. The worst experiences were without doubt the home match against Eastleigh and the away match at Sutton.

All in all though, I think the season was successful. We played some good football, particularly in the first half of the season. We won a lot more games than we lost, and we finished in the play-off places for the second successive season. The real measure of success is that I enjoyed the season and I didn't have to think twice before submitting my season ticket application for next year. As I have said before, most Shots fans do not always expect us to be successful, and we know we have no right to expect us to be successful, but we do believe we have a right to be entertained, and we most certainly have.

I would like to record my sincere congratulations and thanks to the team and everyone who has worked so hard behind the scenes to provide us with another good season.

We've now got three months off for Sir Gary and the team to recuperate, re-group and come back stronger.

Is there any doubt that we'll be back next year, raring to get back on that roller-coaster again?

None whatsoever, and I can't wait. Come on you Shots!

Printed in Great Britain
by Amazon